Studies in Financial Modelling

Jaap Spronk · Benedetto Matarazzo (Eds.)

In Cooperation with the Editorial Board of the Rivista di
Matematica per le Scienze Economiche e Sociali

Modelling for Financial Decisions

Proceedings of the 5th Meeting of the EURO Working Group on "Financial Modelling" held in Catania, 20-21 April, 1989

With 44 Figures

Springer-Verlag

Berlin Heidelberg New York
London Paris Tokyo
Hong Kong Barcelona
Budapest

Prof. Dr. Jaap Spronk
Erasmus University
P.O. Box 1738
NL-3000 DR Rotterdam
The Netherlands

Prof. Dr. Benedetto Matarazzo
Università di Catania
Corso Italia 55
I-Catania
Italia

First published in "Rivista di matematica per le scienze economiche e sociali", Vol. 12, No. 1, 1989

ISBN-13: 978-3-642-76763-0 e-ISBN-13: 978-3-642-76761-6
DOI: 10.1007/978-3-642-76761-6

Softcover reprint of the hardcover 1st edition 1991

Bookbinding: G. Schäffer GmbH u. Co. KG., Grünstadt
2142/7130-543210 – Printed on acid – free paper

CONTENTS

FINANCIAL MODELLING IS BACK IN TOWN

In April 1989, the fifth meeting of the EURO Working Group on Financial Modelling was held in Acireale, Sicily, organized by Benedetto Matarazzo of the University of Catania. The meeting was attended by over 100 participants from fourteen different countries. A large number of papers was presented and dicsussed.

The Catania meeting clearly showed the right of existence of the working group in which not only completed research projects but also ongoing research can be discussed in a relaxed but constructive way. Apparently, there is a need in Europe to strengthen the links between people working in the field of financial modelling. Since 1989, a number of projects undertaken jointly by researchers in different countries have been set up. Since Catania other meetings have been organized in Liège (Belgium), Sirmione (Italy), Groningen (The Netherlands) and Curaçao (The Netherlands Antilles).

This volume was published earlier as a special issue of the Rivista di matematica per le scienze economiche e sociali.

We are grateful to the editorial board of the Rivista for their kind willingness to devote a special issue to this meeting. All papers were referred by two referees. The final acceptance decision were made together with the editorial board of the Rivista. We would like to express our gratitude to the referees for the work they did.

The working group is mainly focussed on the development of tools which support decision makers in the financial area, ranging from treasurers of firms to professional investors (pension funds, mutual funds) and bank managers. The contents of this volume shows a broad variety of applications using techniques and methodologies from various fields such as econometrics, operations research and financial mathematics. Those remembering the practice and theoretical developments of financial modelling in the late sixties and during the seventies and who have since then lost contact with the field may still be a little bit sceptical. And not withhout reason. In the early stages of financial modelling much went wrong. Enormous, complicated models were built with the claim of «realism», requiring sophisticated information systems and access to mainframe computers. As a consequence, financial modelling often was the business of «experts» far more than of decision makers. In fact, the whole approach towards decision making was at the same time «hautain» and somewhat naive. In addition, because of the experts being trained in fields generally different from finance, many models neglected important results from developments in financial theory. Looking backwards it is not much of a surprise that the original optimism towards financial modelling very often turned into frustation. Fortunately, much has changed during the eighties.

First of all, the philosophy and methodology with respect to tools for decision making has been changed towards something which in the field of financial decision making might be labelled as «financial decision support systems». The role of the decision makers has become dominant, both in the development and in the use of the decision support systems.

The developments in both computer hardware and software for computers made and still makes it much easier to individualise decision support systems. In addition, as many of the contributions in this volume show, the results of financial theory are much better taken into account than, say, ten years ago. Ideally, financial modelling would function as a liason between financial theory and practice.

Of course, much work remains to be done. We hope that international cooperation within the framework of the EURO Working Group will contribute to the required development.

Furthermore the editors, also on behalf of the publisher, would like to thank the Editorial Board of the Rivista di Matematica per le Scienze Economiche e Sociali for the kind willingness of transferring the copyright of material which was earlier published in a special issue of the "Rivista".

Benedetto Matarazzo
Jaap Spronk

INFLATION AND FIRM GROWTH: A REASSESSMENT

DANIEL L. BLAKLEY, ARNE DAG STI

Bedriftsokonomisk Institutt
The Norwegian School of Management
P. box 580
N-1301 Sandvika, Norway

Investigations into the impact of inflation on firm growth have resulted in ambiguous conclusions within the economic growth and financial management literature. This paper will attempt to clarify this situation and describe conditions under which firm growth will be helped or hindered by inflaction. This is accomplished by constructing a financial modelling framework which incorporates the findings of earlier research and allows the various effects to be contrasted and cumulatively assessed. Our findings suggest that conditions under which inflation may be beneficial to firm growth do exist but are realistically improbable.

1. Introduction

Does inflation hinder or stimulate growth? The importance of this inquiry to managers and policy makers has generated considerable research effort within both the economic growth and finance literature. There has to date, however, been little agreement either between or within these 2 scenes of academic inquiry as to the overall effect of inflation. Indeed, positive and negative effects of inflation on growth have been identified in both schools leaving the net effect open to debate and speculation.

The overall objective of this research effort is to develop a methodology for analyzing the conflicting nature and cumulative impact of these accepted findings. This will be accomplished via the construction of a modelling framework which will unify micro and macro inflationary considerations. It is believed this is the first attempt to consolidate the theoretical findings from these 2 distinct branches of analysis. A secondary objective is to use the model to describe conditions under which firm growth potential will be positively or negatively influenced by inflation.

One well known result from monetary economic growth theory goes back to James Tobin (1965). Tobin's point of possible non-neutral inflationary effects, working through changes in capital intensity and interest rates, remains as a corner stone finding in modern growth theory. In the literature this non-neutrality result has been termed the Tobin effect. As will be discussed below, increases in capital intensity at the macro-level are analogous at the micro level to decreases in the sales to asset ratio - e.g., the required investment in new assets necessary to support a given increase in sales volume will increase. While this would be expected, ceteris paribus, to decrease firm growth potential, the so-called Tobin-effect may have a secondary impact on the profit rate by lowering real interest expense. This, on the other hand, would have a positive influence on firm growth. Thus, the net effect of inflation on growth is open to debate in the macroeconomic literature.

The original work on the so-called sustainable growth problem in the finance literature was put forth by Higgins (1977). In the absence of taxes, the firm's sustainable growth is determined by additions to retained earnings (via undistributed profits) and the resultant allowable increase in debt to finance asset expansion and sales. Assuming a positive investment in net working capital and constant proportional relationships between sales to assets and profits to sales (both of these factors, explicitly addressed in the growth literature, are assumed exogenous in the sustainable growth formulation), Higgins (1977, 1981, 1984) concludes inflation will reduce sustainable growth. The rational here is that increases in working capital must be financed regardless of whether the cause is real or inflationary growth: to the extent that funds are diverted from investment in productive (fixed) assets, inflation will hinder growth except in the unusual situation where net working capital balances are negative. This intuitively pleasing line of reasoning, however, is at odds with the findings of Johnson (1981). Here, using the sustainable growth model, it is demonstrated that inflation can increase firm growth even if working capital balances are positive.

Thus we observe conflicting evidence concerning the impact of inflation in both the finance and economic growth literature. Furthermore, in economic growth theory working balances and financial policies of the firm pay no role while in the sustainable growth literature the effects of inflation on capital intensity and profit are ignored. This ambiguity has resulted, perhaps not surprisingly, in many researchers simply assuming inflation has a neutral impact. This view can be found in Donaldson (1983, 1985), Ellsworth (1983), Fruhan (1984), Clark et. al. (1985), Harrington and Wilson (1983) among others.

In what follows below we will formulate a theoretical model designed to identify and cumulatively assess the various effects briefly described above. The method used will be to enhance the basic sustainable growth model to include inflation effects on capital intensity and profitability. We will show that by introducing the so-called Tobin-effects into the sustainable growth model we are able to clarify the complex influences of inflation by separating and identifying the different forces that operate on a firm's growth opportunities.

In the next section, we will develop the base model and identify the working capital impact of inflation, which we refer to as the Higgins-effect, on firm growth. Here we will also discuss the contrary results of Johnson and show the dependence of such findings on a misspecification involving the choice of a price deflator. In Section 3, the potential inflationary impact on profit rates and capital intensity (which we refer to below as Tobin-effect 1 and Tobin-effect 2, respectively) is introduced. In the next section we consolidate and isolate these 3 effects and define the sustainable growth equation. The following section will focus on analyzing conditions under which we could expect the positive effect to be outweighed by the negative and vice versa. We close our analysis by discussing possible extensions and caveats and drawing some broad conclusions.

2. Micro Inflationary Considerations

Based on the sustainable growth formulations developed by Blakley et al. (1987), a set of difference equations will now be developed which capture the dynamic relationship between the firm's balance sheet and income statement. After specification of the equations, which reflect the assumptions and identities inherent in standard sustainable growth formulations, a reduced form equation will be derived which defines the level of sales in a given time period. The real rate of sales growth resulting from the solution of the reduced form equation will then be calculated.

Assuming a constant capital structure with a long-run debt to equity ratio of λ, long-term liabilites in time t can be written as

$$L_t = \lambda E_t \tag{1}$$

where E_t is total equity at time t. Without issuing new equity any increase in equity will be determined by the rate of increase in the firm's undistributed profit. Defining δ as the profit retention rate (i.e., 1-dividend payout ratio), equity can be defined as

$$E_t = E_{t-1} + \delta \Pi_t \tag{2}$$

where Π_t is total profit in time t. Assuming no taxes and a constant profit margin on sales, total profit in time t is

$$\Pi_t = \pi S_t \tag{3}$$

where S_t is total sales at time t and π is the profit margin.

Continuing with Higgin's assumptions that depreciation is sufficient to maintain the replacement value of existing assets and that increases in real sales are a constant proportion, θ, of the increase in nominal assets, we can specify

$$\theta = \frac{S_t - (1 + j)\, S_{t-1}}{A^{LT}_{\;t} - A^{LT}_{\;t-1}}$$

and solving for S_t produces

$$S_t = \theta\, (A^{LT}_{\;t} - A^{LT}_{\;t-1}) + (1 + j)\, S_{t-1} \tag{4}$$

where j is the assumed constant, uniform and anticipated rate of inflation and $A^{LT}_{\;t}$ is the firm's net investment in long-term (i.e., productive) assets. (Note the change in real sales has been defined using the current period as the base).

By further assuming current assets and current liabilities will have a constant proportional relationship to nominal sales, we can write net working capital in time t as

$$WC_t = \phi\, S_t \tag{5}$$

where ϕ is the assumed constant proportional relationship between working capital and sales.

Lastly it is necessary to specify the balance sheet identities . Long-term assets, $A^{LT}_{\;t}$, are the difference between total assets, $A^{T}_{\;t}$, and net working capital, WC_t, or

$$A^{LT}_{\;t} = A^{T}_{\;t} - WC_t \tag{6}$$

Further, total assets, $A^{T}_{\;t}$, are the sum of long-term liabilities and equity, or

$$A^{T}_{\;t} = L_t + E_t. \tag{7}$$

We can now derive the reduced form difference equation for sales as a function of previous sales and parameters j, λ, δ, π, θ, and ϕ as (see Appendix 1).

$$S_t = \frac{1 + \theta\, \phi + j}{1 - \theta\{(1 + \lambda)\, \delta\pi - \phi\}} \cdot S_{t-1}$$

We solve this by using standard techniques to get (8).

$$S_t = \left[\frac{1 + \theta\, \phi + j}{1 - \theta\, \{(1 + \lambda)\, \delta\pi - \phi\}} \right]^t \cdot S_0 \tag{8}$$

where S_0 is initial period sales.

The real sales growth can be defined as

$$g^* = \frac{1 + g^*_N}{1 + j} - 1;$$

where

$$g^*_N = \frac{S_t - S_{t-1}}{S_{t-1}} = \frac{1 + \theta\,\phi + j}{1 - \theta\{(1 + \lambda)\,\delta\pi - \phi\}} - 1,$$

and substituting (8) yields

$$g^* = \frac{1 + \theta\,\phi + j}{1 - \theta\,\{(1 + \lambda)\,\delta\pi - \phi\}} \cdot \frac{1}{1 + j} - 1. \tag{9}$$

To investigate the conditions under which inflation will have a neutral impact on growth, it is necessary to find the conditions which result in the first partial derivative of (9) with respect to inflation being equal to zero. The resulting calculating is

$$\delta g^*/\delta j = \frac{1 + \theta\,\phi + j}{1 - \theta\{(1 + \lambda)\,\delta\pi - \phi\}} \cdot \frac{-1}{(1 + j)^2}$$

$$+ \frac{1}{1 - \theta\{(1 + \lambda)\,\delta\pi - \phi\}} \cdot \frac{1}{1 + j} = 0$$

Multiplying each term by

$$\frac{1}{1 - \theta\{(1 + \lambda)\,\delta\pi - \phi\}} \cdot \frac{1}{1 + j}$$

yields

$$1 - \frac{1 + \theta\,\phi + j}{1 + j} = \frac{-\theta\,\phi}{1 + j} = 0,$$

which is true only when $\phi = 0$. Likewise it is clear that inflation will have a positive effect on real growth when $\phi < 0$, and a negative impact when $\phi > 0$.

At this point it will be useful to compare our results to those of Johnson (1981). We have shown above that the Higgins-effect, that is the impact of inflation on growth via the working capital effect, is dependent on ϕ, the net working capital to sales ratio. Assuming as we normally do that the firm will have some positive investment in net working capital, we can say the Higgins-effect is strictly negative. Johnson's results suggest the Higgins-effect is not unique and that plausible conditions exist which would result in inflation stimulating real growth even when $\phi > 0$.

In Exhibit 1 we show a comparison of results using Johnson's methodology in tracing the impact of inflation on sustainable growth (Panel A) and the comparable results generated from the model developed above (Panel B). It can be observed in Panel B that the impact of inflation on sustainable growth is dependent on the value of ϕ. When the firm has positive working capital requirements, for instance when ϕ equals 20% and 5%, inflation proves harmful to real sales growth. Continuing with Panel B, if the firm has negative working capital requirements, as shown in the last column, inflation will increase sustainable growth. Only when the firm has no investment in working capital will inflation be neutral.

The results by Johnson, by comparison, suggest the conditions under which inflation is beneficial include a positive ϕ. Also, it should be noted, the magnitude of any such benefit is greater. The assumptions used in the Johnson analysis are identical to those used above, with one important exception: prior period prices are used as a basis to deflate sales when the change in real sales is defined. More specifically, Johnson defines the relationship between sales and assets as

$$\theta = \frac{S_t/(1+j) - S_{t-1}}{A^{LT}{}_t - A^{LT}{}_{t-1}}$$

which, it is possible to show, results in the real sustainable growth rate of

$$g^*{}_J = \frac{(1+j)(1+\lambda)\,\delta\pi - \phi j}{\theta^{-1} - (1+j)(1+\lambda)\,\delta\pi + \phi(1+j)}$$

With this formulation, Johnson demonstrates that inflation will enhance firm growth whenever $(1+\lambda)\,\delta\pi > \phi$ regardless of the sign of ϕ.

As discussed above, these results can be traced back to the method used to deflate sales using prior period prices as a base. The fundamental problem with this is the change in real sales is being measured with prior period prices that are not comparable to the prices used to value nominal assets: by definition, current nominal assets are valued with current period prices. If we change the deflation procedure so that comparable prices are utilized the Higgins-effect is strictly negative for all cases when net working capital is positive. Theoretical considerations dictate the use of current period base prices, as we have done above, in order to have sales and asset changes measured in comparable values.

Thus we see that contrary to the findings of Johnson, the Higgins-effect is strictly dependent on the sign of net working capital balances. Generally, net working balances can be both positive and negative. Negative working capital can be observed when short-term liabilities are larger than current assets. Even if this case is seldom observed, it is theoretically possible. In this case we get a strictly positive Higgins-effect. Otherwise we will have a strictly negative or neutral Higgins-effect. Stated formally:

Negative Higgins-effect when $\dfrac{-\theta\phi}{1+j} < 0$ or when $\phi > 0$

Positive Higgins-effect when $\frac{-\theta\phi}{1+j} > 0$ or when $\phi < 0$

Neutral Higgins-effect when $\frac{-\theta\phi}{1+j} = 0$ or when $\phi = 0$.

These conclusions follow from the assumptions underlying traditional models of sustainable growth. These assumptions are that the sales-assets ratio θ is positive and the following parameters are held constant:

The debt-equity ratio	$\lambda \geqslant 0$
The profit retention rate	$0 < \delta \leqslant 1$
The profit rate	$\pi > 0$.

One problem with the traditional analysis is that there is, based on research findings in the economic growth literature, strong reason to believe that at least some of the assumed constant parameters vary systematically with inflation. We will now turn our attention in the following section to these considerations.

3. Macro Inflationary Considerations

Economic growth theory as developed by Solow (1956), Tobin (1965) and Feldstein (1976), suggests that a higher inflation rate increases the nominal interest rate and increases the capital intensity-that is the capital/labour ratio. In the absence of taxes, the standard analysis shows that under realistic operating conditions, inflation increases capital intensity, the nominal interest rate and the profit rate but decreases the real interest rate and marginal productivity.

The main results from monetary growth theory relevant to our formulations of the sustainable growth model will be based on the model formulations developed by Martin Feldstein (1976). His basic model can be condensed into the following six equations when we ignore the tax structure in the economy:

A neoclassical production function

$$y = f(k); \qquad f' > 0 \text{ and } f'' < 0 \tag{3.1}$$

where y is output per capita, that is Y/N and k is capital intensity, that is K/N (real assets per capita).

A money demand relation

$$m = L(r+j) \cdot k; \quad L' < 0 \tag{3.2}$$

where m is real demand for money balances per capita. Money demand depends negatively on the nominal interest rate, that is the sum of the real rate (r) and inflation rate (j).

Condition for monetary equilibrium

$$j = (DM/M) - n \tag{3.3}$$

where the anticipated inflation rate is the difference between the growth rate of money (DM/M) and the exogenously determined natural rate of growth for the population and labor stock (n).

Private sector real disposable income is

$$h = y \cdot (1 - \gamma) + n \cdot m \tag{3.4}$$

where h is real disposable income and the parameter γ denotes tax financed government expenditures as a proportion of output.

The Harrod-Domar condition is

$$\sigma(r) \cdot h = n \cdot k + n \cdot m \tag{3.5}$$

where σ is a positive savings rate less than one.

Condition for rational firm behavior

$$f'(k) - dep = r \tag{3.6}$$

where the constant parameter dep denotes the real depreciation rate for real capital.

A standard feature of monetary growth models is that real money demand depends negatively on the nominal interest rate. This is reflected in the portfolio theory specification in (3.2) that money demand per capita m/k depends negatively on the opportunity cost of holding money balances, namely the nominal interest rate. The nominal interest rate is the sum of the real interest rate and the inflation rate.

The inflation rate is assumed to be determined in long-run equilibrium by the money market. This results in an anticipated rate of inflation equal to the difference between nominal money growth and real population growth, as in (3.3). In equation (3.4) the private disposable income per capita consists of two components. The first is the increase in real income after tax. The second is the increase in real monetary wealth.

The fundamental equilibrium condition in the model we find in equation (3.5). We can interpret the left hand side to be savings and the right hand side to be investment necessary to balance the desired savings of the private sector in-long-run equilibrium. The first term is the necessary real investment per capita to keep the additional laborers equipped with the same real capital as the existing labor stock. The second term is the increased investment in liquid wealth (that is real money balances) necessary to keep the public in a balanced state of equilibrium. The last equation of the model stipulates the assumed profit maximizing behaviour of competitive firms: net marginal productivity will be equated with the real cost of capital.

The six equation model is able to determine the endogenous variables y, k, m, r, j and h when the following is assumed to be exogenous:

- Monetary policy DM/M
- Fiscal policy γ
- Population growth n
- Depreciation rate dep.

Using this six-equation model, it has been shown by Feldstein (1976) and Sti (1979) that

$$\mathrm{d}k/\mathrm{d}j = \frac{(1-\sigma)\, nkL'}{B}$$

where

$$B = \sigma\{(1-\gamma) f'' + nL\} - n(1+L) - (1-\sigma)\, nkL' f'' \leqslant 0.$$

From these facts it follows that the sign of dk/dj is the opposite of L'. Thus, when we have a negative interest sensitivity of money demand, as is normally assumed in the macro economy, we find that capital intensity is increased by inflation.

The capital intensity k in the economic growth model and the sales/asset ratio θ in the sustainable growth model have opposite associations with the inflation rate. Inflation drives capital intensity up and the sales/asset ratio down. This can be seen by recognizing that the direct analog of the sales/asset ratio in the economic growth literature is the output/capital ratio, which can be developed to be:

$$Y/K = \frac{Y/N}{K/N} = \frac{y}{k}$$

As can be seen from the figure 1, with a neo-classical production function, an increase in k from k_1 to k_2 will reduce the output-capital ratio to $(y/k)_2$.

Noting in equilibrium that decreases in marginal productivity will drive down the real interest rate, the increase in the nominal rate of interest will be less than the increase in the inflation rate. In as much as the firm's gross profit is influenced by interest payments, we can expect, ceteris paribus, the profit rate to increase with inflation.

In the sustainable growth model, such Tobin-effects would be expected to increase the profit margin and decrease the sales-to-asset ratio. Traditional sustainable growth formulations assume these parameters to be constant and exogenously determined. We have reason to believe from monetary growth theory

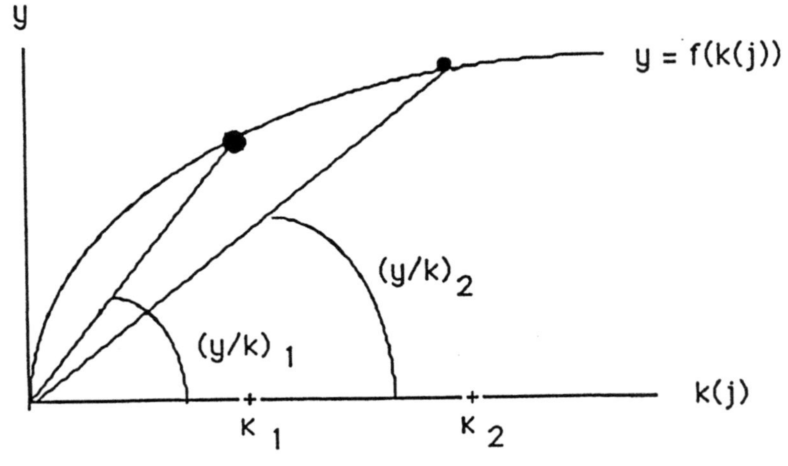

Fig. 1. Relation Between inflation and Capital Intensity.

that in the absence of taxes there are 2 inflationary effects relevant to sustainable growth analysis:

$$\text{Tobin-effect 1 } \pi(j) \text{ with } \frac{\delta\pi(j)}{\delta j} \geqslant 0, \text{ and}$$

$$\text{Tobin-effect 2 } \theta(j) \text{ with } \frac{\delta\theta(j)}{\delta j} < 0.$$

The second effect has a solid theoretical and empirical basis, and is therefore stipulated as strictly negative. The theoretical basis of the first effect is not so strong as for the second, therefore we do not define this relationship as a strict inequality. When it is present it implies inflation will stimulate firm growth.

4. Consolidation of Micro and Macro Considerations

From the results in sections 2 and 3 we can now define the equation for real sustainable growth as

$$g^{**} = \frac{1 + \theta(j)\,\phi + j}{1 - \theta(j) \cdot \{(1 + \lambda)\,\delta\pi(j) - \phi\}} \cdot \frac{1}{1 + j} - 1. \qquad \text{(9M)}$$

Note that this is the same as equation (9) except that we now allow inflation to exert its influence on the parameters θ and π. By differentiating this expression with respect to j we can isolate the various effects. Letting N and D represents the numerator and denominator of the first fraction in (9), we differentiate and set the result equal to zero

$$\delta g^{**}/\delta j = \frac{[\![\phi \, d\phi/dj + 1]\!] D - (1 + \theta \phi + j) [\![\ldots]\!]}{D^2} \cdot$$

$$\cdot \frac{1}{1+j} - \frac{N}{D} \cdot \frac{1}{(1+j)^2} = 0$$

where $[\![\ldots]\!] = [\![\phi \cdot d\theta/dj - d\theta/dj \cdot (1 + \lambda) \, \delta\pi - \theta(1 + \lambda) \, \delta \cdot d\pi/dj]\!]$.

We multiply this expression by $(1 + j) D$ to get

$$[\phi \, d\theta/dj + 1] - \frac{(1 + \theta\phi + j)}{D} \cdot [\phi \, d\theta/dj - d\theta/dj \, (1 + \lambda) \, \delta\pi - \theta(1 + \lambda) \, \delta \, d\pi/dj]$$

$$- \frac{N}{1+j} = 0$$

By manipulating and noting that

$$(1 + g^{**}) = \frac{N}{D} \cdot \frac{1}{1+j}$$

we then arrive at the final expression

$$\underbrace{- \frac{\theta\phi}{1+j}}_{\text{HIGGINS}} + \underbrace{[\theta(1 + \lambda) \, \delta(1 + j) \, (1 + g^{**})] \, \frac{d\pi}{dj}}_{\text{TOBIN 1}}$$

$$\underbrace{+ \{(1 + j) \, (1 + g^{**}) \, [(1 + \lambda) \, \delta\pi - \phi] + \phi\} \, \frac{d\theta}{dj}}_{\text{TOBIN 2}} = 0.$$

or more simply put.

$$\delta g^{**}/\delta j = \text{Higgins-effect} + \text{Tobin-effect 1} + \text{Tobin-effect 2} \tag{10}$$

5. Results

Based on the findings above we can now investigate the various conflicting influences of inflation on firm growth. This will be accomplished by discussing the relative magnitudes of the three effects when the firm has a positive and negative working capital balance.

When the firm has positive net working capital balances, that is $\phi > 0$, then the first term in (10), representing the Higgins effect, is uniquely negative in sign. In the second term, the expression in brackets is strictly positive when the retention rate is positive, which we assume for a firm in growth. The second term, therefore, will have the same sign as the inflation impact on profit margins, that is $d\pi/dj$. Because of its assumed non-negativity, we refer to this influence as the positive Tobin-effect.

Likewise, we will refer to the third and last term in (10) as the negative Tobin-effect. Because the rational firm will not invest in asset expansion unless the funds generated exceed the necessary buildup in working capital, we can assume the product of $(1 + \lambda)\ \delta\pi$ is larger than ϕ. Given this condition, which is necessary for positive growth potential, we see that the third term will have the same sign as the inflation effect on the sales to asset ratio ($d\theta/dj$), which is negative.

In as much as the components of the total effect of inflation on growth are conflicting, we can say our findings are in accord with the ambiguous results of earlier research. However, the various effects are now expressed in such a way that it is possible to explicitly identify the factors which determine their signs and magnitudes. For example, the sign of the Higgins-effect depends only on the sign of ϕ and the magnitude depends on θ and ϕ.

The signs of the Tobin-effects are invariant with respect to possible parameter values, while the strength of the positive effect is directly dependent on λ, δ, and θ and the negative effect on λ, δ, π, and ϕ.

Stated formally, the condition that must be fulfilled in order for the total effect to be positive is specified in (11A) for the case of a positive ϕ.

$$\begin{aligned} &abs\{[\![\theta(1+\lambda)\delta(1+j)(1+g^{**})]\!]\cdot d\pi/dj\} > abs\{-\theta\phi/(1+j)\} + \\ &abs\{\{(1+j)(1+g^{**})\,[\![(1+\lambda)\,\delta\pi-\phi]\!]+\phi\}\cdot d\theta/dj\}\,. \end{aligned} \qquad (11A)$$

On the other hand, when the firm has negative working capital balances the Higgins-effects is uniquely positive and we may observe conditions under which inflation will stimulate growth. This will indeed be the case when the sum of the Higgins-effect and the positive Tobin-effect out-weighs the strength of the nega tive Tobin-effect. Formally, in the case of negative working capital balances we will have a positive inflation effect when (11B) is fulfilled.

$$\begin{aligned} &abs\{-\theta\phi/(1+j)\} + abs\{[\![\theta(1+\lambda)\,\delta(1+j)(1+g^{**})]\!]\,d\pi/dj\} > \\ &abs\{\{(1+j)\,(1+g^{**})\,[\![(1+\lambda)\,\delta\pi-\phi]\!]+\phi\}d\theta/dj\}\,. \end{aligned} \qquad (11B)$$

It should be emphasized, however, that we observe a net inflationary effect that is different from the sign of the Higgins-effect only for cases involving a very small working capital ratio. In other words, the Higgins-effect (that is the working capital ratio) is the dominant determinant of how inflation will impact the growth potential of the firm.

6. Caveats and Extensions

The analysis contained herein can be criticized from at least two points. The first shortcoming concerns the use of a constant proportional relationship between real sales and nominal assets. We have continued with the original Higgins/Johnson formulation despite the fact that a more reasonable formulation would relate real sales to real assets. We have two reasons for doing this. One is that our primary objective here is to clarify some confusing findings in the literature and the best way to accomplish this is to keep in line with the traditional assumptions. Another reason, which perhaps explains the widespread use of this assumption, involves the need to solve simultaneous difference equations to specify the growth rate. Based on the findings of Nell et. al. (1988), which link sales to real assets and demonstrates the dominance of the Higgins effect for all positive growth rates, we do not expect significantly different conclusions if the more theoretically robust formulation is used.

Another possible shortcoming of our analysis is that tax effects have been ignored. It should be noted that the introduction of various tax effects would likely alter our conclusions in significant ways. But before the real-world complexities of taxes are introduced, it is important to understand the inflationary forces in a world without taxes. We feel these forces, at least in the sustainable growth literature, have not been adequately investigated: the falsely stated ambiguity of the Higgins-effect testifies to this. Tax considerations have been introduced into monetary growth theory by Feldstein (1976) and Sti (1979). These insights can now be incorporated into the sustainable growth literature utilizing the more robust formulation developed in this paper.

7. Conclusion

In the sustainable growth literature the primary focus of attention has been the Higgins-effect of inflation through working capital balances. We have demonstrated that firms with positive net working capital balances will be harmed, ceteris paribus, by inflation while those with negative balances will gain. Johnson (1981) overstate both the conditions under which inflation will prove beneficial as well as the magnitude of any such benefits due to a misspecification involving the measurement of real sales (a misspecification, it should be added, also made in the original Higgins model). We have shown the Higgins-effect to be unique and dependent on working capital balances.

Exhibit 1. Real sustainable growth rates*.

	*A. Basic Model Results***				*B. Modified Model Results*			
Working Capital/Sales:	20%	5%	0%	–5%	20%	5%	0%	–5%
Inflation Rate:								
0%	11.64%	17.02%	20.12%	24.59%	11.64%	17.02%	20.12%	24.59%
4	10.30	17.10	21.09	26.97	10.02	16.43	20.12	25.45
8	8.99	17.17	22.08	29.44	8.52	15.88	20.12	26.24
10	8.34	17.21	22.58	30.72	7.81	15.62	20.12	26.62

* The following parameter values are held constant at these values:

$\pi = .055$ $\theta = 3.03$

$\delta = .67$ $\lambda = .50$

** Panel A duplicates Johnson's results, shown in [13, p. 33]. After discussion with Johnson, it has been determined that the her «f» (=1/θ) parameter was incorrectly specified as .30, rather than .33.

We extend the analysis to include several accepted results from monetary growth theory. Inflation increases nominal interest rates, increases capital intensity and possibly the profit margin. The analysis of sustainable growth of the firm is made more complex by the inclusion of the Tobin-effects. But it is possible to formulate the influence of these effects in such a way that we get a clearer and more realistic view of the various channels of influence of inflation on the firm. Our methodology also bears the hope of the future inclusion of tax effects into the analysis.

Appendix 1 - Deduction of the reduced form difference equation for sales

Our basic sustainable growth model is:

$$L_t = \lambda E_t \tag{1}$$

$$E_t = E_{t-1} + \delta \Pi_t \tag{2}$$

$$\Pi_t = \pi S_t \tag{3}$$

$$S_t = \theta [A^{LT}{}_t - A^{LT}{}_{t-1}] + (1 + j) S_{t-1} \tag{4}$$

$$WC_t = \phi S_t \tag{5}$$

$$A^{LT}{}_t = A^T{}_t - WC_t \tag{6}$$

$$A^T{}_t = L_t + E_t \tag{7}$$

Using (6), (7) and (1) gives

$$(1 + \lambda) \cdot E_t = A^{LT}{}_t + WC_t \tag{12}$$

Substituting (5) for WC_t and (2) for E_t into (12) gives

$$A^{LT}{}_t = (1 + \lambda) \cdot [E_{t-1} + \delta\pi \cdot S_t] - \phi \cdot S_t \tag{13}$$

Note that by using (12) we can define E_{t-1} as

$$E_{t-1} = \frac{A^{LT}{}_{t-1} + \phi S_{t-1}}{(1 + \lambda)}$$

which when substituted into (13) yields

$$A^{LT}{}_t = A^{LT}{}_{t-1} + \phi S_{t-1} + [(1 + \lambda) \delta\pi - \phi] \quad S_t \tag{14}$$

Formally, by substituting (14) into (4) for $A^{LT}{}_t$ and solving for S_t we get the desired reduced form equation for sales.

$$S_t = \frac{1 + \theta\phi + j}{1 - \theta[(1 + \lambda) \delta\pi - \phi]} \cdot S_{t-1}$$

GLOSSARY

$L^{LT}{}_t$ = long-term liabilities in time t
E_t = total equity in time t
Π_t = total income in time t
S_t = total sales in time t
WC_t = net working capital in time t
$A^{LT}{}_t$ = long-term (fixed) assets in time t
$A^T{}_t$ = total assets in time t

and:

λ = long-term debt to equity ratio
δ = profit retention rate
π = profit margin on sales
j = uniform rate of inflation
θ = proportion of new real sales to new nominal assets
ϕ = working capital to sales ratio

REFERENCES

[1] B. BALACHANDRAN, N. NAGARAJAN, A. RAPPAPORT: "Threshold Margins for Creating Economic Value", *Financial Management,* (Spring, 1986), pp. 68-77.

[2] D. BLAKLEY, B. DOYLE, L.W. MURRAY, "Reassessing the Impact of Inflation on Su stainable Growth", Working Paper, U. of San Francisco, 1987.

[3] J. J. CLARK, M. T. CLARK, A.G. VERZILLI, "Strategic Planning and Sustainable Growth" *Columbia Journal of World Business,* (Fall, 1985), pp 47-51.

[4] G. DONALDSON, "Financial Goals and Strategic Consequences". *Harvard Business Review,* (May-June, 1985), pp. 57-66.

[5] G. DONALDSON, J.W. LORSCH, *Decision Making at the Top,* (New York, Basic Books, 1983).

[6] R. R. ELLSWORTH, "Subordinate Financial Policy to Corporate Strategy", *Harvard Business Review,* (November-December, 1983), pp. 170-182.

[7] M. FELDSTEIN, "Inflation, Income Taxes, and the Rate of Interest: A Theoretical Analysis", *American Economic Review,* (December, 1976).

[8] W. FRUHAN, "How Fast Should Your Company Grow?" *Harvard Business Review,* (January-February, 1984), pp. 84-93.

[9] D. HARRINGTON, B. WILSON, *Corporate Financial Analysis,* (Plano, TX: Business Publications, Inc. 1983).

[10] R. C. HIGGINS, *Analysis for Financial Management,* (Homewood, IL: Richard D. Irwin, Inc., 1984).

[11] R. C. HIGGINS, "How Much Growth Can a Firm Afford?" *Financial Management,* (Fall, 1977), pp. 7-16.

[12] R.C. HIGGINS, "Sustainable Growth Under Inflation", *Financial Management,* (Autumn, 1981), pp. 36-40.

[13] D. J. JOHNSON, "The Behavior of Financial Structure and Sustainable Growth in an Inflationary Environment", *Financial Management,* (Autumn, 1981), pp. 30-35.

[14] S. NELL, D. BLAKLEY, B. DOYLE, L. W. MURRAY, *Inflation and Firm Growth,* Working Paper, U. of San Francisco, 1988.

[15] R. SOLOW, "A Contribution to the Theory of Economic Growth" *Quarterly Journal of Economics,* (February, 1956).

[16] A. D. STI, "Inflation, Taxes and Economic Growth", *Sosialoekonomen,* (April, 1979).

[17] J. TOBIN, "Money and Economic Growth", *Econometrica,* (October, 1965).

MULTI-FACTOR FINANCIAL PLANNING: AN OUTLINE AND ILLUSTRATION

MARC GOEDHART, JAAP SPRONK
Tinbergen Institute and Dept. of Finance & Investment
Erasmus University Rotterdam
P.O. Box 1738
3000 DR Rotterdam
The Netherlands

This paper deals with the support of strategically oriented financial planning processes in business firms. In handling a financial planning problem, the decision maker has to deal with a number of complications. In this paper special attention is paid to the risk with regard to the outcomes of the financial plan and the existence of multiple, conflicting goals. An interactive approach to financial planning is presented. Risk is modeled by means of so-called multi-factor risk models and multiple goals are explicitly accounted for through the use of an interactive goal programming method. The use of the interactive approach will be numerically demonstrated by means of an exemplary planning problem.

1. Introduction

In this paper, financial planning is seen as a structured process of identification and selection of present and future capital investment projects (including disinvestments) while taking account of the financing of these projects over time This process can be visualized as in figure 1. The firm has to derive its right to exist from the fact that it creates a surplus of value to society. In other words, the sum of contributions from the firm's participants should at least equal the total of effects the firm has in return on these participants. In this view, the firm is continuously managing a set of exchange relations with its participants. Obviously, exchange relations are dynamic: the firm can to a large extent choose its own participants who, in turn, generally have their alternatives outside the firm. This implies that the resultant effect of these relations is dynamic as well. In other words: the firm has to deal with a dynamic goal complex, a multiplicity of goals which vary over time.

Any decision supportive approach to financial planning should, in our opinion, take account of the reasonably well established fact that people are not very good in assessing reliable probabilities to the outcomes of future events. This may be partly explained by pointing at the limitations of the human mind.

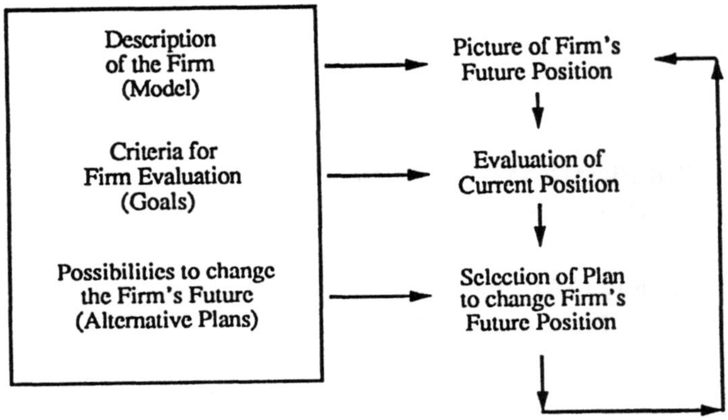

Figure 1. Financial Planning Process

Another reason is of an even more fundamental nature: many future outcomes are contingent on decisions which are still to be made. In the case of capital investment projects, for instance, the future cash flows can generally not be well represented by some probability distribution alone. In addition it is often necessary to describe as well all the «rights» and «duties» connected with the project. For instance, the right to expand or to abandon the project or some legal duty to keep people on the pay-roll even in case it would be more economical to fire them. One might consider the use of decision trees to describe this type of situations. But in most practical cases this is impossible because of the number of possible outcomes being too large and/or because the timing of the potential outcomes (when something will happen) is largely unknown. The picture becomes even more complicated if one realizes that the outcomes of a project are often not only contingent on the future decisions of the decision maker himself, but may also be contingent on the future decisions of the firm's participants, which are in their turn contingent on the firm's decisions. In other words, the way the firm managers its exchange relations influences the uncertainty surrounding the firm's cash flows.

From the above observations it is clear that the alternative plans to be considered by the decision maker are hard if not impossible to evaluate on the *exclusive* basis of the objective adopted by financial thory; the maximization of the shareholders' wealth. One group of problems is formed by the contingencies and the game like nature of at least part of the firm's dynamic goal complex. Furthermore, the firm should not neglect the interest of participants other than the shareholders, even though they may de facto be the most powerful group of participants. But cash flow remains one of the central concepts in developing a financial plan. Shareholdes will evaluate the firm in terms of alternative investment opportunities. An obvious possibility is to invest in the stock market. This gives a clear reason to use the firm's market value as a benchmark for evaluating the firm and its investments. And to close the circle: the firm's market value directly depends on the firm's cash flows and the associated risk. If the firm's cash flows decrease and/or its riskiness increases, its market value will drop. In summary, the firm should for each financial plan try to assess all effects considered to be important by the most influential participants, taking account of the most important contingencies involved.

In this paper we describe a framework for financial planning in the firm which is based on two important developments in financial theory:

a) the use of multi-factor models to describe probability distributions of returns;

b) the revival of the concept of flexibility and its valuation through option pricing theory and contingent claims analysis.

We will show how these two ingredients can be used in a multiple criteria approach to financial planning in which the decision maker can systematically investigate the set of alternative financial plans, taking account of the most important parties, the most important uncertain factors and the most important contingencies, rights and duties involved. Preliminary experiences have given us the conviction that the framework has a good potential to be understood and used in practice. The general ideas behind the proposed framework are outlined in the next section. In section 3 the framework itself is described after which in section 4 some elements of the framework are illustrated by means of a practical example. Our conclusions are summarized in section 5.

2. The Multi-Factor Framework and Contingent Claims

In modeling uncertainty one has to find a compromise between precision on the one hand and comprehensibility and manageability by the model user on the other hand. Very often, uncertain outcomes of decision alternatives (projects, plans, etc.) are modeled as probability distributions defined on the range of possible outcomes. Decision makers are then required to assess the value of some parameters (e.g. mean and variance) of these distributions. In addition, decision makers often have to express their preferences (e.g. utility values) with respect to the uncertain outcomes. The thusly provided information is then used in the formulation of an objective function (e.g. the expected utility of the decision alternatives) or, alternatively, in formulating chance constraints. For the reasons given above we deviate from this approach by assuming that the uncertain phenomena met in financial planning can generally not be modeled precisely. However, following Hallerbach and Spronk [1986], we assume that for many of these phenomena at least some structure can be found by using multi-factor models.

The results of a financial plan (to facilitate the exposition in this section, we take the firm's cash flow as the only relevant outcome variable) will depend on the one hand on the decisions made by the firm and on the other hand on the various forces and influences from its dynamic environment. We assume that, in general, it is very hard if not impossible to define a complete probability distribution over the value of the cash flows which may result. Instead, we assume that the firm is able to define its expectations concerning these cash flows and, in addition, that it is able to assess the sensitivity of these cash flows for unexpected changes in a number of factors which influence these cash flows. Consequently, the effect of a decision can be modeled as an expected level of the cash flows plus a series of sensitivities for unexpected changes in a number of factors influencing these cash flows. The firm does not necessarily know how these factors themselves will change in the future. On basis of this way of modeling, a firm can estimate the firm's aggregate sensitivity (i.e. the sensitivity of all decisions combined) for the various factors it has found to be important. In this way, a given financial plan of the firm can be evaluated in terms of an expected cash flow development accompanied by a vector of sensitivities describing what deviations from this expectation could arise if one or more of the identified factors would get another value than expected. Clearly, the aggregate sensitivities can be treated by the decision makers as goal variables, which can be traded off against each other and against other goal variables, possibly within the framework of a formal multi-criteria analysis (see section 4). Such an analysis might show for instance that the firm's sensitivity for unexpected wage rate changes can be lowered, but at the price of increasing the firm's sensitivity for unexpected changes in the dollar rate. It is conceivable that a firm is also evaluated in other terms than cash flows alone (e.g. employment level, labour relations, market power, etc.). Such a broadened evaluation can be done in a straightforward manner, be it that the amount of calculations increases and that one may want to investigate the interrelations between the evaluation criteria.

After the identification of the most important factors and the assessment of the firm's sensitivity for these factors, i.e. the actual multi-factor risk modeling process, a number of questions remain. These questions concern the choice of the appropriate actions to be taken by the firm when faced with a particular configuration of factor sensitivities. A first question is whether and, if so, how the firm is willing to accept certain exposures to unexpected changes in the factors. Basically, there are two ways to change the firm's aggregate factor sensitivities. The first way is to use contingent instruments such as investment or financing projects that create certain rights or duties, the second is the employment of non-contingent measures.

Non contingent actions resemble «traditional» hedging strategies such as in, for example, an investment portfolio of securities. For a planning problem in a firm such a strategy implies than an unacceptable pattern of factor sensitivities is limited or even neutralized by an investment in a project that generates a series of factor sensitivities of opposite sign. In this manner, both favourable and unfavourable effects of unexpected factor changes on the firm's cash flow can be reduced or perhaps even eliminated. An example of such a strategy of non-contingent hedging is the acquisition of energy plants by a transportation company. The adverse effects of for example oil price increases will be (partly) compensated for by opposite effects of the price rise in the energy producing business, and vice versa.

Contingent instruments give the firm the possibility to eliminate or reduce only the adverse effects of factor changes, and to profit from favourable effects. We distinguish between two kinds of flexibility that may be created by means of contingent instruments: directed flexibility, which has the character of an insurance against some specific risk, and on the other hand undirected flexibility, which will be also referred to as «elbow-room». One possibility to neutralize or to limit a risk beforehand is by «buying an insurance» with respect to this risk (where «buying an insurance» should be understood in a broad sense). For instance, firms often insure themselves against the negative consequences of unexpected changes in factors such as fire or exchange rate fluctuations (the latter can often be insured by buying currency options). On the other hand, the firm can assure itself of the positive effects of unexpected changes in the factors (e.g. by acquiring the exclusive selling rights of a product in development). For this kind of risk handling to be appropriate, it is necessary that management can at least identify the risk factors it wants to be protected from. Another possibility to face risks, instead of buying an insurance, is to create sufficient elbow-room in the firm to be able to react adequately to an unexpected change in some possibly not yet identified factor if and at the moment it occurs. The importance of some elbow-room is illustrated by a comparison of the histories of Pan-Am and Braniff (example from Casey en Bartczak, [1985]). At a certain moment both firms generated a negative net cash flow. Braniff went bankrupt in 1982 while PanAm could survive longer by selling two important assets (Intercontinental Hotel and the PanAm building). An evaluation of PanAm based on a cash flow analysis alone – i.e. without taking account of its «elbowroom» – would clearly have given a wrong answer. Creating elbow-room can be viewed as buying an option. If an unexpected change of a factor materializes, the option holder has the right to use the elbow-room to react to this change. Elbow-room is often labeled as flexibility [1], where a distinction is made between operational and financial flexibility (cf. Kemna [1988]). Examples of operational flexibility are the possibility to quickly adapt production (e.g. with respect to production volume or to product specification) according to the changing needs of the product's consumers. Already twenty years ago, the importance of financial flexibility was stressed by Donaldson [1969], [1984], and in the Netherlands by Diepenhorst [1962]. Examples of financial flexibility are unused reserves (cash surpluses, unused credit facilities), unused debt capacity and the capability to reduce expenditures. Not surprisingly, the creation and maintenance of elbow-room is not without costs: flexibility has its price (cf. Kemna [1988]). In efficient markets we would expect risk handling by creating flexibility to be more expensive than by using non-contingent instruments. For example, in financial markets, we would expect that hedging a currency exposure by means of currency option requires a higher investment than hedging the same position by means of a forward contract. The option strategy gives the buyer the right to exercise his currency option in case of unfavourable currency rate changes, while still enabling him to profit from favourable changes. The forward transaction, however, hedges the currency position against both favourable and unfavourable changes in the currency rate. Once the transaction has been made, the holder of the currency position can no longer profit from favourable currency rate changes. For real markets, an analogous line of reasoning would be valid if those markets were efficient. As this may not always the case, risk handling by creating flexibility need not always be more expensive.

3. Multi-Factor Financial Planning

In the multi-factorial approach to financial planning, the idea of replacing probability distributions by multi-factor representations is combined with the concept of contingent claims and with multiple criteria decision procedures. In broad lines, the resultant approach can be described as follows.

a) Identification of the firm's most important environmental factors. A distinction can be made between operational and financial factors. Operational factors, such as the price of raw materials, labour and the price of energy, relate to the firm's net cash flows. Financial factors relate to the cash flows flowing from and to the suppliers of the firm's capital. Examples are interest rates and risk premiums required by the market.

(1) We would rather use the term "undirected flexibility" for elbow-room, as opposed to "directed flexibility", which refers to the kind of 'insurance' mentioned earlier in the text.

b) Identification of projects, both real and financial. Real projects may vary from stopping a certain production line to the take-over of a competitor. Financial projects may vary from a modest one-year bank loan to a substantial emission of new stock.

c) Calculation of the expected cash flows of the firm as it is. (Obviously, the expected development of other output variables can be calculated as well. For case of exposition hereafter only cash flow is assumed to be relevant). To calculate these expected cash flows, a «base case» policy has to be defined, assuming that the environmental factors defined in (a) will adopt their expected values.

d) Estimation of the expected future cash flows of the projects. Here, the expected incremental cash flows are to be calculated. That is, the difference between the expected cash flows of the firm including the project and the expected cash flows of the firm not including the project (i.e. the expected values calculated in (c). As in (c), the expected incremental cash flows are calculated on the assumption that the environmental factors adopt their expected values.

e) Measurement of the firm's and the projects' sensitivities for unexpected changes in the environmental factors. The effect of the expected changes in the environmental factors has already be included in the expected cash flows calculated in (c) and (d).

f) Identification, specification and, if possible, valuation of the options («rights and duties») available to the firm as it is and of those associated with new projects. The valuation of options is a relatively new area which is producing a stream of exciting results. Notwithstanding the large number of successes in that field (see Kemna [1988], for an overview) a lot of questions remain unanswered. Especially with respect to the valuation of real options one may expect more or less exact answers only in a limited amount of cases. Clearly, options may change the magnitude of the sensitivities of the cash flows. Alternatively, options may limit the effect of one or more unexpected factor movements without changing the sensitivities as such.

g) Both the firm as it is and the projects at hand are described by multidimensional profiles, consisting of the expected values calculated in (c) and (d) and of the sensitivities for unexpected changes in the environmental factors calculated in (e) and if necessary corrected for the effect of the options mentioned in (f). The sensitivities estimated in the preceding steps relate to the cash flows streaming to the suppliers of capital. Given the firm's market value as a primary objective, one should try to find out how the financial market valuates different constellations of risk factors.

h) On basis of these multidimensional profiles of the firm and the projects, the problem is to find the combination of projects which contributes best in terms of the firm's objectives: this is done by IMGP (see Spronk [1981], [1985]), in which the decision maker has the possibility to condition the set of possible project combinations by setting and systematically changing a series of goal constraints.

i) The result of (h) can be a single plan or a set of plans which is subjected to a secondary analysis. For instance, it is possible to investigate how a plan would perform given a constellation of unexpected factor changes (of course, several factor constellations can be investigated). Furthermore, one may want to evaluate the generated plans in terms of objectives which not explicitly included in the model.

4. Illustration

In this section we will address the steps (g) to (i) as indicated in the multi-factorial approach to financial planning. These steps are concerned with the modeling of the firm and its projects in terms of expected values of cash flows and their sensitivities for changes in environmental factors, and furthermore, with the selection of a plan or set of plans and subsequent secondary analysis. In our example, the firm is represented by a financial planning model which covers ten periods. Uncertainty with regard to the firm's cash flows is modeled by means of multi-factor relations. It is assumed that two operational risk factors exist: the oil price level and the wage level, which are both represented by indices. Furthermore, a financial risk factor is embodied in the interest rate level [2] over outstanding debt. Management is to formulate a financial plan over the ten year planning period showing the investment projects undertaken and the way in which these projects will be financed over time.

4.1. Instruments

Three categories of instruments are available to the firm to manipulate its goal variables: the choice of investment projects, the amount of dividends paid out annually and the debt attracted in each year. With regard to the investment projects we assume that the relevant attributes are the annual expected net cash flow, the annual sensitivities for the two indicated operational risk factors and the incremental employment from the project. Incremental employment associated with an investment project can also be negative, which implies a number of dismissals. For simplicity, it is assumed that projects may also be partially adopted, which is defined by:

---

(2) We do not adjust the discounted value of the divided stream for possible changes in the risk free rate of return.

Table 1. Some attributes of the available projects (in $ 1,000).

	Cash Flow										EMP
Project	0	1	2	3	4	5	6	7	8	9	
0	500	550	500	450	460	420	400	480	420	430	-20
1	-100	20	15	9	12	18	15	20	10	20	-40
2	0	0	0	-30	20	12	15	15	25	25	-20
3	-200	25	20	18	16	17	22	15	17	16	-15
4	-100	15	12	11	10	15	16	18	20	20	-16
5	-500	58	50	60	50	55	62	60	55	50	-40
6	0	0	0	-2500	500	550	620	600	550	500	-40
7	0	-150	75	75	75	0	0	0	0	0	10
8	-80	40	10	15	10	20	0	0	0	0	-20
9	0	0	0	0	0	0	0	-100	50	50	-4
10	-100	30	30	30	-50	30	30	30	30	30	10
11	-20	6	7	6	7	0	0	0	0	0	0
12	0	-20	6	7	6	0	0	0	0	0	-15
13	0	0	-20	6	7	6	7	0	0	0	-20
14	0	-80	15	15	15	15	15	15	15	15	-40
15	-200	18	18	18	18	18	20	20	20	20	-15
16	-50	10	20	40	0	0	0	0	0	0	-10
17	-130	20	20	50	50	40	0	0	0	0	-30
18	0	0	0	-130	20	20	50	50	40	0	30
19	-125	15	18	16	10	12	-10	14	-10	20	10
20	-250	50	60	40	30	30	50	40	30	20	-40

$$0 \leqslant x_j \leqslant 1 \quad \text{for } j = 1, \ldots, 20; \tag{1}$$

where j is the project index. However, an integer approach to the project selection problem is also possible within the proposed framework. In table 1 the available investment projects and some of their effects on the model's variables are given.

The second category of instrumental variables in the model is the amount of debt attracted in each period. To finance its capital investments, the firm can choose from a number of large financing projectes such as bond issues. Thus, the financing problem is partly considered as one of selecting the best financing projects. Additional funds can be raised by attracting one-period loans, which are fully repaid at the end of the period. All funds needed for investment are raised either internally from other projects' cash flows, or externally from one-period loans at the prevailing interest rate r_L and bonds issued at a fixed coupon rate.

The bounds pay a fixed annual coupon rate and have a maturity varying from 5 to 9 years, as shown in table [2]. Bond principal is repaid at maturity. In this case we assume that the costs to a firm of financing by means of bonds

Table 2. Financing possibilities by bonds (in $ 1,000)

	Cash Flow								
Bond	0	1	2	3	4	5	6	7	8
0	200	16	16	16	16	16	16	16	216
1	150	11.3	11.3	11.3	11.3	161			
2	300	24	24	24	24	24	324		
3	400	32	32	32	32	32	32	32	432

are higher than the expected costs of financing by a series of short-term loans. But in comparison to the one-period loans, bonds offer the issuing firm a reduction of interest risk. In our model, a substitution of one-period loans by long-term bonds would imply a reduced interest sensitivity and a lower net present value of the cash flow after interest, which is available for dividend payments (see following sections).

In this way, a trade-off arises for the firm in formulating its financial policy: increases of the cash flow to equity can be realized at the cost of facing a higher sensitivity of that cash flow to unexpected changes in the future interest rate. Equity issues and lending facilities are not considered in this example.

Furthermore, the firm can influence its goal variables through dividend policy. The amount of dividend paid out in each period, Div_t, is the third instrument. To smoothen the variability of the dividends management has defined a growth path, which sets an upper bound and a lower bound for the growth rate of the dividend stream:

$$Div_t \leqslant Div_{t-1} \cdot (1 + g^+) \qquad \text{for} \quad t = 1, \ldots, 9; \tag{2}$$

$$Div_t \geqslant Div_{t-1} \cdot (1 + g^-) \qquad \text{for} \quad t = 1, \ldots, 9; \tag{3}$$

where g^+ is the upper, and g^- the lower growth rate level.

4.2. Definitional equations

In the model, the consequences of accepting investment projects for the aggregate net cash flow are figured as follows:

$$\overline{CF}_t = \sum_{j=0}^{20} x_j \cdot \overline{CF}_{jt} \qquad \text{for } t = 0, \ldots, 9; \tag{4}$$

$\overline{CF}_{jt}$: expected net cash flow for project j in period t;

Here, x_0 represents the firm as it is with its existing assets and associated cash flows and factor exposures. Assuming that disinvestments are not possible, x_0 is fixed at 1. The sources and uses of funds constraints are given by:

$$\sum_{j=1}^{20} x_j \cdot \overline{CF}_{j0} + L_0 - Div_0 + \sum_{k=1}^{K} y_k \cdot CF_{k0} = 0; \tag{5}$$

$$\sum_{j=1}^{20} x_j \; \overline{CF}_{jt} + L_t - L_{t-1} \cdot (1 + r_L) - Div_t + \sum_{k=1}^{K} y_k \cdot CF_{kt} = 0; \quad \text{for } t = 1, \ldots, 8; \tag{6}$$

$$\sum_{j=1}^{20} x_j \cdot \overline{CF}_{j9} - L_8 \cdot (1 + r_L) - Div_9 + \sum_{k=1}^{K} y_k \cdot CF_{k9} = 0; \tag{7}$$

The effects of bond issues are modeled with the use of the bond variables y_k and the corresponding – certain – cash flow CF_{kt} created by bond issue k in year t. L_t represents the amount of one-period loans attracted in period t, which is repaid with interest at the expected rate r_L [3] in the following period. In this example, no loans are outstanding at the beginning of the first period or at the end of the last period.

4.3. Goal variables

As argued in section one, management finds itself confronted with a dynamic goal complex. Here, the goal complex is represented by the following goal constraints:

1. Present value of the dividends;
2. Number of dismissals in the planning period;
3. Maximum positive sensitivity of the net cash flow to unexpected changes in the oil price index;
4. Maximum negative sensitivity of the net cash flow to unexpected changes in the oil price index;
5. Average sensitivity of the net cash flow for unexpected changes in the wage rate;
6. Average sensitivity of the cash flow to equity for unexpected changes in the debt rate.

The present value of the dividend stream represents the link with the capital market, or more specifically, with the shareholders. In discounting future divi-

(3) By assuming a certain term structure of interest rates, one should also allow for expected short-term interest rates to vary over time.

dends, the risk free rate of return is used instead of a risk adjusted rate. The present value as calculated in our model only incorporates the time value of money and not a risk premium. Risk is modeled by means of sensitivities for the three indicated risk factors. Therefore, the present value of the dividends is defined as:

$$Pv\ Div = \sum_{t=0}^{9} \frac{Div_t}{(1+r_f)^t} \ ; \tag{8}$$

where r_f is the risk free rate of return and *Pv Div* is to be maximized.

The second goal variable in the model concerns the level of employment in the firm. We assume that management wants to avoid struggles with its employees and that therefore the number of dismissals, Dismiss, during the planning period is to be minimized. This goal variable is derived from the incremental employment ΔEmp_j per investment project x_j in the following way:

$$\sum_{j=1}^{20} x_j \cdot \Delta Emp_j - Admiss + Dismiss = 0 \ \text{ for } Admiss, Dismiss \geqslant 0; \tag{9}$$

Our first goal variable explicitly excluded a risk adjusted discount rate. In this model, risky cash flows from investment projects or financing arrangements are modeled in multi-factor relations (4). The sensitivities from these multi-factor relations lead to the next four goal variables. Three risk factors are thought to influence the firm's cash flows: energy prices, as pictured by an oil price index, wage rates and the interest rate over the firm's debt. As the sensitivities for the first two operational risk factors vary over both projects and years, a method had to be found to summarize these figures. For the oil price sensitivities a mini-max approach combined with a maxi-min approach was chosen. The mini-max approach minimizes the maximal sensitivity for oil price changes over the planning period. Thus, it gives management an impression of the largest possible positive exposure of the net cash flow to oil price movements over the forthcoming ten years for a certain investment plan. In mathematical terms (5):

(4) The approach conceptually resembles a certainty equivalent method for evaluating risky cash flows.

(5) Cash flow sensitivities are defined as the derivative of the stochastic project cash flow with regard to the factor index; e.g.:

$$SensOil_{jt} = \frac{dCF_{jt}}{dOil_t} \tag{10a}$$

$$SensOil_t = \sum_{j=0}^{20} x_j \cdot SensOil_{jt} \qquad \text{for } t = 0, \ldots, 9; \tag{10}$$

$$SensOil^+ \geqslant SensOil_t \qquad \text{for } t = 0, \ldots, 9; \tag{11}$$

and $SensOil^+$ is to be minimized. An analogous method is used with regard to the negative exposure of the cash flow to oil price movements. Now, the minimal sensitivity over the planning period is maximized, or equivalently, the maximal negative sensitivity is minimized:

$$SensOil^- \leqslant SensOil_t \qquad \text{for } t = 0, \ldots 9; \tag{12}$$

We assumed that wage rate changes are always negatively correlated with the net cash flow in the firm: wage rate increases invariably reduce the net cash flow. Therefore, we could suffice with a mini-max approach for the handling of negative wage rate exposures. For illustrational purposes, another method of summarizing the risk associated with wage rate movements was chosen. The average sensitivity for wage rate movements over the ten year planning period constitutes the fifth goal variable, which is to be minimized:

$$WageSens_t = \sum_{j=0}^{20} x_j \cdot WageSens_{jt} \qquad \text{for } t = 0, \ldots, 9; \tag{13}$$

$$\overline{WageSens} = \sum_{t=0}^{9} \frac{1}{10} \cdot WageSens_t; \tag{14}$$

Thus far, two operational risk factors affecting the firm's net cash flow before interest payments were considered. As an example of a financial risk factor the interest rate over the outstanding debt was chosen.. In each year the sensitivity of the cash flow to equity for unexpected changes in the debt rate is simply the amount of one-period loans:

$$SensInt_t = 0.01 \cdot L_t \qquad \text{for } t = 0, \ldots 8; \tag{15}$$

Thus, $SensInt_t$ gives the absolute change in the cash flow to equity for a percentage point change in the interest rate due over the outstanding debt. Interest sensitivity is always positive in our model as we abstracted from the possibility of lending funds. The last goal variable is the average interest sensitivity over the planning period, *SensInt*, which is to be minimized:

$$\overline{SensInt} = \sum_{t=0}^{8} \frac{1}{9} \cdot SensInt_t; \tag{16}$$

4.4. Selection of a Financial Plan

As mentioned earlier, Interactive Multiple Goal Programming (IMGP) is used here to obtain the combination of investment projects, bond issues, annual loans and dividends which best contributes to the firm's objectives. Basically, objectives are modeled as goal constraints in IMGP. By manipulating the goal constraints, the decision maker can systematically condition the set of possible values for the instrument variables. The manipulation of goal constraints takes place in a series of iterations in each of which the decision maker is confronted with a so-called potency matrix. In this matrix, for each goal variable a feasible range is presented defined by an «ideal» and «pessimistic» value. The ideal value for the goal variable in question is the optimum for that individual variable taking the pessimistic values for the other goal variables as constraints to the optimization. The pessimistic values are provided by the decision maker and represent minimally [6] required values. By successively raising these pessimistic values, the decision maker can reach a final solution, or set of solutions, – this depends on the extent to which he conditions the solution space. In each iteration, the decision maker can assess the consequence of a proposed improvement of a certain pessimistic value in terms of reduced ideal values for the remaining goal variables in the next potency matrix. If the costs of the improvement are too high according to the decision maker, the improvement can be reverted. Thus, the trade-offs between various goal variables are revealed. For the case at hand, the first potency matrix is given in table 4 in the column under iteration number 1. The range over which a final solution may be chosen is quite large for some of the goal variables. This holds especially for the number of dismissals and the maximum sensitivity for changes in the oil prices. If desired, the decision maker could even reduce the maximum oil sensitivity to such an extent that it would be negative in each future period. Some other results are shown in table 3 which gives the set of investment projects selected when each of the goal variables is optimized independently to its ideal value in the potency matrix. The table shows that the available projects differ substantially in terms of their contributions to the optimization of the goal variables. For different goal variables, different projects are selected.

The bonds issued and the amount of loans attracted annually for the ideal values in the first potency matrix are summarized in tables 5 and 6. Here, it can be seen that the bond issues are relatively unattractive for the realization of high dividends for financing with one-period loans the reverse argument holds. Starting from the first potency matrix in table 4, we have successively raised

[6] For goal variables to be minimized, the pessimistic values of course represent maximum acceptable values.

Table 3. Investment projects selected when different goal variables are optimized.

	Goal Variable					
Project	Pv-Div	Dismiss.	SensOil-	SensOil+	SensWage	SensInt
0	1	1	1	1	1	1
1	1			1	1	
2	1			1		
3				1		
4				1		
5		0.625	1			
6	1		1		0.05	
7	1	1				0.07
8	1			1	1	
9			1			0.36
10	1	1	1		1	
11	1					
12	1		0.48		1	
13	1			1	0.79	1
14	1		1		0.38	
15		1		0.36		
16	1			1	1	
17	1		0.88		1	0.19
18	1	1		1		0.22
19		1	1		0.45	
20	1			1	1	

Table 4. Some Potency matrices.

		Iteration Number				
Goal Variable	Value	1	2	3		20
Pv-Div	Ideal	3,555.493	3,548.070	3,509.402		3,375.081
	Pessimistic	3,163.327	3,163.327	3,163.327		3,375.000
Dismissals	Ideal	0.000	0.000	0.000		27.897
	Pessimistic	245.000	245.000	*245.000*		28.000
SensOil-	Ideal	-8.000	-8.000	-10.777		-34.975
	Pessimistic	*-143.800*	-50.000	-50.000		-35.000
SensOil+	Ideal	-109.800	-20.000	-20.000		0.085
	Pessimistic	47.000	47.000	47.000		1.000
SensWage	Ideal	1.542	1.542	1.542		17.271
	Pessimistic	75.500	75.500	75.500		17.500
SensInt	Ideal	0.000	0.000	0.000		1.744
	Pessimistic	13.490	*13.490*	5.000		1.750

the pessimistic values for various goal variables. The first lower bound to be raised was the minimal value of the oil sensitivity. The minimal, i.e. the maximum negative, oil sensitivity was reduced from \$ 143,800 to \$ 50,000 for a ten percent change in the oil price. This improvement came at the cost of a lower ideal present value of dividends and a higher maximum sensitivity for oil price changes.

Table 5. Bond issues when different goal variables are optimized.

	Goal Variable					
Period	Pv-Div	Dismiss.	SensOil-	SensOil+	SensWage	SensInt
0		0.03	1	0.53	1	0.19
1		1	1	1	0.86	
2		1	0.86	1	1	0.01
3		1	1	1	0.55	

Table 6. One-period loans attracted when different goal variables are optimized.

	Goal Variable					
Period	Pv-Div	Dismiss.	SensOil-	SensOil+	SensWage	SensInt
0	683			60		
1	752	121	93	21	23	
2	615	18	72	12		
3	3068	39	2520	137	29	
4	2663		2183	67		
5	2278	93	1839	125	10	
6	1773	295	1532	268	215	
7	1130	40	893		10	
8	525	245	782	263	215	

Table 7. Final solution: Some Instrument Values.

Period	Loans	Dividends
0	116	393
1	188	432
2	0	443
3	602	399
4	409	439
5	269	483
6	159	531
7	7	584
8	0	642
9	0	622

Projects	
0	1
1	
2	
3	
4	
5	
6	0.27
7	1
8	
9	
10	1
11	
12	
13	
14	1
15	
16	0.53
17	0.24
18	1
19	0.53
20	

This implies that the range in which the oil sensitivity for each period in the ideal solution would be, was shifted upward. Then, the interest sensitivity was lowered, which caused a further reduction of the present value of the dividend stream and a deterioration of the ideal minimum oil sensitivity. In the following iterations, the minimal levels for the wage rate sensitivity, the present value of the dividends and the number of dismissals were set. In the final iterations, these values were further improved until a set of solutions was obtained which were only marginally different. The «tightening» of the range between pessimistic and ideal solutions for the goal variables is graphically shown for the first

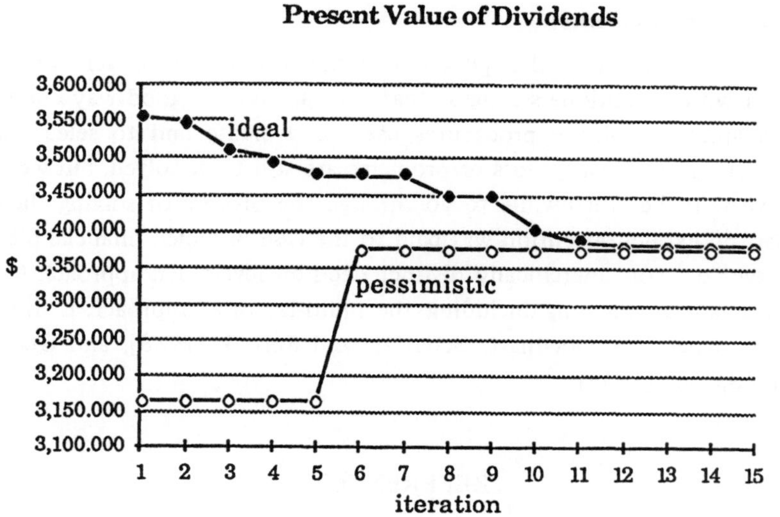

Figure 2. Ideal and pessimistic values for the Present Value of the Dividend stream.

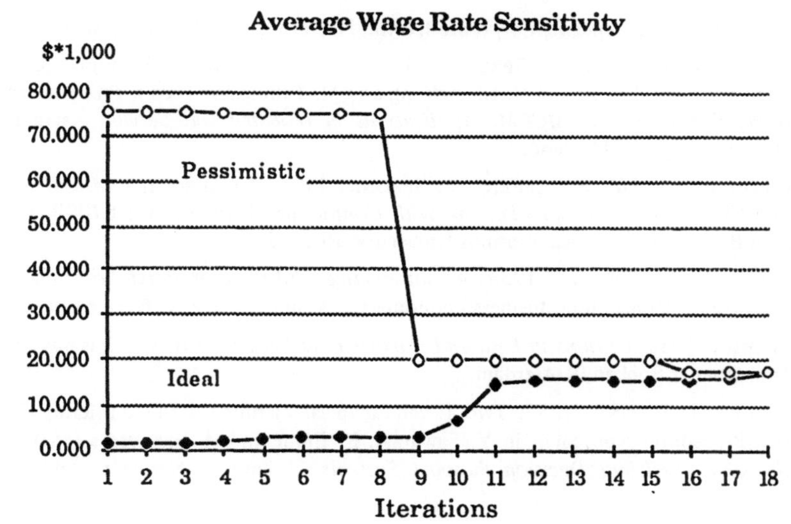

Figure 3. Ideal and pessimistic values for the Interest Sensitivity.

and the sixth goal variable in figure 2 and 3. The final solution is given in table 7 below.

5. Conclusion and Remarks

Although thus far, no real application of the proposed approach was made, discussions with practitioners suggest that «we are on the good way» and have lead to adaptations of the procedures used to evaluate and to select capital investment projects. Clearly, lots of problems are still to be solved, but we strongly believe it to be worthwhile to go through the process of solving them. In this paper, no explicit attention was paid to the case in which financial planning involves two or more hierchically distinct decision levels. An approach to such two-level financial planning including the multi-factorial approach is discussed in another paper (see Goedhart, Schaffers and Spronk [1988], and Goedhart, Peters and Spronk [1989]).

REFERENCES

C.J. CASEY, N.J. BARTCZAK, 1984, Cash Flow - it's not the Bottom Line, *Harvard Business Review,* August-July.

A.I. DIEPENHORST, 1962, *Beschouwingen over de optimale financiële stuctuur van de onderneming,* inaugurale rede, Bohn, Haarlem, (in Dutch).

G. DONALDSON, 1969, *Strategy for Financial Mobility,* Harvard University Press, Boston.

G. DONALDSON, 1984, *Managing Corporate Wealth,* Harvard University Press, Boston.

M.H. GOEDHART, J. PETERS, J. SPRONK, 1989, Two-Level Financial Planning: An Interactive Coordination Mechanism, in V. Changkong and M. Tabucanon (eds.): *Proceedings of the International Conference on MCDM: Applications in Industry and Service.* Asian Institute of Technology, Bangkok, Thailand.

M.H. GOEDHART, J.W.M. SCHAFFERS, J. SPRONK, 1988. *An Interactive Multi-Factor Procedure for Two-Level Financial Planning with Conflicting Goals,* Report 8708/F, Centre of Research in Business Economics, Erasmus University, Rotterdam.

W. HALLERBACH, J SPRONK, 1986, *An Interactive Multi-Factor Portfolio Model,* Report 8610/F, Centre for Research in Business Economics, Erasmus University, Rotterdam.

A.G.Z. KEMNA, 1988, *Options in Real and Financial Markets,* PhD thesis, Erasmus University Rotterdam, Donner Boeken, Rotterdam.

J SCHAFFERS, J. SPRONK, 1987, Two Level Financial Planning with Conflicting Goals, An Interactive Procedural Approach, in Y. Sawaragi, K. Ihoue and H. Nakayama (eds), *Towards Interactive and Intelligent Decision Support Systems,* Volume 1, Springer, Heidelberg, pp. 270-279.

J. SPRONK, 1981, *Interactive Multiple Goal Programming: Applications to Financial Planning,* Martinus Nijhoff, Boston.

J. SPRONK, 1985, Financial Planning with Conflicting Objectives, in G. Fandel and J. Spronk (eds.), *Multiple Criteria Decision Methods and Applications,* Springer, Berlin, pp. 269-288.

J. SPRONK, 1989, Multi-Factorial Financial Planning, in: Lockett, A.G. and G. Islei (eds.), *Improving Decision Making in Organisations,* Springer, Heidelberg.

A SURVEY AND ANALYSIS OF THE APPLICATION OF THE LAPLACE TRANSFORM TO PRESENT VALUE PROBLEMS

ROBERT W. GRUBBSTRÖM
Linköping Institute of Technology
Department of Production Economics
S - 58183 Linköping, Sweden

JIANG YINZHONG
Beijing Institute of Light Industry
Department of Management
100037 Beijing, P.R. of China

This article provides an overview of the current position with regard to the application of the Laplace transform to Present Value problems. The limitations of the use of the Laplace transform are discussed and some ideas for future possible research are presented.

1. Introduction

The method of the Laplace transform has been in widespread use as a valuable tool to deal with problems concerning linear systems involving integro-differential equations with constant coefficients, ordinary, partial and difference equations, etc. ever since P.S. Laplace first proposed this technique in about 1820. In the area of economics and management, the Laplace transform has been applied to the evaluation of payments [1-12, 16-20], to reliability and maintenance strategies [40-45], to utility function analysis [46], to the choice of investments [55, 56], to assembly line and queueing system problems [57, 62-64], to the theory of system and element behaviour [48], to the investigation of the dispatching aspect of job-shop scheduling [61], for assessing econometric models [47], and to many other areas. Also, to some extent, the transform has been used to study dynamical economic systems, such as inventory (and work-in-progress) processes [49-51, 57-60]. The purpose of this paper is mainly to review and discuss the application of the Laplace transform to Present Value problems. Our interest in the Laplace transform is quite practical and we wish to encourage the application of the Laplace transform to solve a wider range of problems concerning economic and managerial issues. In a separate paper [68] we have presented the use of the related z-transform method.

The definition of the Laplace transform is as follows. Let $f(t)$ be a continuous real function defined for all $t \geq 0$. The function $\mathcal{L}\{f(t)\}$, given by the expression

$$\mathcal{L}\{f(t)\} = \int_0^\infty e^{-st} f(t) \mathrm{d}t = F(s) \tag{1}$$

is defined as the Laplace transform of $f(t)$. Traditionally the function is written either $\mathcal{L}\{f(t)\}$, to show its dependence on the function $f(t)$, or as $F(s)$, indicating that it is a function of the complex variable $s = \beta + i\omega$ where β is a real part and i the imaginary unit $\sqrt{-1}$. The original function $f(t)$ is called the inverse transform of $F(s)$. There is a unique, one-to-one relationship between $f(t)$ and $F(s)$.

In the following sections, a survey of the application of the Laplace transform to present value problems will be given firstly. Then we shall discuss and explain reasons for the limitations of the use of the Laplace transform in some aspects. Finally, we provide three explicit examples of its applications and present some ideas for future possible research.

2. Survey

One of the recurring problems in the economic analysis of engineering projects, finance, capital planning or investment is to find the present value (present worth) of a given cash flow $C(t)$ for a given rate of discount r . The concept of the present value of a cash flow allows the monetary transactions with different amounts and timing to be compared in equivalent cash units. The ultimate in present value analysis is perhaps the concept of a continuous cash flow with continuous compounding. In this case, the present value can be solved by several techniques. One of the very elegant methods is using the Laplace transform which can map a cash flow function which is continuous or discrete in the time domain to a present value function continuous in the interest rate domain. The present value integral, $V(r)$, is identified as the Laplace transform of the cash flow $C(t)$, that is

$$V(r) = \int_0^\infty e^{-rt} C(t) \mathrm{d}t = [\mathcal{L}\{C(t)\}]_{s=r} \tag{2}$$

This idea was first put forward by Grubbström [1] who also suggested the application of Laplace transforms to stochastic as well as to deterministic economic processes, a forerunner to this article being [2]. In 1986, 19 years later, Buser set forth a similar idea in a short note in the *Journal of Finance* [25]. Two early applications of the Laplace transform to financial problems are reported by Pistoia in 1960 [26] and by Levi in 1961 [27]. These treatments do not identify the Laplace transform and the Net Present Value Function; instead the transform is used in a traditional manner for solving a capital accumulation integral equation where interest is added to capital after a constant time lag.

Following the work in [1], many scientists have made contributions to the solution of present value problems. Buck and Hill [3, 4] used the Laplace transform techniques for developing the present value formulae for a few continuously discounted deterministic cash flows which occur as impulses at certain known points in time or are continuous functions of time. Beenhakker [18] recommended the use of the Laplace transform to compute present values of time functions considered for time profiles of investment outlays and production outputs while giving a sensitivity analysis of the present value of a project. Beenhakker also presented pairs of some truncated functions and present value transforms in the case of a continuous stream of payments in [18].

In a deterministic present value analysis, all the parameters in the cash flow functions are non-probabilistic. In practice, however, uncertainties may exist on the function parameters designating the time of occurrence or the amount of the cash flow. Then it is often needed a present value risk analysis which may be performed using some statistics, such as expected value, variance, skewness, kurtosis, etc., of the present value probability distribution function. Reisman and Rao [5] exploited the Laplace transform properties and obtained the expected value of a sequence of revenues, discounted continuously with respect to time by means of $E\{e^{-rt}\}$ which is the Laplace transform of the probability density function of the stochastic time interval t. An example applying this result to a cash flow associated with a tandem queueing system interpreted as a production line is given in Section 4 below. Rosenthal [6], using Laplace transforms, extended the work of Young and Contreras [12] to obtain expressions for the variance of the present value of a lump sum impulse cash flow at an uncertain time and uniform continuous cash flows of uncertain duration. Since the distribution can be described by its mean and variance, and the mean and variance can be obtained by Laplace transforms after knowing the functional form of the cash flows, Zinn et al. [7], in view of the Central Limit Theorem, put forth a probabilistic approach to determine the probability distribution (defined by its mean and variance) of the net present value of an investment alternative having probabilistic initial investment, net return, economic life and salvage value.

Based on a decomposition of the Laplace transform method and theorems on products and sums of moments for independent random variables, Tanchoco et al. [8] extended the work of Young et al. [12], Rosenthal [6] and Zinn et al. [7] to nonuniform cash flows and higher moments of present value. Knowing the continuous cash flow function and continuous discounting rate, the present value is first obtained by using Laplace transforms, which is then decomposed into a few standard forms. The derivation of the statistics of these standard forms is performed on the assumption that the coefficients (or parameters) of alternative cash-flow time series are independent random variables with known probability density functions. Finally, the statistics of present value are obtained by recombining the statistics of the individual standard forms. This methodology lays the general mathematical structure and closed-form solutions to present value risk analysis. Moreover, Grubbström [19] used the concept of the double-sided Laplace transform to develop an expression for the expected present value and its variance for a payment stream given in nominal payments where the payments are affected by a stochastic inflation rate.

The computation of the moments is useful since an approximation of a probability density function in general requires the knowledge of its moments. It is clear, however, that a finite set of moments does not necessarily specify a unique probability density function from which the moments arose [11, 13] even though some theorems are available which establish sufficient conditions for the uniqueness of the distribution when all of its moments are known [14]. So a precise analytic determination of the probability density function of the net present value, in some sense, is preferable. Using the Laplace transform method, Perrakis and Henin [9] provided a computational technique for the evaluation of the distribution of the net present value of an investment. Assuming that the initial cash outlay be deterministic, the magnitudes of the cash inflows be nonnegative random variables with known distributions, and the lengths of the intervals between successive cash inflows be independently distributed and independent of the magnitude of these inflows, the final results are presented in the form of Laplace transforms of probability densities, and these transforms can directly yield all moments of the distributions. For the distribution of the present value, let

$$W_n = \sum_{k=1}^{n} X_k e^{-rt_k} = \sum_{k=1}^{n} X_k e^{-r\sum_{l=1}^{k}\tau_l} \tag{3}$$
$$\tau_i = t_i - t_{i-1} \quad (i = 1, 2 \ldots, n;\ t_0 = 0)$$

If considering it as a stochastic process, the following outcome can be obtained from the Laplace transform techniques

$$\begin{aligned} \bar{b}_1(s) &= \bar{b}(s), \\ \bar{b}_{i+1}(s) &= \bar{b}(s) \int_0^{\infty} g(t)\bar{b}_i(se^{-rt})\mathrm{d}t, \quad i = 1, \ldots, n-1 \end{aligned} \tag{4}$$

$$\bar{\omega}_n(s) = \int_0^{\infty} \bar{b}_n(se^{-rt})g(t)\mathrm{d}t \tag{5}$$

where upper cases denote distributions, lower cases densities and bars the corresponding Laplace transforms. Here $g(t)$ is the probability density function of the random variable τ_i, $B_i(x)$ $(i = \overline{1, n})$ is the distribution of the inflow $X_i's$ and $b_i(x)$ is the associated density. $\bar{\omega}_n(s)$ is the Laplace transform of the distribution of W_n, the present value of independent cash inflows. The moments of the distribution can be obtained by expanding the transform into a Taylor series. In [9] it is assumed that the project terminates after a predetermined number n of cash flows. Perrakis and Sahin [10] relaxed this assumption and substituted instead of n a fixed planning horizon T. Based on the similar conditions mentioned in [9], all the distributions can still be given in the forms of the

Laplace transforms of their densities and all moments of the distributions may be derived directly by repeated differentiation of the transforms. Barnes et al. [11] also employed Laplace transforms while applying integral transform theory to obtain analytically the probability density function of the present value of independently and identically distributed cash flows. Suppose the returns $R_n (n = \overline{1, N})$, restricted to non-negativity, to be independent random variables governed by probability density functions $f_n(R_n)$ of arbitrary form. We then have

$$\mathcal{L}_t\{f_n(R_n)\} = \int_0^\infty f_n(R_n) e^{-tR_n} \mathrm{d} R_n$$

$$\mathcal{L}_t\{h(\rho_n R_n)\} = \mathcal{L}_{\rho_n t}\{f_n(R_n)\}$$

$$\mathcal{L}_t\{g(Q)\} = \prod_{n=1}^{N} \mathcal{L}_{\rho_n t}\{f_n(R_n)\}, \text{for fixed } N \tag{6}$$

$$E[Q^k] = (-1)^k \frac{\partial^k \left[\prod_{n=1}^{N} \mathcal{L}_{\rho_n t}\{f_n(R_n)\}\right]}{\partial t^k}\Bigg|_{t=0}$$

$$g(Q) = \lim_{T\to\infty} \frac{1}{2\pi i} \int_{\beta - iT}^{\beta + iT} e^{tx} \mathcal{L}_t\{g(Q)\} \mathrm{d} t$$

where

$\rho_n = (1 + r)^{-n}$ (here r is the corresponding discrete discount rate);

$y_n = \rho_n R_n$ and $h(y) = \frac{1}{\rho_n} f_n\left(\frac{y}{\rho_n}\right)$ which is the probability density function associated with y,

$Q = \sum_{n=1}^{N} \rho_n R_n$ with associated density function $g(Q)$,

t is the parameter of the transform space.

Recognizing that the sum of independent random variables in the time domain corresponds to the product of their transforms, Barnes et al. obtained the transform of the probability density function of the random cash flows in the transform domain.

Apart from the applications mentioned above, the Laplace transform method appears especially well-suited to the discounting of periodic cash flows, i.e. cash flows which occur repeatedly each and every period over a given planning horizon [16]. Consider a periodic sequence of cash flows, a cash flow function $f(x, t)$ where x and t are scale and time variables respectively, Gurnani [17] presented a methodology, based on Laplace transforms, to formulate a closed form expression for the present value of periodic cash flows. For continuous cash flows, the present value is

$$PV_T\{f(x,t)\} = \frac{1 - e^{-rT}}{1 - e^{-r\tau}} \int_0^\tau e^{-rt} f_1(x,t) \mathrm{d} t \tag{7}$$

where T is the length of a planning horizon, τ is the time interval during which the cash flow function completes one cycle, r is the nominal annual compounding rate and $f_1(x,t)$ is defined as the function representing the first period of $f(x,t)$. Based upon Eq. (7), Fleischer [16] assessed the relative efficacy of the transform method for discounting periodic cash flows by means of comparisons of the transform method and a conventional enumeration method by using computer simulation. In Section 4 we apply the Laplace transform technique to periodic cash flows associated with the *MAPI* method for equipment replacement problems.

Finally, we wish to point out that the Laplace transform of the cash flow time function is particularly useful when the cash flow profiles may be described by linear differential equations in time. Examples are given in [2, 51, 52, 58] and in Section 4 below. This technique provides us with the possibility to solve for the NPV algebraically without having to solve the differential equations in the first place.

In the example of [52], the cash flow profile is considered as the result of two competing mechanisms, the positive cash flow from production gains competing against the negative cash flow from investment expenditures. Assuming the rate of expenditure, C_i, to be proportional to the difference between the final and actual investment, we have

$$C_i = \frac{dI}{dt} = K_i(I_\infty - I), t \geq 0 \tag{8}$$

where K_i is a constant. The cash flow from production and sales accrues after its start-up at a later stage and it is assumed that the rate of change of this cash flow is proportional to the difference between the final and actual cash flow rate,

$$\frac{dC_p}{dt} = K_p(C_\infty - C_p), t \geq T_0 \geq 0 \tag{9}$$

where K_p also is a constant. The net cash flow rate C_n covering the investment profile as well as the production profile may then be approximated by the simple difference

$$C_n = C_p - C_i \tag{10}$$

Note that the two terms in Eq. (10) are modelled by ordinary linear differential equations, and the net present value, $NPV(r)$, can then be easily computed by the Laplace transform of the equations on the assumption that the project lifetime be infinite,

$$NPV(r) = \frac{K_p C_\infty e^{-rT_0}}{r(r+K_p)} - \frac{K_i I_\infty}{r+K_i} \tag{11}$$

3. Analysis

In the foregoing we have reviewed the application of the Laplace transform to the problems of present value analysis. However, recalling from the survey we made, it appears that there exist some restrictions which limit the applicability of the Laplace transform in the area of economics and management. In this section, we shall attempt to discuss and explain reasons (at least partially) for the limitations of the use of the Laplace transform, mainly from the existence of the Laplace transform, integrability, the transform inversion and nonlinear problems.

Existence

Before using the Laplace transform, we must pay careful attention to the question that the integral of Eq. (1), in fact, does exist because it is of no significance if the Laplace transform of a function $f(t)$ does not exist. To do this, it is necessary to know the criteria which can be used to examine the existence of the Laplace transform.

We now introduce a class of functions which is referred to as class $\mathcal{A}$ for which the Laplace transform exists. A function $f(t)$ is said to belong to class $\mathcal{A}$, namely $f(t)\epsilon\mathcal{A}$ if $f(t)$ is of some exponential order as $t \to \infty$ and is piecewise continuous over every finite interval of $t \geq 0$. When $f(t)\epsilon\mathcal{A}$, $\mathcal{L}\{f(t)\}$ exists, provided s is large enough [53]. The condition that $f(t)\epsilon\mathcal{A}$ is sufficient to ensure the existence of the Laplace transform. Furthermore, a general condition of the existence of the Laplace transform can also be given by the following statement [15]. If $f(t)$ is continuous and satisfies a bound of the form,

$$|f(t)| \leq Me^{\alpha t} \tag{12}$$

for some constants α and M as $t \to \infty$ and if

$$\int_0^T |f(t)|\mathrm{d}t < \infty \tag{13}$$

for every finite T, then the integral (1) exists and converges absolutely and uniformly for $Re(s) > \alpha$. The above conditions for the existence of the transform of a function are elementary and practical for most of our applications. Obviously, according to these conditions, for instance functions which contain $e^{t^k}(k > 1)$ cannot be used as functions depicting the characterization of cash flows if we want to use the Laplace transform to solve present value problems, because these functions are not of exponential order, or in other words, they can grow more rapidly than $Me^{\alpha t}$ as $t \to \infty$. Especially, the nominal annual cost-of-capital r in the present value analysis is chosen as a positive real number. The conditions for the existence of the integral in Eq. (2) might become more strict since it is possible that the functions concerning $e^{\alpha t}(\alpha \geq 0)$ will not satisfy $|f(t)| \leq Me^{rt}$ when $\alpha \geq r$. For instance, the Laplace transform of the function

$$f(t) = cte^{\alpha t} \quad (c \text{ is a constant}) \tag{14}$$

does only exist for $\alpha < r$. As a result, the conditions for the existence, in particular, the convergence of the Laplace transform restricts its use to a certain class of cash flow functions.

Integrability

Integrability here contains two meanings. One is whether the simple decomposition of the functions, such as cash flow functions, can be obtained. Another is whether the integrand, $f(t)e^{-st}$ or $C(t)e^{-rt}$, can be integrated analytically.

Tables of special Laplace transforms have been available for a long time. The calculation will become easy if we can decompose complex functions into simple ones, the Laplace transforms of which can be found in the tables. In most cases, however, it is impossible directly to make use of the Laplace transform tables for very complex functions. We have to integrate to solve the problem. But it is sometimes difficult to take the integral of more complex functions and even the integrand cannot be integrated analytically, such as the Weibull function

$$f(t) = \frac{\beta}{\eta}\left[\frac{t-T_s}{\eta}\right]^{\beta-1} e^{-\left[\frac{t-T_s}{\eta}\right]^{\beta}} \tag{15}$$

although the Laplace transforms for these complex functions may exist. It is obvious that the difficulties resulting from the integration, to some degree, can restrict the use of Laplace transforms. The non-integrable functions usually can be evaluated numerically. Nevertheless, expressions for the nonintegrable models will not be found in a closed form. In [54] are shown a number of present value expressions of cash flows including both integrable and nonintegrable models. In Table 1 we list the Laplace transform pairs of a few nonintegrable functions which may be considered for time profiles of cash flows. In this table, $Ei(x)$ is the exponential integral function represented by

$$Ei(x) = \int_{-\infty}^{x} \frac{e^{t}}{t}\mathrm{d}t = -\int_{-x}^{\infty} \frac{e^{-t}}{t}\mathrm{d}t \quad (x > 0) \tag{16}$$

and $\mathrm{erf}(z)$ is the error function given by

$$\mathrm{erf}(z) = \frac{2}{\sqrt{\pi}}\int_0^{z} e^{-t^2}\mathrm{d}t = 1 - \mathrm{erfc}(z) \tag{17}$$

Note that the error function has the following relation to the normal probability function $\varphi(t)$

$$\int_0^{x} \varphi(t)\mathrm{d}t = \frac{1}{2}\mathrm{erf}\left(\frac{x}{\sqrt{2}}\right) \tag{18}$$

Therefore the value of $\mathrm{erf}(z)$ can be evaluated by using the normal probability function table.

Table 1. Laplace Transform pairs.

Model	Present Value	
Reciprocal	$-e^{ar}Ei(-ar)$	$n=1$
	$1/a + re^{ar}Ei(-ar)$	$n=2$
$\dfrac{1}{(t+a)^n}$	$a^{1-n}e^{ar}En(ar)$	$n \geq 3$
$(a>0; n=0,1,2,\ldots)$	$En(x) = \int_1^{\infty} \dfrac{e^{-xt}}{t^n} dt$	
Logarithmic		
$\ln(t+1)$	$-\dfrac{e^r}{r}Ei(-r)$	
Rayleigh distribution		
$\dfrac{t}{\alpha^2}e^{\frac{-1}{2}(\frac{t}{\alpha})^2}$	$1-\sqrt{\dfrac{\pi}{2}}r\alpha e^{\frac{1}{2}(\alpha r)^2}\,\mathrm{erfc}\left(\dfrac{\alpha r}{\sqrt{2}}\right)$	
Normal distribution		
$\dfrac{1}{\sigma\sqrt{2\pi}}e^{-\frac{(t-\mu)^2}{2\sigma^2}}$	$\dfrac{1}{2}\exp\left\{\dfrac{(r\sigma)^2-2r\mu}{2}\right\}\mathrm{erfc}\left\{\dfrac{r\sigma^2-\mu}{\sigma\sqrt{2}}\right\}$	
$(\mu \gg \sigma)$		
Truncated Normal distribution		
$\dfrac{1}{K\sigma\sqrt{2\pi}}\exp\left\{-\dfrac{(t-\mu)^2}{2\sigma^2}\right\}$	$\dfrac{\exp\left\{\dfrac{(r\sigma)^2-2r\mu}{2}\right\}}{1+\mathrm{erf}\left(\dfrac{\mu}{\sigma\sqrt{2}}\right)}\mathrm{erfc}\left\{\dfrac{r\sigma^2-\mu}{\sigma\sqrt{2}}\right\}$	
$K=\int_{-\infty}^{\frac{\mu}{\sigma}}\dfrac{1}{\sqrt{2\pi}}e^{\frac{-1}{2}t^2}dt$		

$Ei(x)$ is given by Eq. (16) and $\mathrm{erf}(x)$ by Eq. (17).

Transform Inversion

The inversion of the Laplace transform appears to be of limited value to present value analysis since the integral of the present value is just the Laplace transform of the cash flow. However recall from the foregoing section that the distributions of the present value in risk analysis are sometimes given in the forms of Laplace transforms of probability densities, such as in [9-11]. For analytical expressions of the distributions, the transforms need to be inverted into the real domain. Similar problems may arise regarding other aspects of economics and management. Starting with $F(s)$, the inverse transform $f(t)$ is given by the established inversion formula

$$f(t) = \lim_{T\to\infty}\frac{1}{2\pi i}\int_{\beta-iT}^{\beta+iT} e^{st}F(s)\,ds \tag{19}$$

or alternatively

$$f(t) = \frac{e^{\beta t}}{\pi} \int_0^{\infty} [\mathrm{Re}\{F(s)\}\cos(\omega t) - \mathrm{Im}\{F(s)\}\sin(\omega t)]\,\mathrm{d}\omega \tag{20}$$

where $s = \beta + i\omega$ and where β can be any real number greater than α, and

$$\begin{aligned} \mathrm{Re}\{F(s)\} &= \int_0^{\infty} e^{-\beta t} f(t)\cos(\omega t)\,\mathrm{d}t \\ \mathrm{Im}\{F(s)\} &= -\int_0^{\infty} e^{-\beta t} f(t)\sin(\omega t)\,\mathrm{d}t \end{aligned} \tag{21}$$

In the strict sense of the concept of uniqueness of functions, the inverse Laplace transform is not unique because there exist null functions $N(t)$ for which $\int_0^T N(t)\,\mathrm{d}t = 0$ for all positive T. However if we confine ourselves to functions $f(t)$ which are sectionally continuous in every finite interval $0 \leq t \leq N$ and of exponential order for $t > N$, a given function $F(s)$ cannot have more than one inverse transform $f(t)$ that is continuous for each positive t [21].

The transform inversion of a function of s can be carried out by using the function decomposition and the Laplace transform tables. It is usually true, however, that a given problem will not easily yield transforms in just the tabulated form, such as the probability density functions of present values given in the foregoing. Direct use of Eqs. (19) or (20) can be cumbersome. In such a case, the relatively efficacious approach may be the numerical inversion of the Laplace transforms by using computers. Some numerical inversion methods can be found in [22-24]. In practice, however, we often hope to obtain reasonable estimates of the principal characteristics for the system under consideration. But in the numerical approach it is difficult to study the structure of the solution or to examine explicit parametric relationships. Moreover the numerical round-off and cancellation errors limit the accuracy of the related results from time to time. No doubt, all of these possible drawbacks can exert some influence on the use of the Laplace transform.

Nonlinear Problems

A nonlinear problem is one which cannot be described by a linear mathematical model, such as a linear differential or difference equation. Many nonlinear problems may exist in the area of economics and management. In [28], for example, is given a model of management goal setting. The function of the firm is expressed by the following nonlinear differential equations including a sinusoidal interaction term with the environment,

$$\begin{cases} \dfrac{dy}{dt} = \omega \\ \dfrac{d\omega}{dt} = \dfrac{1}{M}\{-P_{\max}\sin(y + x_0) - D\omega + P_{\max}\sin(x_0)\} \end{cases} \tag{22}$$

where $y = x - x_0$ in which x is a quantity indicating the quality aspects of products. P_{max} is the maximum demand. $\sin(x)$ is a coefficient describing the success of the quality segmentation. $P_{max} \cdot \sin(x)$ is the volume of market demand the firm satisfies by existing business activities. $P_{max} \cdot \sin(x_0)$ is the planned and actual production volume or production goal. M and D are two constant coefficients describing the strength of the counteractive effects of the competitors in the market and the effectivity of marketing to dampen fluctuations respectively. Solutions for different values of y can be found with the help of certain methods, such as the second-order Runge-Kutta method. However, the ordinary Laplace transform defined in the foregoing section does not seem possible to use to deal with such nonlinear problems. Even in a simpler case, suppose that the relationship between the rate of expenditure and the investment described in Eq. (8) is a nonlinear, first-order differential equation, then the ordinary Laplace transform does not work either. Why?

The key to this question is because the ordinary Laplace transform is one of linear integral transformations which are represented by the equation

$$T\{f(t)\} = \int_a^b K(t, s) f(t) \mathrm{d} t \tag{23}$$

where $K(t, s)$ denotes a function of the variable t and a parameter s, and $f(t)$ is defined on a finite or infinite interval $a < t < b$. A transformation $T\{f(t)\}$ is linear if for every pair of functions $f_1(t)$ and $f_2(t)$ and for each pair of constants C_1 and C_2 it satisfies the following relation

$$T\{C_1 f_1(t) + C_2 f_2(t)\} = C_1 T\{f_1(t)\} + C_2 T\{f_2(t)\} \tag{24}$$

or in other words, the transform of a linear combination of two functions is the same linear combination of the transforms of the two functions if the transformation is linear. It seems obvious that such functions like $\{f(t)\}^n (n > 1)$ cannot satisfy this linear relationship. Furthermore, if we let $a = 0$ and $b = \infty$ and $K(t, s) = e^{-st}$, the transformation in Eq. (23) will become the Laplace transform. Under certain conditions, this linear integral transformation can guarantee a one-to-one correspondence between a time function and its Laplace transform. In addition, we can also explain the question from another aspect. According to the theorem of the Fourier integral, the Fourier integral of a function $\varphi(t)$, which satisfies the conditions of the theorem, can be expressed as follows,

$$\varphi(t) = \frac{1}{2\pi} \int_{-\infty}^{\infty} \int_{-\infty}^{\infty} \varphi(\tau) e^{-i\omega\tau} e^{i\omega t} \mathrm{d}\omega \mathrm{d}\tau \tag{25}$$

Let

$$G(\omega) = \int_{-\infty}^{\infty} \varphi(t) e^{-i\omega t} \mathrm{d} t \tag{26}$$

then

$$\varphi(t) = \frac{1}{2\pi}\int_{-\infty}^{\infty} G(\omega)e^{i\omega t}\mathrm{d}\omega \tag{27}$$

It should be noted that the relation between $\varphi(t)$ and $G(\omega)$ is reciprocal, that is, $G(\omega)$ can be represented by $\varphi(t)$, not $\{\varphi(t)\}^n$ ($n > 1$) or any other forms, and $\varphi(t)$ can also be expressed by $G(\omega)$, not by other forms. Taking the Fourier transform to the function $\varphi(t)u(t)e^{-\beta t}$ ($\beta > 0$) where $u(t)$ is the unit step function defined as

$$u(t) = \begin{cases} 0 & t < 0 \\ 1 & t \geq 0 \end{cases} \tag{28}$$

then

$$G_\beta(\omega) = \int_{-\infty}^{\infty} \varphi(t)u(t)e^{-\beta t}e^{-i\omega t}\mathrm{d}t = \int_0^{\infty} f(t)e^{-st}\mathrm{d}t \tag{29}$$

where $s = \beta + i\omega$ and $f(t) = \varphi(t)u(t)$. Further let

$$F(s) = G_\beta\left(\frac{s-\beta}{i}\right) \tag{30}$$

Then we obtain

$$F(s) = \int_0^{\infty} f(t)e^{-st}\mathrm{d}t \tag{31}$$

which is just the Laplace transform of the function $f(t)$. Note that the conditions which the Laplace transform has to satisfy , obviously are similar to those of the Fourier transform. As a result, we can see that non-linearity conditions have limited the domain of the use of the ordinary Laplace transform.

Apart from the reasons given above, the application of the Laplace transform to economic analysis may also be faced with the following difficulties, as López Léautaud pointed out in [30]. One is that the objective of the decision-maker has not been duly clarified and the input/output behaviour of the "components" of the economic system are not thoroughly known with absolute certainty. The reason for this is that human behaviour has not been deterministically modelled and all "subcomponents" are human beings.

4. Three explicit examples

This section we devote to illustrating some highlights of the applications described in the foregoing. First we demonstrate the *periodic cash flow* application by taking the MAPI method as an example. Secondly, we choose an *uncertain cash flow* taken from an assembly line optimization model and show how properties of the distribution functions are captured. As a third example we demonstrate short-cuts made available when the cash flow associated with a production system is given by *linear differential equations.*

Periodic cash flows - the MAPI method

According to the MAPI method [69], the cash flow associated with a piece of equipment (a machine) is made up of a basic investment outpayment $-G$, a salvage value inpayment S at the end of its life time T, and a hypothetical linearly increasing outpayment stream capturing the obsolescence of this equipment as compared to technically and commercially more modern equipment becoming available on the market. The slope of the linear stream $-g$ is called the *inferiority gradient.* It is assumed that G, S and g are positive constants and that at the end of the life cycle of each machine it is replaced by a similar machine having the same parameters. The problem is to determine the optimal value of T which maximizes the net present value of the total sequence of cash flows from all machines. The corresponding hypothetical constant stream of outpayments yielding this maximum NPV is called the *adverse minimum.*

For an individual machine its cash flow discounted to its time of procurement is:

$$NPV_0 = -G + Se^{-rT} - \frac{g}{r^2}(1 - e^{-rT}) + \frac{gT}{r}e^{-rT} \tag{32}$$

Here Laplace transform theory has been made use of in several ways. The first two terms are Dirac impulses located at $t = 0$ and $t = T$. The third term is made up of a linear outflow $-gt$ starting at $t = 0$ and a linear inflow $g(t-T)$ starting at $t = T$ cancelling the linear increase of the former flow. The fourth term is a step function amounting to gT located at $t = T$. This term cancels the remainder of the two linear flows from $t = T$ and onwards.

The net present value of the entire sequence of machines NPV is the Laplace transform of a sequence of impulses, each of magnitude NPV_0 located at $t = 0, t = T, t = 2T, \ldots$:

$$NPV = NPV_0(1 + e^{-rT} + e^{-2rT} + \ldots) = \frac{NPV_0}{1 - e^{-rT}} \tag{33}$$

Inserting NPV_0 from Eq. (32) and differentiating with respect to T provides the optimization condition for the life cycle. An approximate solution may be shown to be $T = \sqrt{2(G-S)/g}$ having the adverse minimum $\sqrt{2g(G-S)} + r(G+S)/2$.

Uncertain cash flows - an assembly line model

We consider an assembly line modelled as a series of N one-server queueing stations in tandem similar to the one described in [57]. At each station the service time $T_k, k = 1,2,\ldots,N,$ is stochastic having an exponential distribution with the mean $1/\mu_k$. At the end of the line (after station N) an inpayment amounting to the product price p is obtained. At station k an outpayment c_k (a variable cost) is made for each product treated there. At the first station products (material) arrive at independent stochastic intervals having negatively exponential distributions with a common mean of

$1/\lambda$. The $M/M/1$ character of the first station ensures that the release intervals also will be exponentially distributed with the same mean and this follows straight through the entire system. Hence the mean time a product spends at station k will be $1/(\mu_k - \lambda)$.

The net present value of an individual product $l, l = 0, 1, 2, \ldots,$ will be made up of outpayments $c_1, c_2, \ldots, c_N$, and an inpayment p discounted to its arrival time at the first station:

$$NPV_l = pe^{-r\sum_{k=1}^{N}\tau_k} - \sum_{j=1}^{N} c_j e^{-r\sum_{k=1}^{j}\tau_k} \tag{34}$$

where τ_k is the stochastic time the product spends at station k. Under the assumptions of independence between the service times, the different τ_k will also be stochastically independent. The expected net present value of an infinite sequence of products will then be:

$$E(NPV) = \sum_{l=0}^{\infty} E(NPV_l) \cdot E(e^{-r\sum_{i=0}^{l} t_i}) = \sum_{l=0}^{\infty} E(NPV_l) \cdot \prod_{i=0}^{l} E(e^{-rt_i}) \tag{35}$$

where t_i is the stochastic inter-arrival time between products $i-1$ and i, applying the convention $t_0 = 0$. Using Laplace transform theory we have:

$$E(e^{-rt_i}) = [\mathcal{L}\{f_i\}]_{s=r} = \lambda/(\lambda + r) \tag{36}$$

where f_i is the probability density of t_i, i.e. $\lambda e^{-\lambda t_i}$. Also from Eq. (34) we take a typical term having a factor:

$$E(e^{-r\sum_{k=1}^{j}\tau_k}) = \prod_{k=1}^{j} E(e^{-r\tau_k}) = \prod_{k=1}^{j} [\mathcal{L}\{g_k\}]_{s=r} \tag{37}$$

where g_k is the probability density function of τ_k. For the $M/M/1$ system considered, the sum of the queueing and service times τ_k will have an exponential density $(\mu_k - \lambda) \cdot$ $\cdot e^{-(\mu_k - \lambda)\tau_k}$. Using Laplace transform methodology once again we have:

$$[\mathcal{L}\{g_k\}]_{s=r} = (\mu_k - \lambda)/(r + \mu_k - \lambda) \tag{38}$$

$$E(NPV_l) = p\prod_{k=1}^{N} \frac{\mu_k - \lambda}{r + \mu_k - \lambda} - \sum_{j=1}^{N} c_j \prod_{k=1}^{j} \frac{\mu_k - \lambda}{r + \mu_k - \lambda} \tag{39}$$

Since all products have equal $E(NPV_l)$, the expected net present value of an infinite sequence of products in Eq. (35) reduces to:

$$E(NPV) = E(NPV_l) \sum_{i=0}^{\infty} \left[\frac{\lambda}{\lambda + r} \right]^i = (1 + \lambda / r) E(NPV_l) \tag{40}$$

The mean service rate μ_k may be interpreted as the capacity of station k and the expected NPV from Eq. (40) can be balanced against the additional NPV of investment in capacity together with operating and maintenance expenses at each station by maximizing the composite $E(NPV)$ with respect to each μ_k. This also provides an evaluation principle for work-in-progress along the assembly line as well as a rule for allocating a mean overcapacity increasing as value is added to the products queueing to be processed.

Linear differential equations - production system behaviour

As a third example we choose a simple production-inventory system similar to those given in [2]. An additional related example of more complexity is treated in [58]. Our over-simplified example here is designed to illustrate the short-cut made available when the cash flow is modelled in terms of linear differential equations.

We consider a one-product production system in which the deviation of the production rate $P(t)$ from a reference level $\hat{P}$ is assumed proportional to the negative deviation of the current inventory level $L(t)$ from its reference level $\hat{L}$ after a delay T:

$$P(t + T) - \hat{P} = \alpha(\hat{L} - L(t)), \quad t \geq 0 \tag{41}$$

where α is a positive constant. The demand rate is exogenously given as $D(t)$. Since inventory is the time integral of the difference between production and demand, we have the two equations:

$$\begin{aligned} \mathcal{L}\{P\} - \hat{P}/s &= \alpha(\hat{L}/s - \mathcal{L}\{L\})e^{-sT} \\ s\mathcal{L}\{L\} - L(0) &= \mathcal{L}\{P\} - \mathcal{L}\{D\} \end{aligned} \tag{42}$$

where $L(0)$ is inventory at time $t = 0$. Assuming the revenue inpayment stream to be pD, the production outpayment stream to be cP, and the outpayment stream for inventory holding to be hL (apart from capital costs taken care of by the discounting), where $p, c,$ and h are positive constants, the Laplace transform of the relevant cash flow is:

$$\mathcal{L}\{C\} = p\mathcal{L}\{D\} - c\mathcal{L}\{P\} - h\mathcal{L}\{L\} \tag{43}$$

Solving for $\mathcal{L}\{P\}$ and $\mathcal{L}\{L\}$ in Eq. (42), we obtain the net present value as:

$$\begin{aligned} NPV = [&p\mathcal{L}\{D\} - \beta(\alpha c e^{-sT} - h) \cdot (\mathcal{L}\{D\} - L(0)) - \\ &- \beta(\hat{P} + \alpha \hat{L} e^{-sT}) \cdot (c + h/s)]_{s=r} \end{aligned} \tag{44}$$

where $\beta = 1/(s + \alpha e^{-sT})$ and r is the continuous interest rate.

We may note that the NPV expression here has been obtained by using algebraic rules of Laplace transform theory only, thereby avoiding the necessity to solve the original dynamical relationships.

5. Future possible research

Based on the above survey and analysis, some research that might be carried out in the future is suggested below. An interesting line to take would be to investigate the possibilities of extending the Laplace transform, a simple and powerful tool in linear system analysis, to the domain of nonlinear system analysis in the area of economics and management. The theory of linear systems has been developed over many years into a unified collection of results on the basis of the application of linear mathematics. In theory and practice, attention is increasingly being directed to nonlinear systems. Now analysts have been striving to use the Laplace transform for solving nonlinear problems of one kind or another. Some progress in this research area has been made [31-39, 65]. For example, an operational method, called multi-dimensional Laplace transform (MDLT), for solving a large class of nonlinear problems has been attempted by Lubbock and Bansal [35], Mullineux et al. [31], Koh [33] and Karmakar [38]. The basic idea in the use of MDLT is to express the transform of nonlinear terms in the dependent variable $f(t)(f(t) \equiv 0$ for $t < 0)$ in terms of the Laplace transform $F(s)$ of $f(t)$ according to (1). For terms, such as $\{f(t)\}^n$, this is achieved by introducing a set of artificial independent time variables $t_1, t_2, \ldots t_m (m \geq n)$ into the function such that

$$f(t) \equiv f(t_1, t_2, \ldots t_m), \text{ whenever } t = t_1 = t_2 = \ldots = t_m \tag{45}$$

The multi-dimensional Laplace transform of $f(t)$ is defined as

$$\begin{aligned} \mathcal{L}_m\{f(t)\} &= \int_0^\infty \cdots \int_0^\infty f(t_1, \ldots, t_m) e^{(-s_1 t_1 - \ldots - s_m t_m)} \mathrm{d}t_1 \ldots \mathrm{d}t_m = \\ &= F(s_1, \ldots, s_m) \end{aligned} \tag{46}$$

The inversion of MDLT is given by

$$\begin{aligned} &\mathcal{L}_m^{-1}\{F(s_1, \ldots, s_m)\} = \\ &= \frac{1}{(2\pi i)^m} \int_{l_1} \int_{l_m} F(s_1, \ldots, s_m) e^{(s_1 t_1 + \ldots + s_m t_m)} \mathrm{d}s_1 \ldots \mathrm{d}s_m \end{aligned} \tag{47}$$

with $t_1 = t_2 = \ldots = t_m = t$ and l_i being the infinite line

$$\mathrm{Re}(s_i) = C_i(\text{a positive constant}) > \mathrm{Re}\begin{bmatrix}\text{Poles of } F \text{ treated} \\ \text{as a function of } s_i\end{bmatrix}$$

A number of applications of MDLT to nonlinear systems have been made, mainly in the area of electrical and control engineering [35-39]. Moreover, Dasarathy [32] also obtained the exact solution of a class of nonlinear systems by introducing a modified form of the Laplace transform which he termed as the D-transform. However, since there are no universal mathematical methods for the solution of a variety of nonlinear problems, different methods of approach are often developed for different types of nonlinear systems, and each approach has its own limitations and drawbacks, the development of the related methods based on the Laplace transform and their applicability to nonlinear system analysis indeed face real difficulties. Whether the application of the Laplace transform can be extended to nonlinear systems in economics and management needs further research. Other possible work would include the investigation of the existing problems of the transform inversion in present value analysis, the survey of the application of the Laplace transform to equipment replacement analysis, etc..

6. Acknowledgements

The authors wish to thank Ms. Susanne Gavatin and Ms. Pia Jonsson for all their help in the preparation of this manuscript and to Professor Lorenzo Peccati, University of Turin, for pointing out some interesting early Italian references.

References

[1] GRUBBSTRÖM, R.W.,1967. On the application of the Laplace transform to certain economic problems. *Management Science*, **13** (7): 558-567

[2] GRUBBSTRÖM, R.W.,1966. *Värdering av information i feedbackslingan vid en lagerstyrd produktionsprocess*, Dept of Industrial Economics and Management, Royal Institute of Technology, Stockholm.

[3] BUCK, J.R., and HILL, T.W., 1971. Laplace transforms for the economic analysis of deterministic problems in engineering. *The Engineering Economist*, **16** (4): 247-263.

[4] BUCK, J.R., and HILL, T.W., 1975. Additions to the Laplace transform methodology for economic analysis. *The Engineering Economist*, **20** (3): 197-208.

[5] REISMAN, A. and RAO, A.K., 1973. *Discounted cash flow analysis: stochastic extensions.* Publication #1 , Engineering, Economy Division, AIIE, Atlanta, Georgia.

[6] ROSENTHAL, R.E., 1978. The variance of present worth of cash flows under uncertain timing. *The Engineering Economist*, **23** (3): 163-170.

[7] ZINN, C.D., W.G. LESSO and B. MOTAZED, 1977. A probabilistic approach to risk analysis in capital investment projects. *The Engineering Economist*, **22** (4): 239-260.

[8] TANCHOCO, JOSE M.A., J.R. BUCK and L.C. LEUNG, 1981. Modeling and discounting of continuous cash flows under risk. *Engineering Costs and Production Economics*, **5** (3): 205-216.

[9] PERRAKIS, S., and HENIN, C., 1974. The evaluation of risky investments with random timing of cash returns. *Management Science*, **21** (1): 79-86.

[10] PERRAKIS S., and SAHIN, I., 1976. On risky investments with random timing of cash returns and fixed planning horizon. *Management Science*, **22** (7): 799-809.

[11] BARNES, J.W. and ZINN, C.D. and ELDRED, B.S., 1978. A methodology for obtaining the probability density function of the present worth of probabilistic cash flow profiles. *AIIE Transactions*, **10** (3): 226-236.

[12] YOUNG, D. and CONTRERAS, L.E., 1975. Expected present worths of cash flows under uncertain timing. *The Engineering Economist*, **20** (4): 257-268.

[13] JOINER, B.L. and ROSENBLATT, J.R., 1971. Some properties of the range in samples from Tukey's symmetric Lambda distributions. *JASA*, **66**: 394-399.

[14] FELLER, W., 1966. *An introduction to probability theory and its applications.* Vol II, John Wiley & Sons, Inc., New York.

[15] BELLMAN, R.E. and ROTH, R.S., 1984. *The Laplace transform.* World Scientific Publishing Co Pte Ltd.

[16] FLEISCHER, G.A., 1981. Assessing the relative efficacy of the transform method for discounting periodic cash flows. 1981 *ASEE annual conference proceedings*, 71-74.

[17] GURNANI, C., 1982. Present worth analysis of deterministic periodic cash flows. *The Engineering Economist*, **27** (2): 101-126.

[18] BEENHAKKER, H.L., 1975. Sensitivity analysis of the present value of a project. *The Engineering Economist*, **20** (2): 123-149.

[19] GRUBBSTRÖM, R.W., 1979. *Mean and variance of the net present value of a payment stream after correction for a stationary stochastic inflation rate.* Working paper WP-71, Department of Production Economics. Linköping Institute of Technology, Sweden.

[20] ALMOND, B. and REMER, D.S., 1979. Models for present-worth analysis of selected industrial cash flow patterns. *Engineering and Process Economics*, **4**: 455-466.

[21] SPIEGEL, M.R., 1965. *Schaum's outline of theory and problems of Laplace transforms.* McGraw-Hill Inc., New York.

[22] MILLER, M.K. and GUY, W.T., 1966. Numerical inversion of the Laplace transform by use of Jacobi polynomials. *SIAM Journal on Numerical Analysis*, **3** (4): 624-635.

[23] CRUMP, K.S., 1976. Numerical inversion of Laplace transforms using a Fourier series approximation. *Journal of the Association for Computing Machinery*, **23** (1): 89-96.

[24] HOSONO, T., 1981. Numerical inversion of Laplace transform and some applications to wave optics. *Radio Science*, **16** (6): 1015-1019.

[25] BUSER, S.A., 1986. Laplace transforms as present value rules: A note. *The Journal of Finance*, Vol. XLI, No. 1: 243-247.

[26] PISTOIA, A., 1960. *Qualche considerazione su uno schema di operazione finanziaria che prevede il reinvestimento degli interessi*, Istituto di Matematica Finanziaria dell' Università di Torino, **84**.

[27] LEVI, E., 1961. Problemi di ritardo in matematica finanziaria, *Giornale Istituto Italiano Attuari*: 194-202.

[28] MALASKA, P. and KINNUNEN, T., 1986. A model of management goal setting and its dissipative structure. *European Journal of Operational Research*, **25**: 75-84.

[29] CHURCHILL, R.V., 1958. *Operational Mathematics*, McGraw-Hill Inc., New York.

[30] LÓPEZ LÉAUTAUD, JOSÉ L., 1972. Comment on: "Laplace transforms for the economic analysis of deterministic problems in engineering" by J.R. Buck and T.W. Hill. *The Engineering Economist*, **17** (2): 137-138.

[31] MULLINEUX, N., and REED, J.R. and RICHARDSON, R.G., 1973. Multi-dimensional Laplace transforms and non-linear problems. *Int. J. Elect. Enging. Educ.*, **11**: 5-17.

[32] DASARATHY, B.V., 1971. D-transforms and non-linear systems analysis. *Journal of Sound and Vibration*, **15** (2): 269-273.

[33] KOH, E.L., 1975. Association of variables in n-dimensional Laplace transform. *Int. J. Systems Sci.* **6** (2): 127-131.

[34] FLOWER, J.O., 1976. A note on the application of operational methods to certain non-linear problems. *Int J. Elect. Enging. Educ.*, **13**: 219-223.

[35] LUBBOCK, J.K. and BANSAL, V.S., 1969. Multidimensional Laplace transforms for solution of nonlinear equations. *Proc. IEE*, **116** (12): 2075-2082.

[36] JOSHI, S.G. and SRINIVASAN, P., 1978. Application of Laplace transform technique to the solution of certain third-order non-linear systems. *Journal of Sound and Vibration*, **57** (1): 41-50.

[37] BUSSGANG, J.J. and EHRMAN, L. and GRAHAM J.W., 1974. Analysis of nonlinear systems with multiple inputs. *Proceedings of the Institute of Electrical and Electronics Engineers*, **62**:1088-1119.

[38] KARMAKAR, S.B., 1980. Approximate analysis of non-linear systems by Laplace transform. *Journal of Sound and Vibration*, **69** (4): 597-602.

[39] SATO, H. and ASADA, K., 1988. Laplace transform transient analysis of a non-linear system. *Journal of Sound and Vibration*, **121** (3): 473-479.

[40] SRINIVASAN, S.K. and GOPALAN, M.N., 1973. Probabilistic analysis of a two-unit system with a warm standby and a single repair facility. *Operations Research*, **21** (3): 748-754.

[41] SMITH, D.R., 1978. Optimal repair of a series system. *Operations Research*, **26** (4): 653-662.

[42] TAKARAGI, K. et al., 1985. A probability bound estimation method in Markov reliability analysis. *IEEE Transactions on Reliability*, **R-34** (3): 257-261.

[43] WELLS, C.E., 1985. An adaptive estimation procedure using the Laplace transformation. *IIE Transactions*, **17** (3): 242-251.

[44] SHANTHIKUMAR, J.G., 1986. First failure time of dependent parallel systems with safety periods. *Microelectronics and Reliability*, **26** (5): 955-972.

[45] GOPALAN, M.N. and NAGARWALLA, H.E., 1986. Cost-benefit analysis of a 1 out of n: G system with variable repair and preventive maintenance rates. *International Journal of Quality & Reliability Management*, **3** (3): 26-32.

[46] BROCKETT, P.L. and GOLDEN, L.L., 1987. A class of utility functions containing all the common utility functions. *Management Science*, **33** (8): 955-964.

[47] VALLÉE, R. and NICOLAU E., 1983. Econometric models and generalized Laplace transforms. *Econ. Comput. Econ. Cybern. Stud. Res.*, **18** (4): 79-82.

[48] GRUBBSTRÖM, R.W. and LUNDQUIST, J., 1975. *Theory of Relatively closed systems and applications.* Production-Economic Research in Linköping, Profil 2, Linköping.

[49] GRUBBSTRÖM, R.W., 1980. A principle for determining the correct capital costs of work-in-progress and inventory. *Int. J. Prod. Res.*, **18** (2): 259-271.

[50] GURNANI, C., 1983. Economic analysis of inventory systems. *Int. J. Prod. Res.*, **21** (2): 261-277.

[51] GRUBBSTRÖM, R.W., 1986. "On the dynamics of a simple multi-stage production-inventory system with production rates depending on inventory levels". In Chikán, A., (Ed.), *Inventory in theory and practice*, Elsevier, Amsterdam: 539-561.

[52] ASBJØRNSEN, O.A., 1983. Project evaluation and cash flow forecasting by stochastic simulation. *Modeling, Identification and Control*, **4** (4): 237-254.

[53] WILLIAMS, J., 1973. *Laplace transforms*. George Allen & Unwin Ltd.

[54] REMER, D.S. et al., 1984. The state of the art of present worth analysis of cash flow distributions. *Engineering Costs and Production Economics*, **7**: 257-278.

[55] GRUBBSTRÖM, R.W., 1982. *On the choice of investments under the condition of different borrowing and lending rates*. Research Report RR-82, Department of Production Economics, Linköping Institute of Technology.

[56] GRUBBSTRÖM, R.W., 1981. *On the traditional investment problem*. Working Paper WP-95, Department of Production Economics, Linköping Institute of Technology.

[57] GRUBBSTRÖM, R.W., 1976. *On the balancing of queueing costs and capacity costs along the assembly line*. Proceedings, the Fifth International Seminar on Algorithms for Production Control and Scheduling, Karlovy Vary.

[58] GRUBBSTRÖM, R.W., and LUNDQUIST, J., 1977. The Axsäter integrated production-inventory model interpreted in terms of the theory of relatively closed systems, *Journal of Cybernetics*, **7**: 49-67.

[59] GRUBBSTRÖM, R.W. and THORSTENSON, A., 1986. Evaluation of capital costs in a multi-level inventory system by means of the annuity stream principle. *European Journal of Operational Research*, **24** (1): 136-145.

[60] THORSTENSON, A., 1988. *Capital costs in inventory models - A discounted cash flow approach*. Production-Economic Research in Linköping, Profil 8, Linköping.

[61] CHENG, T.C.E., 1985. Analysis of job flow-time in a job-shop. *J. Opl. Res. Soc.*, **36** (3): 225-230.

[62] SIVAZLIAN, B.D., 1979. Approximate optimal solution for a D-policy in an M/G/1 queuing system. *AIIE Transactions*, **11** (4): 341-343.

[63] KOTIAH, T.C.T., 1978. Approximate transient analysis of some queuing systems. *Operations Research*, **26** (2): 333-346.

[64] HARRISON, J.M., 1975. A priority queue with discounted linear costs. *Operations Research*, **23** (2): 260-269.

[65] WEBER, E., 1956. *Complex convolution method applied to non-linear problems*. Proceedings of the Symposium on Non-linear Circuit Analysis, Polytechnic Institute of Brooklyn, New York, Vol. 6: 409-427.

[66] DOYON, L.R., 1981. Stochastic modeling of facility security-systems for analytical solutions. *Computers & Industrial Engineering*, **5** (2): 127-138.

[67] GIBLEY, R.A. and SUNDSTROM, R., 1975. Some important applications of Laplace transforms. *Proceedings of the American Institute for Decision Sciences*, P. 93.

[68] GRUBBSTRÖM, R.W. and JIANG, Y., 1989, *The z-transform - An approach to present value analysis*, Working Paper WP-158, Dept. of Production Economics, Linköping Institute of Technology, Linköping.

[69] TERBORGH, G., 1949. *Dynamic equipment policy*, New York.

TAX EFFECTS IN THE DUTCH BOND MARKET

G.H.M.J. KREMER
Erasmus University Rotterdam

In this paper an analysis of the Dutch bond market is made. The technique used is linear programming. Given the fact that coupon income and capital gains are taxed differently and that some investors are tax-exempt in the Netherlands, it is shown that there are overpriced bonds in the market. This is as can be expected. But it is found that there are bonds that a rational investor would never hold in his portpolio, whatever the tax rate the investor has to pay on coupon income. Given the fact that the Dutch bond market is very illiquid for some bonds, an analysis of the effects of bid-ask spreads is made. It is shown that the effect of these spreads cannot explain the existence of bonds that are overpriced. It is not clear where these remaining overpricings stem from.

The pricing of default risk free bonds in a frictionless market is straightforward. Future cash flows generated by the bonds are discounted by the spot rates that correspond to the timing of the cash flows. Applying the term structure to the market gives bond prices that represent the present values of the cash flows generated in the market. If, however, taxes are introduced, pricing becomes more difficult. In this case the bond prices should represent the present value of the after tax cash flows. In the Netherlands, as in the UK or the USA, this is impossible. Coupon income is taxed at the marginal tax rate of the investor, capital gains are tax exempt. The progressive taxation of coupon income ensures that different investors can have different marginal tax rates. So calculating the after tax cash flows in the Dutch bond market is impossible.

An investor buying a bond has to consider, given his marginal tax rate, whether to buy the bond directly or mimicking the cash flows generated by that bond by a portfolio consisting of other bonds. The portfolio then gives him comparable cash flows.

EXAMPLE. two zero-coupon bonds, the first matures at t_1, the second matures at t_2. The two spot rates corresponding to the maturity dates are $r_1 = 10\%$ and $r_2 = 12\%$.

	time	t_1	t_2	bond price
cash flow	bond 1	1	0	0.909
	bond 2	0	1	0.797

A bond having a coupon of 10 % and maturing at t_2 has different values to different investors. A tax exempt investor calculates on an after tax basis the value at 96.78. An investor with a marginal tax rate of 50% calculates the value at 88.25. Remember that capital gains are not taxed. The 50% paying investor has the choice of buying the bond or buying a portfolio consisting of 5 zero coupon bonds maturing at t_1 and 105 zero coupon bonds maturing at t_2. The price of this portfolio is 88.25. If the price of the 10% bond is 96.78 the 50% tax paying investor will not rationally buy the 10% bond. He will only buy the portfolio of the zero coupons. The tax exempt investor is indifferent between the portfolio and the bond. So the marginal tax rate of 50% does not belong to the clientele of the 10% bond.

It is clear that if a bond is mimickable, that is if there is a porfolio that gives comparable after tax cash flows, then if the portfolio price is lower than the bond price the bond will not rationally be bought by an investor with the specific marginal tax rate. The bond is called dominated. The tax rate for which the bond is dominated does not belong to the clientele of the bond. This idea will be presented in detail in the next section.

The model

In this paper only bonds are used that are default risk free, noncallable and non-extendable. So the investor knows timing and amount of all future cash flows. For each bond a portfolio is built that, on an after tax basis, generates cash flows that are at least as high as the cash flows of the bond and that are received at the same moment. The porfolio has the lowest possible price. Now if the portfolio has a lower price than the bond that is dominated, a rational investor prefers the porfolio over the bond if he interested in the cash flow pattern of the bond. The model is a linear programming model:

$$\min_{x_i} p_{\text{port}} = \sum_{i=1}^{n} p_i x_i \qquad \text{(LP)}$$

s.t.

$$\sum_{i=1}^{n} c_{it} \quad x_i \geq c_{0t} \quad t = 1, \ldots, T$$

$$x_i \geq 0 \quad i = 1, \ldots, n$$

with

x_i	=	weight in port. of bond i.
c_{it}	=	after tax cash flow of bond i at time t.
p_i	=	price of bond i.
p_{port}	=	price of portfolio
c_{0t}	=	cash flow of bond to be mimicked at time t
n	=	number of bonds in the market that can be part of port.
T	=	time of last cash flow of bond to be mimicked

Short sales are not allowed. If it is possible to short a bond in the market this would imply arbitrage between a dominated bond and its dominating portfolio. This then would imply a market that is not in equilibrium and never will be. See also Schaefer [1982b] and Dermody and Prisman [1988]. This argument agains short sales is in its nature positive, the model here presented is simply intended to be a tool for decision making. But also without using positive arguments it is possible to disallow short sales in the Dutch bond market; it simply is not possible to short a bond for a long time. The market is too rigid to allow short sales over a longer period of time.

Examining the dual problem gives a good insight into the process of searching a dominating portfolio.

$$\max_{d_t} \quad \sum_{t=1}^{T} c_{0t} d_t \tag{DP1}$$

s.t.

$$\sum_{t=1}^{T} c_{it} \quad d_t \leq p_i \quad i = 1, \ldots, n$$
$$d_t \geq 0 \quad t = 1, \ldots, T$$

with

d_t	=	dual variable
c_{it}	=	after tax cash flow of bond i at time t.
p_i	=	price of bond i.
p_{port}	=	price of portfolio
c_{0t}	=	cash flow of bond to be mimicked at time t
n	=	number of bonds in the market that can be part of port.
T	=	time of last cash flow of bond to be mimicked

The dual variables can be interpreted as discount factors. So solving the LP-problem means calculating discount factors for which the present value of the bond is as high as possible with the restriction that the present values of the other bonds in the market can be at most as high as their prices. For some bonds the present value will be lower than the price; they will not be used in the mimicking portfolio. In this respect the presented method differs from the well-known technique in which a pay-off of 1 is created at a certain moment in time, for the presented method uses only a subset of all the bonds traded in the market.

The after tax cash flows are calculated using a specific marginal tax rate. If the model is used in a positive setting, the discount factors correspond to the term structure. But in this case it is clear that a term structure for the total market does not exist. Every marginal tax rate has its own term structure. Again, in this paper it is not intended to estimate term structures. But for more information on this see Schaefer [1981] (in which this model is explained is detail) and Dermody and Prisman [1988].

Complementary slackness

The model presented so far contains some simplifying implicit assumptions. Examining complementary slackness makes this clear.

$$\text{CS1:} \quad x_i \left[\sum_{t=1}^{T} c_{it} d_t - p_t \right] = 0$$

If the present value of a bond, calculated by using the calculated discount factors, is less than the bond price, it will not be used in the mimicking portfolio. It is not certain, however, that the bond itself is dominated.

$$\text{CS2:} \quad d_t \left[\sum_{i=1}^{n} c_{it} x_i - c_{0t} \right] = 0$$

If there is excess cash flow in period t then money has no marginal value for that period. This is clearly unrealistic. So an extra posibility has to added.

For an investor, it is always possible to keep a dollar received at period t until period $t + 1$ and then use this dollar to enlarge the cash flow generated by the mimicking portfolio. By keeping the dollar (without interest!) he can use it on a later date. This implies nonnegative forward rates in a positive model. In the model here presented it means a non-increasing discount function. So $d_t \geq d_{t+1}$.

EXAMPLE. An investor has to chose between a bond and a portfolio. The cash flows are as given

		t_1		t_2	
cf	portfolio	12		8	
cf	bond	10		10	
$cf_{\text{port}} -$	cf_{bond} =	+2	$\rightarrow$	$-2+2$	$= 0$

The excess cash flows ot t_1 are used to cover the deficit ot t_2.

The dual problem now looks like

$$\max_{d_t} \sum_{t=1}^{T} c_{0t} d_t \qquad \text{(DP2)}$$

s.t.

$$\sum_{t=1}^{T} c_{it} d_t \leq p_i \qquad i = 1, \ldots, n$$

$$1 \geq d_1 \geq d_2 \geq \ldots \geq d_T \geq 0$$

In this model excess cash flow can be used on a later date. In order to cover a potential deficit for the first cash flow period an investor can also include an amount of cash in his portfolio.

In solving the model DP2 is used. This turned out to be preferable to solving LP or a modified version of it.

The data

This paper intends to uncover the effectiveness of dominance in the Dutch bond market. So as many bonds as possible are used. In total there were 69 government bonds that were not callable or extendable. Of these 69 bonds 3 were perctuals and by this not mimickable by a portfolio of non-perpetuals. Three marginal tax rates were used, 0% is applicable to pension funds [(1)], 48% is applicable to companies and 72% is applicable to individuals in the highest tax bracket. Companies can deduct accrued interest paid when the bond is bought at the end of the fiscal year. Usually, however, tax covenants are used in order to deduct the interest directly.

Data of three wednesdays in june 1984 are used. Between 6-6-1984 and 13-6-1984 nothing special happened in the bond market, between 13-6-1984 and 20-6-1984 however, coupon payments and restitution of face value were made. So the effect of time can be studied in the sample used.

Quotations were used. It is certain that these quotations are usually incorrect. This is due to asynchronous quotations, bid-ask spreads, liquidity of the bonds and transaction costs. See the appendix for a more detailed study. But in general it can be concluded that prices paid when actually purchasing a bond will increase due to the above mentioned effects. For the Dutch bond market a mispricing of 2% for an individual a bond is extreme. This will result in an incorrect dominance of 2.5% at its maximum, but usually the effects are not so severe. However, these effects have to be considered when analyzing the results. Dropping incorrect quotations is not a valid solution, for it would corrupt the results of this study. A more detailed analysis of these effects is very difficult, for most important traders on the bond market receive preferential treatment on transaction costs.

The results

In table 2 the result are given. For each marginal tax rate, day and bond δ is given, with

$$\delta = \sum_{i=1}^{n} p_i x_i + s_0 - p_0$$

[(1)] Up till this date pension funds are not taxed at all in the Netherlands. Some plans are under development to change this situation.

with s_0 the amount of cash in the portfolio. The bond is dominated if $\delta < 0$. In this case buying the dominating portfolio is cheaper. For only 66 bonds δ is listed, the perpetuals are not analysed. Looking at the result carefully some very interesting effects can be seen.

1) The magnitude of the dominances is slightly stronger than the results found in Schaefer [1982]. There are two possible explanations for this. Firstly the quotations are not totally reliable, but see the appendix. Secondly, the range of coupons is in this study greater. This effect will increase dominance effects in the market.

2) A number of bonds is dominated for all marginal tax rates used in this paper. This is a very strange effect. If investors are rational then no trade would take place in these bonds.

3) Bonds with relatively high coupons are dominated for the high marginal tax rates. This implies that investors in these tax brackets will not buy the bonds but their dominating portfolio instead. The bonds they will choose from are the bonds with $\delta > 0$.

4) On 20-6 the situation is changed dramatically. For a number of bonds coupons and part of the face value is paid. The cash flow pattern in the market changes and this has a profound effect on the dominating portfolio. Especially the payments of part of the face value seems to be very important because the money received is tax exempt.

Viewing the results confirms the intutional ideas. Bonds with high coupons are usually of no interest to investors with high marginal tax rates. These bonds are bough by the tax exempt investors. Secondly the passing of time is more important than usually is assumed. Coupon payments can severely disrupt tax clienteles and dominances. Thirdly, the strange effect of no clientele for some 20 bonds in the market at 6-6 and 13-6 is puzzling. No explanation can be given for this.

Conclusions

In this paper an already tested model is applied to the Dutch bond market. The results are in line with the results from the UK (Schaefer [1982]), altough some questions are raised about the efficiency of the market. Further research has to be done on these effects. The model should be used with caution, small dominances can be the result of misquotations. Big dominances (4% and upwards) are potentially interesting opportunities for trade. The reason that these dominances can exist in the market may lie in the fact that bond portfolio management in the Netherlands is usually very static. The market is heavily influenced by the pension funds. These investors are very reluctant to sell parts of their bond portfolios. So bond swapping hardly ever occurs. This reluctance is induces by the fact that bonds are valued on the balance sheet not by their price but by face value. Buying high coupon bonds can be profitable, but the effects show in the books as a loss. The bonds may be the best buy in the market for the pension fund, but the cash outflow is larger than the increase in value for the bonds.

The effects of the passing of time are clearly to be seen. This effect is not yet described in literature.

REFERENCES

G.M. COSTANTINIDES and J.E. INGERSOLL, 1984: *Optimal Bond Trading with Personal Taxes*, The Journal of Finance 299-335.

C.D. DERMODY and E.Z. PRISMAN, 1988: *Term Structure Multiplicity & Clientele in Markets with Transaction Costs & Taxes*, The Journal of Finance 893-911.

J.V. JORDAN, 1984: *Tax Effects in Term Structure Estimantion*, The Journal of Finance 393-406.

R.H. LITZENBERGER and J. ROLFO, 1984: *Arbitrage Pricing, Transaction Costs and Taxation of Capital Gains*, Journal of Financial Economics 337-351.

R.H. LITZENBERGER and J. ROLFO, 1984: *An International Study of Tax Effects on Government Bonds*, The Journal of Finance 1-22.

S.M. SCHAEFER, 1981: *Measuring a Tax-Specific Term Structure of Interest Rates in the Market for British Government Securities*, The Economic Journal 415-438.

S.M. SCHAEFER, 1982a: *Tax-Induced Clientele Effects in the Market for British Government Securities*, Journal of Financial Economics 121-159.

S.M. SCHAEFER, 1982b: *Taxes and Security Market Equilibrium*, in W.F. Sharpe en C.M. Cootner (eds), Financial Economics: Essays in Honour of Paul Cootner, Englewood Cliffs, NJ: Prentice Hall 159-177.

Appendix

Analysis of mispricing

The quotations used are usually not correct. There are four reasons for this.

1) asynchronous quotations. The quotations are not made at the same moment. For a very illiquid bond the quotation can be several days old. So trading on this quotation is not possible.

2) Bid-ask spread. An investor has not to pay the quotation but the ask price of the trader. This ask price is usually higher than the quotation.

3) Liquidity. Many bonds are very illiquid. Buying such a bond will mean paying extra in order to find a seller. For very large transactions it can be impossible to find a seller. In the paper it is presumed that bonds can always be bought.

4) transaction costs. An investor has to pay transaction costs if he wants to buy bonds. These costs will increase the price of the bonds.

The effect 1) has an indeterminate effect on the price of a bond, the effects 2) to 4) will increase the price of the bond. It will be presumed that the sum of the effects will increase the price of a bond.

A sensitivity analysis of DP2 reveals that the dominating portfolio will still mimick the bond but that the prices change. In order to find a limit on the effect is using the wrong quotations an analysis of the maximum effect is made.

p_i quotation used
p_{ih} proper quotation for trade

The difference is

$$\pi_i = p_{ih} - p_i \geq 0$$

as was assumed above. The price of the portfolio was calculated at

$$p_{\text{port}} = \sum x_i p_i$$

The correct price is, however

$$p_{\text{port h}} = \sum x_i p_{ih}$$

$$p_{\text{port h}} - p_{\text{port}} = \sum x_i p_{ih} - \sum x_i p_i = \sum x_i \pi_i$$

So the price of the portfolio will higher than calculated. For dominance the difference between the prices of the portfolio and the bond were calculated.

$$D = p_{\text{port } h} - p_{0h} = \sum x_i \pi_i - \pi_0$$

It is clear that the dominances found in this paper are influenced by the values of $\pi_i, i = 0, \ldots, n$. It is very hard to calculate the values of π_i. But it is possible to get an idea about the total effect. Assume that there are π_{min} and π_{max} so that

$$\pi_{\text{min}} \leq \pi_i \leq \pi_{\text{max}} \qquad \text{for all} \qquad i = 0, \ldots, n$$

then

$$D = \sum x_i \pi_i - \pi_0 \leq \sum x_i \pi_i - \pi_{\text{min}} \leq \sum \pi_{\text{max}} - \pi_{\text{min}}$$

so

$$D \leq \pi_{\text{max}} \left(\sum x_i\right) - \pi_{\text{min}} \leq \pi_{\text{max}} \left(\sum x_i\right)$$

The mispricing for the portfolio is at its maximum and for the bond at its minimum. Now it depends on π_{max} if the dominance remains intact. From results not presented in this paper follows that

$$0.77 < \sum x_i < 1.25$$

From this it is clear that in the worst case a overvalueing of dominance by 2.5 can be found. The assumption that $\pi_{\max} = 2$ is extreme, however. If it is assumed that $\pi_i = \pi$, so all mispricing are equal, the,

$$D = \sum x_i \pi_i - \pi_0 = \pi \left(\sum x_i - 1 \right) \lessapprox 0.25\,\pi$$

This would mean that in the case of $\pi = 1$, an overvalueing of .25 would occur.

In both cases many of the dominances remain intact, so the model still is useable, even if the wrong quotations are used.

THE CONTINUOUS QUOTATIONS AT AN AUCTION MARKET

THOMAS LANDES
Department of
Statistics and Econometrics

OTTO LOISTL
Department of
Finance and Banking

Faculty of Economics
University of Paderborn
Post Box 1621
D - 4790 Paderborn

The paper embodies the first attempt to describe the explicit activities of the market participants within the rules of the stock market organisation: They are making offers to buy or to sell and they are accepting such offers with matching quantities and prices.

The approach is based on a Markov - Process. The high dimensional state space is an explicit description of the market place: The change of the state space is governed by the attached probability transition rates which are themselfes determined by the behavioural attitudes of the market participants.

I . Introduction

Nowadays, the stock markets are characterized by the technological improvements of the last decade. There is an increase in data volume and in trading volume. The number of trades increased too. For the big international companies there are several thousands of trades and of price quotations every day. The individual price quotation can no longer be taken as a unique market clearing equilibrium price. We have to regard the dynamics of the stock market and have to incorporate the continuous quotations and the individual's processing of the information disclosed by the market performance. The interaction between the individual agents has to be modelled, where the institutional rules are regarded by the market participants. We propose a model for the continuous quotations at an auctions market. In this first step we assume that there is only one security to be traded, but that there are many agents.

With regard to the formal apparatus we rely on the concept of synergetics, which gains increasing attention for modelling complex economic systems [1]

[1] cf. Arthur (1988), pp. 23.

It is especially appropriate to incorporate selforganizing activities. The stock market seems to be such a system. A basic approach is developed in Loistl/Landes (1989) with a broad discussion of the economic aspects. The following presentation is a clarified version concentrating on the formal analytical aspects. It incorporates the further insight we gained by the comments made at the presentation especially at both the meetings of the Euro Working Group on Financial Modelling in Catania (Spring (1989)) and Liège (Autumn (1989)).

II. The analytical model

1. General description of the model

Our model is a Markov process $(\mathbf{Z}_t)_{t\geqslant 0}$ on the probability space (S, Σ, P) in continuous time with values in the discrete countable set $\mathscr{Z}$, the *state space.* To be more precise, we assume that the process is a homogeneous conservative Markov chain. This means that the following three conditions are fulfilled.

1. The transition probabilities are time homogeneous, i.e., depend only on the time difference:

$$P(\mathbf{Z}_t = \mathbf{z}' \mid \mathbf{Z}_s = \mathbf{z}) = P_{t-s}(\mathbf{z}, \mathbf{z}'), \quad s \leqslant t \tag{1}$$

and the $(P_t)_{t\geqslant 0}$ form the transition semigroup i.e. the Chapman Kolmogorov equation holds

$$P_{t+s}(\mathbf{z}, \mathbf{z}'') = \sum_{\mathbf{z}'} P_t(\mathbf{z}, \mathbf{z}') P_s(\mathbf{z}', \mathbf{z}'') \tag{2}$$

2. The *transition semigroup* $(P_t)_{t\geqslant 0}$ is continuous from the right at 0, i.e.,

$$\lim_{t\to 0} P_t(\mathbf{z}, \mathbf{z}') = \begin{cases} 1 & \mathbf{z} = \mathbf{z}' \\ 0 & \mathbf{z} \neq \mathbf{z} \end{cases}. \tag{3}$$

so that the *transition rates* exist:

$$w(\mathbf{z}, \mathbf{z}') = \lim_{t\to 0} \frac{1}{t} P_t(\mathbf{z}, \mathbf{z}') < \infty, \quad \mathbf{z} \neq \mathbf{z}' \tag{4}$$

$$w(\mathbf{z}, \mathbf{z}) = \lim_{t\to 0} \frac{1}{t} (P_t(\mathbf{z}, \mathbf{z}) - 1) = -w(\mathbf{z}) \leqslant -\infty \tag{5}$$

3. The condition of being conservative is fulfilled:

$$\sum_{z' \neq z} w(z, z') = w(z) < \infty. \tag{6}$$

In our modelling, there will be only finitely many possible transitions in each state so that (6) is an immediate consequence of the formula of total probability.

As we deal with a conservative Markov chain, the transition semigroup satisfies the *forward Kolmogorov equations.*

$$\begin{aligned} \frac{d}{dt} P_t(z, z'') &= \sum_{z'} P_t(z, z')\, w\,(z, z'') \\ &= \sum_{z' \neq z''} P_t(z, z')\, w(z', z'') - P_t(z, z'')\, w\,(z'') \end{aligned} \tag{7}$$

From this, we deduce the evolution equation for the distribution of $\mathbf{Z}_t$ at time t, $P_t(z) = P(\mathbf{Z}_t = z)$, the so called master equation

$$\frac{d}{dt} P_t(z) = \sum_{z' \neq z} P_t(z')\, w\,(z', z) - P_t(z)\, w\,(z). \tag{8}$$

It is now our task to describe the state variables $z \in \mathscr{Z}$, the transitions and the corresponding transition rates.

2. *The state variables*

The state of the market is described by a collection of variables forming the vector $\mathbf{z} \in \mathscr{Z}$, the *state variable.* We distinguish between public variables – i.e. disclosed to each agent – and individual variables influencing one individual agent only.

Due to bounded rationality, the agents in our model do not base their decisions on the full information of the whole past of the process. We rather assume that the relevant information is conglomerated in a few information variables, namely: the *current price* p of the asset, being the price of the last call; the *call status* ω of the market, consisting of the *last actor* and the *type of the call;* the *market power* m*;* the *price trend* p^T, the price difference between the current price and the price at the last trend reversal. These variables constitute the public variables.

The individual variables are, for each agent $i \in I = \{1, \ldots, N\}$, his current estimation $\hat{p}_i$ of the future (end of period) price of the asset dynamically adjusted during the trading session. This estimation is the decision basis of the agent:

He will buy the stock, if $\hat{p}_i > p$ and he will sell the stock, if $\hat{p}_i < p$. His individual variables are further the stock holding x_i and his capital y_i measured as integer multiples of certain basic units. The initial value of $\hat{p}_i$ is just his assessment $\hat{p}_i^{ext}$ of the intrinsic value of the asset. The distribution $\hat{\mathbf{p}}^{ext} = (\hat{p}_i^{ext})_{i \in I}$ reflects the market's assessment of the fundamental value of the asset. All these variables are shown in the following listing.

$$\mathbf{z} = (p, \omega, m, p^T, \mathbf{x}, \mathbf{y}, \hat{\mathbf{p}}) \in \mathscr{Z} = \mathbb{N} \times \Omega \times M \times \mathbb{Z} \times \mathbb{Z}^I \times \mathbb{Z}^I \times \mathbb{N}^I \tag{9}$$

$$p = \text{ current price} \in \mathbb{N} = \text{set of positive integers} \tag{9.1}$$

$$\omega = (i_\omega, c_\omega) = \text{call status} \in \Omega = I \times C \tag{9.2}$$

$$i_\omega = \text{last actor} \in I = \{1, \ldots, N\} \tag{9.2.1}$$

$$c_\omega = \text{type of last call} \in C = \{-1, 0, 1\} \tag{9.2.2}$$

$$m = \text{market power} \in M = \text{countable subset of real numbers} \tag{9.3}$$

$$p^T = \text{price trend} \in \mathbb{Z} = \text{set of integers (multiples of price unit)} \tag{9.4}$$

$$\mathbf{x} = (x_i)_{i \in I} = \text{stock distribution} \in X = \mathbb{Z}^I \tag{9.5}$$

$$\mathbf{y} = (y_i)_{i \in I} = \text{capital distribution} \in Y = \mathbb{Z}^I \tag{9.6}$$

$$\hat{\mathbf{p}} = (\hat{p}_i)_{i \in I} = \text{price expectation distribution} \in \mathbb{N}^I \tag{9.7}$$

The values 1, -1, 0 of the variable c_ω encode the types ask, bid, trade of the call. The codest ± 1 are chosen in accordance to the fact, that demand gives a price signal in the positive direction while supply gives a downwards directed price signal.

3. Transitions and actions

In each state $\mathbf{z} \in \mathscr{Z}$, each agent has to choose among finitely many alternative actions. Each such action is either a reevaluation of the estimation $\hat{p}_i$ or a call to the market. When carried out it is considered as the occurrence of an event causing a specific transition of the state $\mathbf{z}$ of the market. Vice versa, each transition of the state $\mathbf{z}$ is caused by exactly one action. So, there is a one-to-one correspondence between transitions and actions. We thus describe the transitions by means of possible actions.

To this aim, let us fix an agent $i \in I$ and a state $\mathbf{z} \in \mathscr{Z}$. One possible action is to reevaluate the price estimation $\hat{p}_i$. This is an adjustment of $\hat{p}_i$ by ± 1 where an adjustment by -1 is not admissible when $\hat{p}_i = 1$. This reevaluation, formally described by $v = (i_v, \delta_v)$, $i_v = i$ = adjusting agent, $\delta_v = \pm 1$, corresponds to the transition

$$\hat{p}_{i_v} \to \hat{p}_{i_v} + \delta_v \tag{10}$$

while all other components of **z** remain unchanged.

More complicated is the situation for the other alternatives, namely to give a call e of type c_e, i.e., to offer an *ask* ($c_e = 1$) or a *bid* ($c_e = -1$) or to *accept* ($c_e = 0$) a previous offer, the latter meaning to agree in a *trade*. Such a call can be formally described by the tripel

$$e = (i_e, c_e, p_e), \tag{11}$$

$$i_e = i \in I: \text{ calling agent} \tag{11.1}$$

$$p_e \in \{p - 1, p, p + 1\}: \text{ the price cried out to the market} \tag{11.2}$$

$$c_e \in C = \{-1, 0, 1\}: \text{ call type.} \tag{11.3}$$

Such a call causes the following transition:

$$p \mapsto p + \Delta p, \ \Delta p := p_e - p; \tag{12.1}$$

$$\omega \mapsto (i_e, c_e) \tag{12.2}$$

$$m \mapsto (1 - \lambda)\, m + c_e - \epsilon\, c_\omega\, (1 - |c_e|) \tag{12.3}$$

$$x_{i_e} \mapsto x_{i_e} + c_e, \ x_{i_\omega} \mapsto x_{i_\omega} - c_e \tag{12.4}$$

$$y_{i_e} \mapsto y_{i_e} - c_e\, p_e, \ y_{i_\omega} \mapsto y_{i_\omega} + c_e\, p_e \tag{12.5}$$

$$p^T \mapsto \begin{cases} \Delta p & \text{if } p^T * \Delta p < 0 \text{ and } p^T * c_e < 0 \\ p^T + \Delta p & \text{otherwise} \end{cases} \tag{12.6}$$

All other components of **z** remain unchanged.

The transition of the market power consists in a downscaling $m \mapsto (1-\lambda)m$ $(0 \leqslant \lambda < 1)$ of the past combined with an adding of the signal coming from the present call: An ask forces an increase, a bid a decrease of m by 1 (corresponding to the nature of m as being a kind of demand surplus) while a trade cancels at least a part ϵ $(0 \leqslant \epsilon \leqslant 1)$ of the preceding offer. The parameter λ is called the *oblivion factor,* the parameter ϵ the *cancellation factor.* If $\lambda > 0$, then $|m|$ is bounded by $1/\lambda$.

The price trend transition is to be understood in the following way: The price trend is the difference between the actual price and the price at the last trend reversal. If both the type of the call and the price difference are opposite to the price trend, then a trend reversal occurs so that the new price trend is given by Δp, while in the other cases the trend continues so that p^T changes by Δp.

We have to observe that not every call is possible for an agent i in a given state **z**. There are a number of restrictions:

(13.1) An acceptance can only follow an offer, i.e.

if $c_\omega = 0$ then $c_e \in \{-1, 1\}$

(13.2) Only price changings of at most one unit are considered:

$\Delta p = p_e - p \in \{-1, 0, 1\}$

(13.3) A trade has the same price as the preceding offer:

if $c_e = 0$ then $\Delta p = 0$

(13.4) After an offer, the same agent can only make a call of the same type

if $c_\omega \neq 0$ and $c_e\, c_\omega \leqslant 0$ then $i_e \neq i_\omega$

(13.5) The asset can only be bidden or sold when the agent owns at least one unit of the asset:

$c_e = -1$ only if $x_{i_e} > 0$

if $c_\omega = 1$ then $c_e = 0$ only if $x_{i_e} > 0$

(13.6) Credit is allowed up to a share σ_c $(0 \leqslant \sigma_c < 1)$ of the value of the stock holding of the agent. So, the agent will only ask or buy when his credit after the (potential) transaction does not overdraw the limit:

$c_e = 1$ only if $y_{i_e} - p_e \geqslant -\sigma_c\, p_e\, (x_{i_e} + 1)$

if $c_\omega = -1$ then $c_e = 0$ only if $y_{i_e} - p_e \geqslant -\sigma_c\, p_e (x_{i_e} + 1)$

(13.7) After an ask (bid) the price in the next call cannot fall (raise):

if $| c_\omega | = 1$ then $\Delta p \neq c_\omega$

(13.8) The agent only asks or buys (bids or sells) at prices below (above) his price estimation:

$(c_e = 1)$ or $(c_e = 0$ and $c_\omega = -1)$ only if $\hat{p}_{i_e} > p_e$

$(c_e = -1)$ or $(c_e = 0$ and $c_\omega = -1)$ only if $\hat{p}_{i_e} < p_e$

(13.9) If the agent's credit limit is overdrawn, then (besides the limitation (13.6)) the limitation (13.8) is suspended and he is forced to ask or buy:

if $y_{i_e} < -\sigma_c\, p_e\, x_{i_e}$ then:

$c_\omega = -1 \Rightarrow c_e = 0$

$c_\omega \in \{0, 1\} \Rightarrow c_e = 1$

4. Transition rates and master equation

In our model we assume that the agents act «instantaneously independent» and that the reevaluation and call processes are also instantaneously independent. This means that two different actions cannot occur at exactly the same time instant (only with probability 0), so that it is enough to model the transition rates for the transitions caused by each single action only. We call these transition rates the specific reaction rates $w\,(A,\, \mathbf{z})$ of the corresponding actions A in state $\mathbf{z}$. As these are positive, we use the following modelling

$$w(A, \mathbf{z}) = W(A) \exp\ \Phi(A; \mathbf{z}) \tag{14}$$

$$\text{where } W(A) = \begin{cases} W_E & \text{if } A \text{ is a call (Explicitely observable event)} \\ W_V & \text{if } A \text{ is a reevaluation (Value adjustment)} \end{cases} \tag{15}$$

The constants W_E and W_V are called the reagibility parameters of the call and reevaluation process, respectively. The function Φ is the so called motivation potential for the corresponding action.

As it is well known from the theory of Markov chains, that the probability that the next action will be A is proportional to $w(\mathrm{A}, \mathbf{z})$, our modelling reflects the principle:

The higher the motivation for an action, the higher the probability of its execution.

It is also known that the waiting time of the process is just the minimum of the «reaction times» of all actions, the latter being the waiting time of a process in which only one transition, namely that corresponding to the action, is possible. These reaction times are independent and exponentially distributed with mean $1/w\ (A, \mathbf{z})$. So our modelling also reflects the principle:

The higher the motivation for an action, the shorter its expected reaction time.

These observations justify the choice of the name *motivation potential.* We assume that each motivation potential is additively decomposed into a number of specific potentials. This decomposition is structurally different for the two kinds of actions, calls or reevaluations. So, we discuss them separately.

We begin with the motivation potential for a reevaluation

$$\Phi_V(v, \mathbf{z}) = \delta_v \{\bar{\Phi}_V^{ext}(\mathbf{z}) + \bar{\Phi}_V^{inf}(\mathbf{z}) + \bar{\Phi}_V^{pot}(\mathbf{z}) + \bar{\Phi}_V^{trd}(\mathbf{z})\} \tag{16}$$

decomposed into four components, which are explained in the following:

When the agent i enters the market, he has a certain prior price expectation, the intrinsic value $\hat{p}_i^{ext}$ determined by the external factors as already described above. His actual price expectation $\hat{p}_i$ then differs from this intrinsic value $\hat{p}_i^{ext}$ caused by new informations from inside the market. But this deviation $D\hat{p}_i^{int}$ does not vary freely, i.e. a speculator will not want to depart too far in his price expectation from the externally determined value. This means that the value $\hat{p}_i^{ext}$ behaves like the base of a spring whose end is connected to $\hat{p}_i$. In other words, the first component of the motivation potential called the *external potential* $\Phi_V^{ext} = \delta_v\ \bar{\Phi}_V^{ext}$ attracts $\hat{p}_i$ closer to $\hat{p}_i^{ext}$ and the stronger, the larger the deviation $D\hat{p}_i^{int}$ is in absolute value. In order to be more flexible in our model, we allow the dependence of $\bar{\Phi}_V^{ext}$ on $|\ D\hat{p}_i^{int}\ |$ to be linear or stronger or weaker than linear, i.e. $\bar{\Phi}_V^{ext}$ is proportional to a power of $|\ D\hat{p}_i^{int}\ |$:

$$\bar{\Phi}_V^{ext}(\mathbf{z}) = \eta_{ext} \,|\, \hat{p}_{i_v}^{ext} - \hat{p}_{i_v} |^{K} * \operatorname{sign}(\hat{p}_{i_v}^{ext} - \hat{p}_{i_v}). \tag{17}$$

The parameter $K > 0$ is the degree of the external force, where $K = 1$ correspondends to the linear case.

A good deal of the internal market information is given by the actual price p. Each agent tends to fit his price expectation to this market information. This feature is modelled by the *information potential* $\bar{\Phi}_V^{inf} = \delta_v \, \Phi_V^{inf}$ attracting $\hat{p}_i$ closer to $|\, \hat{p}_i - p \,|$ the stronger the larger the deviation. Here we propose a linear setting so that

$$\bar{\Phi}_V^{inf}(\mathbf{z}) = \eta_{inf} (p - \hat{p}_{i_v}) \tag{18}$$

The market information potential favours the value adjustment $v = (i, \operatorname{sign}(p - \hat{p}_i))$ of agent i in the direction of $p - \hat{p}_i$, i.e. closer to p, while it suppress the opposite value adjustment with the same power proportional to $|\, p - \hat{p}_i \,|$.

The last two components pay regard to the information concerning the activities at the market of the recent past being stored in the variables «market power» and «price trend».

The *market power potential,* $\Phi_V^{pot} = \delta_v \, \bar{\Phi}_V^{pot}$ represents the influence of the market power m on the price expectations of the speculators: if there exists a demand pressure ($m > 0$), then the price expectations rise rather than fall, while in case of a supply pressure ($m < 0$) they fall rather than rise; and the stronger the market power in absolute value the greater the rise or fall. Again a linear model is chosen:

$$\bar{\Phi}_V^{pot}(\mathbf{z}) = \eta_{pot} \, m. \tag{19}$$

The *price trend potential* $\Phi_V^{trd} = \delta_v \, \bar{\Phi}_V^{trd}$, models the effect of the information contained in the price trand p^T on the price expectations. Obviously, a positive price trend favours upwards value adjustments and suppresses downwards ones, while a negative price trend has just the opposite effect. The power varies synchronously with the absolute value of the price trend, where we propose a linear setting:

$$\bar{\Phi}_V^{trd}(\mathbf{z}) = \eta_{trd} \, p^T \tag{20}$$

The coupling parameters $\eta_{ext}, \eta_{inf}, \eta_{pot}, \eta_{trd} \geqslant 0$ measure the influence of the corresponding potential.

The motivation potential for a *call* is also decomposed into four components:

$$\Phi_E(e; \mathbf{z}) = \Phi_E^{ip}(e; \mathbf{z}) + \Phi_E^{mc}(e; \mathbf{z}) + \Phi_E^{cl}(e; \mathbf{z}) + \Phi_E^{gt}(e; \mathbf{z}). \tag{21}$$

The first and most important component of Φ_E is the *individual preference* potential Φ_E^{ip} stemming from the individual price expectation. The more the price expectation $\hat{p}_{i_e}$ of the agent i_e differs from the called price p_e in absolute value, the higher the motivation of i_e for the call c_e; that is, the higher the transition rate of the event (i_e, c_e, p_e). So the individual preference potential Φ_E^{ip} is assumed to be proportional to the absolute value of the difference between the price expectation and the called price.

The call under consideration is admissible only if the sign of $\hat{p}_{i_e} - p_e$ is the same as the sign of the call-type of the call [+1 for an ask or a purchase, − 1 for a bid or sale]. This sign can be obtained formally by

$$\operatorname{sign}(c_\omega\, c_e) = \begin{cases} c_e & \text{if } c_e \neq 0 \\ -c_\omega & \text{if } c_e = 0 \end{cases} = c_e - (1 - |c_e|)\, c_\omega \tag{22}$$

But if the credit limit of agent i_e is overdrawn, a call of positive signi is forbidden while a call of negative sign can occur even if $\hat{p}_{i_e} \geqslant p_e$: individual preferences must leave behind credit responsibilities.

So,

$$\Phi_E^{ip}(e; \mathbf{z}) = \begin{cases} 0 & \text{if } y_{i_e} < -\sigma_c\, p_e\, x_{i_e},\ \operatorname{sign}(c_\omega\, c_e) = -1, \hat{p}_{i_e} \geqslant p_e \\ \alpha_{c_\omega c_e} |\hat{p}_{i_e} - p_e| & \text{otherwise} \end{cases} \tag{23}$$

The coupling parameter $\alpha_{c_\omega c_e}$ which may depend on the special call sequence $c_\omega c_e$ as indicated, measures the agent's individual confidence in his own estimation.

The second component is the *market climate potential* Φ_E^{mc} induced by the market power m. If there is a demand pressure ($m > 0$) then further asks are forced, leading to raising prices, while a supply pressure ($m < 0$) favours further bids. However, this force would seem rather bounded, i.e. it has a saturation bound, because it should not overcompensate the individual preference potential by much. So we propose the following model

$$\Phi_E^{mc}(e; \mathbf{z}) = \gamma_{c_\omega c_e}(1 - \exp(-\beta_{c_\omega c_e} |m|))\, \operatorname{sign}(c_\omega\, c_e)\, \operatorname{sign}(m) \tag{24}$$

This bounded modelling also takes into account the phenomenon that beyond a certain bound doubts about the actual tendency arise and a possible trend reversal is expected.

The sign of the market climate potential is modelled by the combination of the sign functions appearing on the right hand side of the formula. The term sign $(c_\omega c_e)$ is positive (negative) exactly in case of a demand-(supply-) type call, so that the product of the to sign functions is positive (= + 1) if market force and call type are of the same kind and negative (= − 1) if they are of opposite kind.

The γ-parameter controls the scaling in the Φ_E^{mc} -direction, i.e. the global strength (to be precise the least upper bound of the strength) of the market climate potential. The β-parameter controls the scaling in the m-direction. Large values of β correspond to steep curves, small values to gently sloped curves.

The slope of the curve at the origin is given by the product of β and γ.

The third component of Φ_E is the *credit limitation potential* Φ_E^{cl}, which takes into account the sales pressure stemming from surpassed credit limitations.

This pressure is the stronger the further the credit amount surpasses the limit:

$$\Phi_E^{cl} = \begin{cases} -\theta(y_{i_e} + \sigma_c\, p_e\, x_{i_e}) \text{ if } y_{i_e} < -\sigma_c\, p_e\, x_{i_e}, \text{ and sign } (c_\omega\, c_e) = -1 \\ 0 \qquad\qquad\qquad \text{otherwise} \end{cases} \tag{25}$$

The credit pressure parameter θ measures the influence of the credit limitation potential.

The last component is the *general tendency part* Φ_E^{gt} given by the parameter $\xi_{c_\omega c_e}$ which may be positive, zero or negative. It is introduced because certain call sequences might be preferred to others, i.e., appear more often.

To write down the master equation we introduce the following notation:

(26) $E_i(\mathbf{z})$: set of possible calls $e = (i, c_e, p_e)$ of agent i in state $\mathbf{z}$ according to the rules (13.1) to (13.9)

(27) $T_e\mathbf{z}$: state after the transition of $e \in E_i(\mathbf{z})$ in state $\mathbf{z}$. That is $e \in E_i(\mathbf{z})$ causes the transition $\mathbf{z} \mapsto T_e\mathbf{z}$.

(28) $\overleftarrow{E}_i(\mathbf{z}) = \{(e, \mathbf{z}') \mid e \in E_i(\mathbf{z}'), T_e\mathbf{z}' = \mathbf{z}\}$

(29) $T_i^\pm$ $\mathbf{z}$: state after the transition of $v = (i, \pm 1)$ in state $\mathbf{z}$.

(30) $w_i^\pm(\mathbf{z}) = w((i, \pm 1); \mathbf{z})$: corresponding transition rate.

Then the master equation has the following form

$$\begin{aligned} \frac{d}{dt} P_t(\mathbf{z}) = & \sum_i \Big\{ \sum_{(e,\mathbf{z}')\in\overleftarrow{E}_i(\mathbf{z})} w(e, \mathbf{z}')\, P_t(\mathbf{z}') - \sum_{e\in E_i(\mathbf{z})} w(e, \mathbf{z})\, P_t(\mathbf{z}) \Big\} \\ & + \sum_{i:\bar{p}_i > 1} \Big\{ w_i^+(T_i^-\mathbf{z})\, P_t(T_i^-\mathbf{z}) - w_i^-(\mathbf{z})\, P_t(\mathbf{z}) \Big\} \\ & + \sum_i \Big\{ w_i^-(T_i^+\mathbf{z})\, P_t(T_i^+\mathbf{z}) - w_i^+(\mathbf{z})\, P_t(\mathbf{z}) \Big\} \end{aligned} \tag{31}$$

We do not write down the master equation in its explicit form in the full extent. It is very complicated on account of the various restrictions. It gives not much insight in its structure also. But now we leave to look at the possibilities to solve the master equation to extract the economic implications of our model.

5. The solution of the master equation

Even if the master equation is linear, it is practically impossible to obtain an explicit solution because of its very high dimension. Moreover, we are interested at first in the evolution of the marginal distribution of the price p or even of some of its parameters only. Therefore we suggest to solve the master equation by performing Monte Carlo simulations at this stage of the discussion.

To this aim, we want to choose the simulation procedure as close as possible to the real (modelled) process. By this, we mean that reevaluations, as they are not observed by the other agents, should not influenced directly the decisions of the other agents. This principle should also apply to the simulations. In fact, this can be done as the following observations show.

Given any $\mathbf{z} \in \mathscr{Z}$, we denote by

$$\mathscr{Z}(\mathbf{z}) = \{\mathbf{z}' \mid w(\mathbf{z}, \mathbf{z}') > 0\} \tag{32}$$

the set of all states the process can jump to from $\mathbf{z}$ in one step. Let further for each $\mathbf{z}' \in \mathscr{Z}(\mathbf{z})$ the set

$$\mathscr{Z}(\mathbf{z}, \mathbf{z}') = \{\mathbf{z}'' \in \mathscr{Z}(\mathbf{z}) \cap \mathscr{Z}(\mathbf{z}') \mid w(\mathbf{z}, \mathbf{z}'') = w(\mathbf{z}', \mathbf{z}'')\} \tag{33}$$

be the collection of all states, which can be reached in one transition from both $\mathbf{z}$ and $\mathbf{z}'$ with the same transition rates, i.e. for which the transition rate does not change if a transition from $\mathbf{z}$ to $\mathbf{z}'$ occurs.

We start with independent exponentially distributed random variables $T_{0,\mathbf{z}}$ with parameters $w(\mathbf{z}_0, \mathbf{z})$, $\mathbf{z} \in \mathscr{Z}(\mathbf{z}_0)$, let T_0 be the minimum of all $T_{0,\mathbf{z}}$ and define $\mathbf{z}_1$ to be the element of $\mathscr{Z}(\mathbf{z}_0)$ this minimum is attained at, i.e. we have

$$t_{0,\mathbf{z}_1} = t_0 = \min\{t_{0,\mathbf{z}} \mid \mathbf{z} \in \mathscr{Z}(\mathbf{z}_0)\} \tag{34}$$

when $t_{0,\mathbf{z}}$ are the realizations of $T_{0,\mathbf{z}}$ and t_0 is the realization of T_0. To explain how to proceed, we assume states $\mathbf{z}_0$ and $\mathbf{z}_\upsilon \in \mathscr{Z}(\mathbf{z}_{\upsilon-1})$, $\upsilon = 1, \ldots, k$, and random variables $T_{\upsilon,\mathbf{z}}$ with realizations $t_{\upsilon,\mathbf{z}}, \mathbf{z} \in \mathscr{Z}(\mathbf{z}_\upsilon)$, $\upsilon = 0, \ldots, k-1$, to be already constructed so that the minimum t_υ of the $t_{\upsilon,\mathbf{z}}$ is attained at $\mathbf{z}_\upsilon$, $\upsilon = 0, \ldots, k-1$. The induction step is then performed in the following way.

We define the random variables

$$T_{k,\mathbf{z}}, \mathbf{z} \in \mathscr{Z}(\mathbf{z}_k) \setminus \mathscr{Z}(\mathbf{z}_{k-1}, \mathbf{z}_k),$$

to be independent, exponentially distributed with parameters $w(\mathbf{z}_k, \mathbf{z})$ and independent of all previous $T_{\upsilon,\mathbf{z}}$, $\upsilon = 0, \ldots, k-1$. The surplus potential waiting times

$$t_{k,\mathbf{z}} = t_{k-1,\mathbf{z}} - t_{k-1}, \quad \mathbf{z} \in \mathscr{Z}(\mathbf{z}_{k-1}, \mathbf{z}_k) \tag{35}$$

of the remaining states which are reachable in one step from $\mathbf{z}_k$ are then considered to be the realizations of random variables $T_{k,\mathbf{z}}$, i.e. these random variables are defined in this way. We again let T_k be the minimum of all $T_{k,\mathbf{z}}$ and, finally, define $\mathbf{z}_{k+1}$ to be the state the minimum t_k of the realizations $t_{k,\mathbf{z}}$ of $T_{k,\mathbf{z}}$, $\mathbf{z} \in \mathscr{Z}(\mathbf{z}_{k-1})$ is attained at. One can show, [(2)] that for each $\upsilon \geqslant 0$ the $T_{\upsilon,\mathbf{z}}$, $\mathbf{z} \in \mathscr{Z}(\mathbf{z}_\upsilon)$, are independent, independent from $T_{\upsilon-1}$ (for $\upsilon \geqslant 1$) and exponentially distributed with parameters $w(\mathbf{z}_\upsilon, \mathbf{z})$.

So the distribution of the paths simulated in this way is the correct distribution governed by the master equation. In our case, this means that the simulation can be performed as follows. In the beginning, the initial state $\mathbf{z}_0$ has to be generated either by a value fixed for each simulated path or by a simulated value corresponding to a fixed distribution. Then, at $t = 0$ and after each call, new reaction times are computed for each agent i and each admissable action A_{ij}, $j = 1, \ldots, n_i(\mathbf{z})$, (a reevaluation $(i, \pm 1)$ or a call $(i, c_e, p_e) \in E_i(\mathbf{z})$) according to the formula

$$\Delta t_{ij} = \text{reaction time } (A_{ij}, \mathbf{z}) = -\ln(\text{random})/w(A_{ij}, \mathbf{z}) \tag{36}$$

where random is a random number from a uniform distribution on (0, 1). Agent i then chooses his potential action A_i^* as that action for which the reaction time is minimal. The probability for choosing A_{ij} as A_i^* equals $w(A_{ij}, \mathbf{z}) \,/\, w_i(\mathbf{z})$, where

$$w_i(\mathbf{z}) = \sum_{j=1}^{n_i(\mathbf{z})} w(A_{ij}, \mathbf{z}) \tag{37}$$

is the reaction rate of the agent i. The corresponding reaction time $\Delta t_i = \min_j \Delta t_{ij}$ is then the realization of an exponential distribution with mean $1/w_i(\mathbf{z})$. Finally, the potential action $A^* = A^*_{i*}$ of the agent i^* with minimal reaction time is executed at time $t + \Delta t^*$

$$\Delta t^* = \Delta t_{i*} = \min_i \Delta t_i. \tag{38}$$

Again the probability that agent i is the next actor is proportional to his reaction rate, namely $w_i(\mathbf{z}) \,/\, w(\mathbf{z})$,

$$w(\mathbf{z}) = \sum_{i=1}^{N} w_i(\mathbf{z}) = -w(\mathbf{z}, \mathbf{z}) \tag{39}$$

and the waiting time Δt^* is the realization of an exponential distribution with mean $1/w(\mathbf{z})$. If A^* is a call then the simulation proceeds as above with simulation of reaction times for each agent and each action. But if A^* is a reevaluation of agent i^*, then a new reaction time and potential action must only be computed

(2) Cf. Loistl/Landes (1989), p. 100.

for agent i^*, the potential actions of the remaining agents remain the same but with rest reaction time $\Delta t_i := \Delta t_i - \Delta t^*$. The next actor is then again elected as the one with minimal reaction time.

In this way, the simulation runs until a preassigned time is reached. For each parameter constellation, L paths p_t^ℓ, $0 \leqslant t \leqslant t_{max}$, $\ell = 1, \ldots, L$, are simulated (in our simulations $L = 100$) and the marginal distributions

$$\hat{P}_t(p) = \frac{1}{L} \# \{\ell \mid p_t^{(\ell)} = p\} \tag{40}$$

are estimated from the simulated path for a set $t_k = k / K \, t_{max}$, $k = 0, \ldots, K$, of time instants.

III. Numerical illustration

1. Design of computation

The implication of the model will be demonstrated by numerical examples. We report the results mainly by graphical representation. The following diagrams are organized in a uniform shape. They exhibit in the upper right and the lower left quadrant three-dimensional graphs, in the lower right and the upper left corner however tables. The table in the upper left corner presents the scenario of the market atmosphere described by the distribution of the intrinsic value, by the behavioural parameters and by the amount of the opening quotation. The microstructure is due to an open outcry market, where sellers compete against sellers and buyers against buyers.

In every simulation there are assumed 100 agents acting at the market place. The other explicit parameter values are at least partly different in every simulation. There have been investigated many constellations. In the following, the results of only three different scenarios will be presented.

The three-dimensional (time, value estimate and frequency) diagram in the lower left corner exhibits the adjustment of the value estimates due to the market performance during the market session. It starts with the graphical representation of all the market participants' a priori estimation of the intrinsic value $\hat{\mathbf{p}}^{ext}$, condensed as a frequency distribution. The exact figures describing the frequency distribution are given in the first two lines of the table in the upper left corner. The diagrams shows along the time axis how this distribution changes on the average of the 100 calculations performed within every simulation.

The three-dimensional (time, price quotation, frequency) diagram in the upper right corner shows in the same manner the distribution of the prices quoted. It exhibits first the opening quotation, that is also reported in the last line of the upper left corners' table. The diagram describes the price quotations of the 100 simulations by means of their frequency distribution during the time running. The actual quotations occur at different points of time, but the distributional frequency is as a crossection over all the runs noted at equidistant time points. The reported value might therefore not represent an actual quotation but might be the result of an interpolation between two actual quotations occuring at time points different from the time points when the distribution is computed.

The table in the lower right corner describes the results by means of the mean numbers for occurence of every activity. There are reported the average demand, supply and acceptance activities, discerning whether the activity causes an increase, a decrease of the price, or leaves it unchanged. The statistic of the acceptances reports, if the foregoing call was a demand or a supply, too.

The number of value adjustments is also reported. In this first approach there are only changes of one unit possible, like quotations at the stock market which change at least by one unit. In our model, changes at a multiple of one unit are expressed by the speed of sequence of activities. With regard to the same time span there are quite different changes possible.

In this early stage of investigation model we apply a simple (truncated) normal distribution, expressing a more or less unique estimation of the intrinsic value.

Simulation of market performance. Case 1.

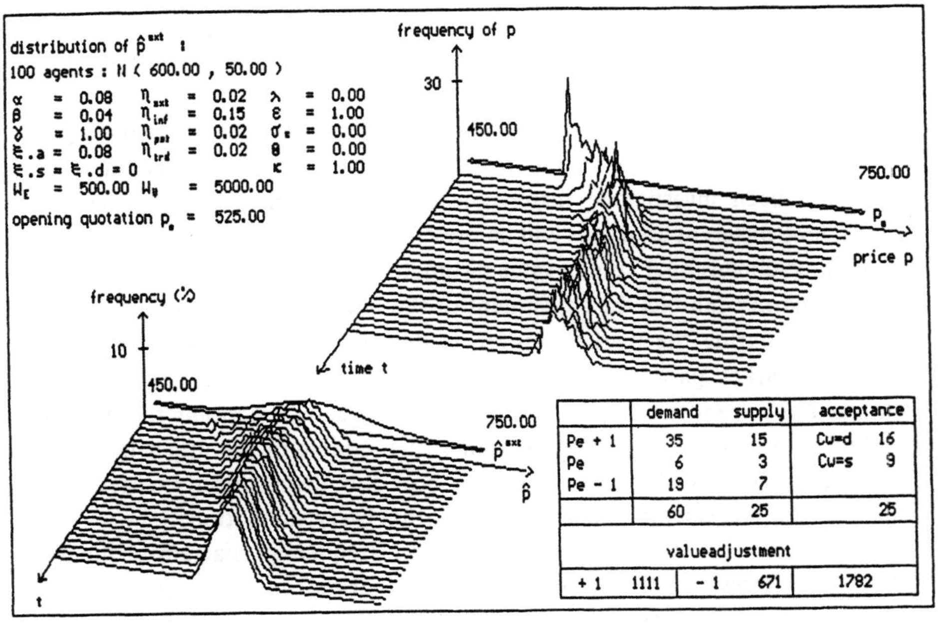

Simulation of market performance. Case 2.

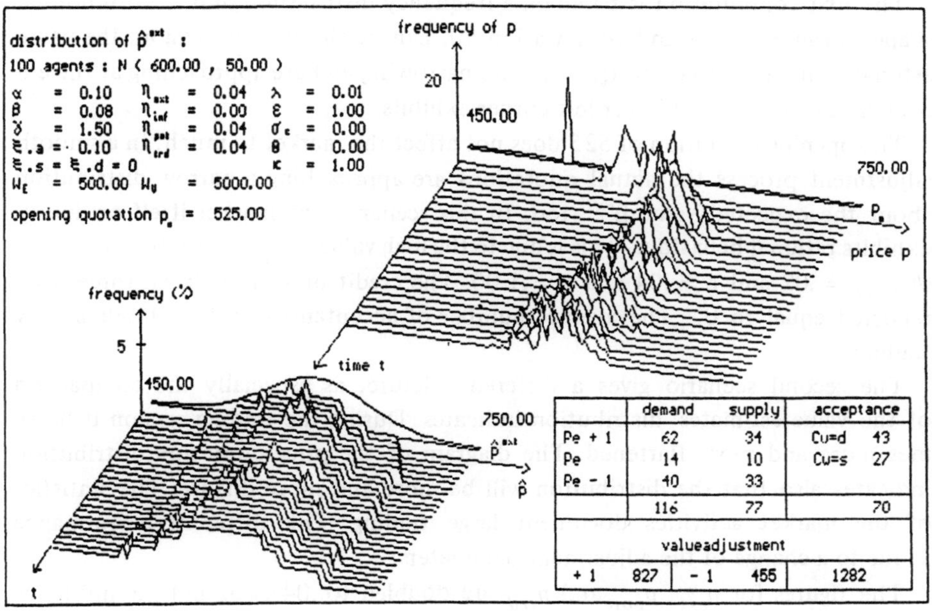

Simulation of market performance. Case 3.

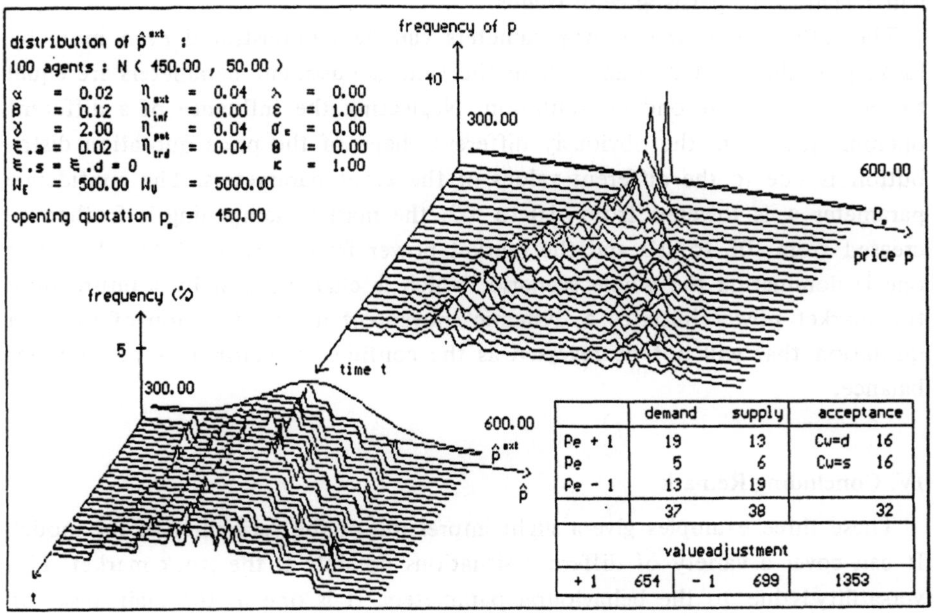

2. The results

The first computation is based on a frequency distribution of $\hat{\mathbf{p}}^{ext}$ with normal shape, mean = 600, standard deviation 50. During the trading session, the value estimates of the market participants are narrowing and are approaching at the expected value $\hat{\mathbf{p}}^{ext}$ as the lower left corner exhibits.

The opening quotation of 525 does not affect the market to much: In a smooth adjustment process the actual quotations are approaching a narrow distribution about the expected value $\hat{\mathbf{p}}^{ext}$ too. In this scenario, the market itself obviously exhibits rational behaviour. This is due to the high value of $\eta_{inf} = .15$, the low values of $\eta_{ext} = .02$ and $\beta = .04$ and $\gamma = 1.00$. The credit pressure is in all three cases reported equal to 0. The average number of acceptances of 25 exhibits a slow trading.

The second scenario gives a different picture, as especially the comparison of the value estimates' distribution indicates. During the trading session it becomes more and more flattened. The diagram of the price quotation distribution indicates also that the distribution will be more and more diffuse. The statistics of the market activities document large trading. This different performance is due to a change of the adjustment parameters:

The figures for η_{ext}, η_{pot} and η_{trd} are doubled to .04 each and the influence of the market performance is neglectable with $\eta_{inf} = 0$ compared to $\eta_{inf} = .15$, in the first simulation. The factor for the market potential is increased from .04 to .08 and the confidence in the own price estimation α also increased from .08 to .10. The market power factor γ was also increased from 1.00 to 1.50 which lead to the persistance of trends.

The influence of the event-parameters can be demonstrated even more by looking at the third diagram, where the value adjustment parameters are equal to values of the second computation. Neglecting the influence of a different opening quotation, the obviously different shape of the price quotation distribution is due to the different values of the event parameters. The confidence parameter α is lowered from .10 to .02, the market dampening is further increased from .08 to .12 and the market power from 1.50 to 2.00. The latter one is dominating the whole scenario, which is characterized by a bifurcation: the market power initiates a dynamic movement in the direction of the first quotation that will not be reversed as the confidence factor does not counter balance.

IV. Concluding Remark

These three examples give a slight impression of the variability of the model. It can cover a variety of different situations possible at the stock market. This versatility is due to the behavioural parameters. It is one of the main tasks on the current research stage to investigate this topic, esp. if the set of parameters can be reduced referring to the postulate of parsimonious modelbuilding. A further step will be to introduce different parameter sets for the individual market participants and increasing the number of parameters comparably. But compared to the amount of parameters, e.g. the modern weather forecast requiries, we have a parsimonious model. And last but not least, as we try to model at the microlevel such a versatile phenomenon like the stock market, we should not be blamed too much, if we came out with a simple structured, but also highly flexible approach.

REFERENCES

W.B. ARTHUR (1988): *Self-Reinforcing Mechanisms in Economics,* in: P.W. Anderson, K.J. Arrow, D. Pines (ed.): The Economy As An Evolving Complex System, Vol. 5, Santa Fe Institute Studies in the Sciences of Complexity, p. 9-31.

O. LOISTL, T. LANDES (ed.) (1989): *The dynamic pricing of financial assets,* Hamburg, McGraw Hill 1989.

A NEW PERSPECTIVE ON DYNAMIC PORTFOLIO POLICIES

ELISA LUCIANO

Università Cattolica del Sacro Cuore,
Milano, Italy

The paper starts from the preceeding paper by L. Peccati in this issue. The original model is enriched with corporate taxes and reinvestment possibilities.

The decomposition of NPV is used to study an optimal dynamic reinvestment policy.

A generalization of the model is outlined and a numerical example is provided in an appendix.

The purpose of this paper is to obtain portfolio policy prescriptions in a riskless, multiperiod framework, using dynamic optimization techniques and future value evaluation.

First of all, we extend to a world with taxes and reinvestments an intra-period, inter-period decomposition of discounted cash flow originally proposed by Peccati (1989) (1). For the purpose of our discussion we rephrase it in terms of future value.

Then, we combine this decomposition with the discrete maximum principle. The joint use of the two instruments allows us to determine optimal decision in a dynamic framework. With this approach in fact we revisit a classic issue in finance, namely debt-equity mix with corporate taxes. We study also the optimal allocation of retained earnings between the investment itself (reinvestment) and alternative assets.

The plan of the paper is as follows.

Section one briefly summarizes Peccati's notation and some of his results, to be used in what follows.

Section two revises the previous model with reference to an economy where corporate taxes are imposed, and profits can be reinvested as well as rerouted.

Dynamic optimization is then used in order to define rational financial policies within our context: this is the subject matter of section three.

In section four a generalization of the problem is outlined.

Section five summarizes and suggests further extensions.

The appendix provides a numerical example.

---

(1) Peccati L., Multiperiod Analysis of a Levered Portfolio, paper presented at the Fifth Meeting of the Euro Working Group on Financial Modelling, Catania, Italy, April 20-21, 1989.

1. THE SIMPLER MODEL

In a world without taxes Peccati (1989) takes into consideration an investment – call it I – with discounted cash flow

(1)
$$G(\Phi) \equiv \sum_{s=0}^{N} f_s \, \Phi(s, 0),$$

where i) the cash flow at time s, f_s, $s = 0, 1, \ldots, N$, is meant to be positive (negative) whenever it represents a money inflow (outflow), ii) f_0 is assumed to be negative, and iii) the discount factors $\Phi(s, 0)$ are particular cases of

$$\Phi(s, t) \equiv \prod_{u=t}^{s-1} 1/(1 + R_u), \qquad (s > t),$$

R_u being the interest rate on alternative assets in the period $(u, u + 1)$.

I – as well as its alternative – can be thought of as a single asset or as a portfolio: in the latter case, its composition is given.

An internal financial law Φ^* for the investment I (from now on *IFL*) is defined as a solution of the equation

$$G(\Phi^*) = 0.$$

Corresponding to it interest rates ρ_s exist, which generalize the standard notion of internal rate of return:

$$\Phi^*(s, t) \equiv \prod_{u=t}^{s-1} 1/(1 + \rho_u), \qquad (s > t).$$

With reference to the investment *I* the notion of outstanding capital is introduced too: the outstanding capital at time s, w_s, is recursively defined as

(2)
$$w_s \equiv w_{s-1} \,(1 + \rho_{s-1}) - f_s.$$

In addition, w_0 is taken to be $-f_0$, so that

$$w_s = \sum_{u=s+1}^{N} f_u \, \Phi^*(u, s),$$

and $w_N = 0$.

Solving for f_s in (2) and substituting in (1) we obtain the following representation for $G(\Phi)$ in terms of outstanding capitals:

(3)
$$G(\Phi) = \sum_{s=1}^{N} w_{s-1}(\rho_{s-1} - R_{s-1}) \, \Phi(s, 0).$$

Especially if the investment I is thought of as a purely financial instrument a sequence of operating cash costs and/or revenues may exist [(2)]: let us call Ω_s these sums, $s \geqslant 1$, with $\Omega_s < 0$ representing costs, $\Omega_s > 0$ revenues. Let $\psi(\Phi)$ be their present value:

$$\psi(\Phi) \equiv \sum_{s=1}^{N} \Omega_s \Phi(s, 0) \equiv \sum_{s=1}^{N} \omega_s w_{s-1} \Phi(s, 0), \tag{4}$$

i.e. define $\omega_s \equiv \Omega_s / w_{s-1}$, $s \geqslant 1$.

The investment I is financed by a mix of debt and equity, since a share θ_0 of the outflow at time zero is supposed to be borrowed from debt holders, while the rest $(1 - \theta_0)$ comes from shareholders. As a counterpart an amount a_s out of $f_s + \Omega_s > (<) \; 0$ is paid to (by) debt holders, while $f_s + \Omega_s - a_s > (<) \; 0$ to (by) equity holders. The latter evaluate each cash flow as if they invested it in the investment with rate of interest R_s. Consequently, if $a_0 \equiv -D_0$, D_0 being the initial debt, the net discounted cash flow for shareholders is

$$\Gamma(\Phi) \equiv f_0 - a_0 + \sum_{s=1}^{N} (f_s + \Omega_s - a_s)\, \Phi(s, 0).$$

As concerns debt, if the rate of return required by creditors during the period $(s-1, s)$ is δ_{s-1}, the evolution of debt over time is represented by

$$D_s \equiv D_{s-1}(1 + \delta_{s-1}) - a_s, \tag{5}$$

where D_s is evidently the corporate debt as $s+$, and the payments a_s are such that

$$D_s = \sum_{u=s+1}^{N} a_u \prod_{t=s}^{u-1} 1/(1 + \delta_t) \equiv \sum_{u=s+1}^{N} a_u H(u, s).$$

According to (2) and (5), the ratio of debt to the outstanding capital

$$\theta_s \equiv D_s / w_s,$$

referred to as leverage, may vary over time.

The evolution of leverage over time, as well as the changes in interest rates, motivate the following splitting up of $\Gamma(\Phi)$:

$$\Gamma(\Phi) = G(\Phi) + \psi(\Phi) + \sum_{s=1}^{N} \theta_{s-1} w_{s-1} (R_{s-1} - \delta_{s-1})\, \Phi(s, 0), \tag{6}$$

which is obtained from (3) and (4). This splitting up points out the overall leverage effect, and can be rewritten as

---

(2) If I is an industrial investment, it seems to be more logical to think of f_s as rents.

$$\Gamma(\Phi) = \sum_{s=0}^{N-1} \tau_s(\Phi) = \tag{7}$$

$$= \sum_{s=0}^{N-1} w_s[(1-\theta_s)(\rho_s - R_s) + \theta_s(\rho_s - \delta_s) + \omega_{s+1}]\,\Phi(s+1, 0),$$

which not only puts into evidence the role of debt, but also of the other sources of funds. In fact the contribution to the overall discounted cash flow of each period $(s, s+1)$, $\tau_s(\Phi)$, shows up in (7) as the sum of three addenda, due to equity $(w_s - D_s)$, debt (D_s) and working capital (Ω_s) respectively [3].

The splittings up (6) and (7) prove to be very helpful in defining the rate of return of investments and in determining the role played in their formation by debt and equity.

Our purpose is now to use these decompositions in a normative instead of a descriptive sense. Therefore, we need first of all to enrich the model with tax payments and reinvestment opportunities.

2. THE MODEL WITH REINVESTMENTS AND TAXES

In this section we develop the model summarized above in order to add corporate taxes and reinvestment opportunities. In the meanwhile, we restate it in terms of future values.

Let us assume for the time being that no taxes exist, and compute the future value of Peccati's decomposition:

$$\Gamma(\Phi)/\Phi(N,0) \equiv f_0 - a_0 + \sum_{s=1}^{N} (f_s + \Omega_s - a_s)\,\Phi(s,0)/\Phi(N,0) =$$

$$= \sum_{s=0}^{N-1} w_s[(1-\theta_s)(\rho_s - R_s) + \theta_s(\rho_s - \delta_s) + \omega_{s+1}]\,\Phi(s+1,0)/\Phi(N,0).$$

Under Peccati's hypotheses, the net cash flow for equity holders at s is invested from s on in the asset with rate of return R_u, $u = s, s+1, \ldots, N-1$.

Let us suppose instead that a share $1 - b_s$ of the net (i.e. after cash costs or revenues, interest and principal payment) profits matured in $(s-1, s)$ is reinvested, while a share b_s only is employed at R_u, $u = s, s+1, \ldots, N-1$. Formally, the net cash flow for equity at time s, invested at the interest rate R_u, $u = s, s+1, \ldots, N-1$, is

(3) Each addendum in turn is proportional both to the amount of capital to which it pertains and to the difference between its rate of return through I (ρ_s for debt and equity, 1 for working capital) and its cost (opportunity cost R_s and zero for equity and working capital respectively, effective cost δ_s for debt).

$$b_s(f_s - a_s + \Omega_s), \quad s = 1, 2, \ldots, N,$$

while the capital invested in I in $(s, s+1)$ amounts to the capital at s increased by $(1 - b_s)(f_s - a_s + \Omega_s)$.

In turn, the presence of this additional investment calls for a redefinition of the *IFL* of I and of its outstanding capital. For the sake of convenience, let us define directly the rates of return corresponding to the *IFL*, i.e. the rates ρ_s, $s = 0, 1, \ldots, N-1$, such that

$$\sum_{s=0}^{N} \left[f_s + \sum_{u=1}^{s-1} (1 - b_u)(f_u - a_u + \Omega_u)\, \rho_{s-1} \right] \prod_{i=0}^{s-1} (1 + \rho_i)^{-1} = 0.$$

Correspondingly, let us call outstanding capital the quantity

$$w_s \equiv \sum_{t=s+1}^{N} \left[f_t + \sum_{u=1}^{t-1} (1 - b_u)(f_u - a_u + \Omega_u)\, \rho_{t-1} \right] \prod_{i=s}^{t-1} (1 + \rho_i)^{-1},$$

which obeys to the recurrence relation

$$\text{(8)} \qquad w_s \equiv w_{s-1}(1 + \rho_{s-1}) - f_s - \sum_{u=1}^{s-1} (1 - b_u)(f_u - a_u + \Omega_u)\, \rho_{s-1},$$

with initial condition $w_0 = -f_0$ and final value $w_N = 0$.

Then, since the rate of return of $(1 - b_s)(f_s - a_s + \Omega_s)$ is evidently ρ_u, $u = s, s+1, \ldots, N-1$, as defined above, the value at N of the net cash flow $f_s - a_s + \Omega_s$ is

$$(f_s - a_s + \Omega_s)\,[b_s/\Phi(N, s) + (1 - b_s)/\Phi^*(N, s)].$$

Consistency requires that b_0 is zero, so that equity in $(0, 1)$ is $(1 - b_0)(f_0 + - a_0) = f_0 - a_0$. Also, we impose that $b_N = 1$, i.e. that N represents the ending point not only of the original investment, but also of the reinvestments stemming from it.

When taxes are imposed the net cash flow for equity holders at time s becomes

$$\text{(9)} \qquad f_s + \Omega_s - a_s - t_{s-1}(\rho_{s-1} w_{s-1} + \Omega_s - \delta_{s-1} D_{s-1}), \quad s \geqslant 1,$$

where t_{s-1} is the corporate tax rate for profits gained in $(s-1, s)$ and interest payments $\delta_{s-1} D_{s-1}$ are assumed to be tax deductible. At time 0 the net cash flow for equity remains $f_0 - a_0$.

Using our former definition of outstanding capital and rate of return corresponding to the *IFL*, this cash flow can be written as

$$\{w_{s-1}[1 + \rho_{s-1}(1 - t_{s-1})] - w_s - \sum_{u=1}^{s-1} (1 - b_u)(f_u - a_u + \Omega_u)\, \rho_{s-1}\} +$$

$$- (a_s - \delta_{s-1} D_{s-1}) - (\delta_{s-1} D_{s-1})(1 - t_{s-1}) + \Omega_s(1 - t_{s-1}).$$

This representation puts into evidence the nature of the cash flow itself: the first addendum in fact represents the after tax variation in the outstanding capital, the second is the principal repayment to debt holders, and finally the third and fourth are the net burden of interest payments and cash costs or revenues.

The last formula enlights also the net rate of return of I in $(s - 1, s)$: $\rho_{s-1}(1 - t_{s-1})$. In order to get a correct evaluation of the net future value of the cash flows from I, we must use this rate of return to compound their reinvested share. Accordingly, we define the compound factors:

$$\mu^*(s, N) = \prod_{u=s}^{N-1} (1 + \rho_u(1 - t_{cu})), \quad s < N.$$

and analogously the compound factors for the share rerouted to the alternative investment:

$$\mu(s, N) = \prod_{u=s}^{N-1} (1 + R_u(1 - t_{cu})), \quad s < N.$$

Finally, we denote with β_s the weighted average of $\mu(s, N)$ and $\mu^*(s, N)$:

$$\beta_s \equiv b_s\, \mu(s, N) + (1 - b_s)\, \mu^*(s, N).$$

With these definitions, the value for shareholders of the investment I at N is

$$\Gamma(\mu, \mu^*) =$$

$$= (f_0 - a_0)\, \mu^*(0, N) +$$

$$+ \sum_{s=1}^{N} [f_s + \Omega_s - a_s - t_{s-1}(\rho_{s-1} w_{s-1} + \Omega_s - \delta_{s-1} D_{s-1})]\, \beta_s.$$

By substituting in this formula the recurrence relations for w_s and D_s, as well as the definitions of the leverage ratio and of ω_s, the future value of I can be decomposed into N addenda, which we will show in a moment, after having introduced some additional symbols.

The part of the future value of I which pertains to the period $(s, s + 1)$, which will be denoted with $\tau(\mu, \mu^*)$, is due to the simultaneous contributions of equity, retained earnings, debt and working capital.

The contribution of equity $(w_s - D_s)$ is:

$$(w_s - \theta_s)\{[b_{s+1}(1 + \rho_s(1 - t_s)) - b_s(1 + R_s(1 - t_s))]\, \mu(s + 1, N) +$$

$$+ (b_s - b_{s+1})(1 + \rho_s(1 - t_s))\, \mu^* (s + 1, N)\},$$

which can be written as $(w_s - \theta_s)\ k_s$.

The quota from retained earnings is:

$$- \sum_{u=1}^{s} (1 - b_u)(f_u - a_u + \Omega_u)\, \rho_s\, \beta_{s+1}\,,$$

while that of debt (D_s) amounts to:

$$\theta_s\, w_s\, (\rho_s - \delta_s)(1 - t_s)\, \beta_{s+1}.$$

Finally, working capital (cash costs or revenues Ω_s) contributes with:

$$\omega_{s+1}\, w_s (1 - t_s)\, \beta_{s+1}.$$

We then have the following decomposition of the future value of I:

$$\Gamma(\mu, \mu^*) = \sum_{s=0}^{N-1} \tau_s(\mu, \mu^*) = \tag{10}$$

$$= \sum_{s=0}^{N-1} w_s \{(1 - \theta_s)\, k_s + [\theta_s(\rho_s - \delta_s)(1 - t_s) + \omega_{s+1}(1 - t_s)]\, \beta_{s+1}\} +$$

$$- \sum_{u=1}^{s} (1 - b_u)\ (f_u - a_u + \Omega_u)\, \rho_s\, \beta_{s+1}.$$

The fact that $\tau_s(\mu, \mu^*)$ is the sum of four contributions, due to equity capital, retained earnings, debt capital and cash costs or revenues (4), allows us to rewrite the future value of I in the following way:

$$\Gamma(\mu, \mu^*) = \tag{11}$$

$$= E(\mu, \mu^*) + R(\mu, \mu^*) + \psi(\mu, \mu^*) + \sum_{s=0}^{N-1} \theta_s\, w_s\, (\rho_s - \delta_s)(1 - t_s)\, \beta_{s+1}\,,$$

where

---

(4) In Peccati's model (see (7) above, to which (10) reduces when $t_s = 1 - b_s = 0$, $s = 0, 1, 2, \ldots, N$) the contribution to the $(s, s + 1)$ addendum of discounted cash flow of each source of capital was the product of the capital in question times its spread: rate of return through I (ρ_s or one) minus cost (true or opportunity).

Under our hypotheses the contribution is still the product of the amount of capital times its spread, but: i) as concerns equity, the spread is in terms of compound factors instead of rates, ii) as regards reinvestments, the opportunity cost does not appear.

$$E(\mu, \mu^*) = \sum_{s=0}^{N-1} w_s(1 - \theta_s)\, k_s,$$

describes the equity role in the formation of the future value of I,

$$R(\mu, \mu^*) = -\sum_{s=0}^{N-1} \sum_{u=1}^{s} (1 - b_u)(f_u - a_u + \Omega_u)\, \rho_s\, \beta_{s+1},$$

is the contribution of reinvestments,

$$\psi(\mu, \mu^*) = \sum_{s=0}^{N-1} \omega_{s+1}\; w_s\,(1 - t_s)\, \beta_{s+1} = \sum_{s=1}^{N} \Omega_s(1 - t_{s+1})\, \beta_s,$$

evidences the role of working capital.

Finally, the fourth addendum in (11) puts into evidence the leverage effect in the presence of taxes: when $b_s = 1$, $s = 1, 2, \ldots, N$, this effect can be compared with the one in the model without taxes (see (7) above). If the net return of assets does not change with respect to the previous model [(5)], debt increases the profitability of the investment even more than above. As expected, there is a tax shield on debt, which is proportional in each period to the cost of debt, to its amount and to the tax rate [(6)].

An alternative representation of the future value of I, which can be compared with the splitting up (6) above, is:

(12) $$\Gamma(\mu, \mu^*) = G(\mu, \mu^*) + R(\mu, \mu^*) + \psi(\mu, \mu^*) - \Delta(\mu, \mu^*),$$

where

(13) $$G(\mu, \mu^*) = \sum_{s=0}^{N-1} w_s\, k_s,$$

(14) $$\Delta(\mu, \mu^*) = \sum_{s=0}^{N-1} \theta_s\, w_s\, [-\beta_s + (1 + \delta_s\,(1 - t_s))\, \beta_{s+1}].$$

This formulation puts into evidence the role of assets on the one side (G), liabilities (R, ψ and Δ) on the other: the comparison with the future value of the decomposition (6) can be done as above.

---

(5) i.e. if the net rate of interest corresponding to the IFL now ($\rho_s(1 - t_s)$) is the same as the net rate earned in the previous model (ρ_s, which was also a gross rate).

(6) In fact, when i) $b_s = 1, s = 1, 2, \ldots, N$, ii) $\rho_s(1 - t_s)$ amounts to ρ_s in the previous model, the tax shield on debt is $D_s\, \delta_s\, t_s$.

3. OPTIMAL PORTFOLIO POLICIES

The purpose of this section is to show how the splitting up of future value (10) can be used in order to optimize financial decisions concerning the amount of capital invested in I and in other assets and their sources.

We will take into consideration first of all the optimal choice of debt for a given asset policy (section 3.1). Then we will analyze the opposite issue, i.e. fixing an optimal reinvestment path for given external financing (section 3.2).

3.1. Optimal debt path

For given asset policy and initial debt, shareholders may be interested in choosing the debt path – i.e. the values of a_s, $s = 1, 2, \ldots, N$ – which maximize the net future value of I.

This choice is constrained, since i) creditors are likely to fix a minimum due payment, ii) in any case, no more than the whole debt with interests is given back: this sum represents a maximum due payment.

Formally, the problem is that of maximizing the future value of I by a proper choice of the instalments $a_1, a_2, \ldots, a_N$:

$$\max_{a_1, \ldots, a_N} \Gamma(\mu, \mu^*),$$

subject to the constraints

$$a^{sm} \leqslant a_s \leqslant a^{sM},$$

i.e. a_s between a minimum (a^{sm}) and a maximum (a^{sM}) level, where

$$a^{sM} = -\sum_{u=0}^{s-1} a_u \prod_{t=u}^{s-1} (1 + \delta_t), \tag{15}$$

which means that at most the whole debt is paid back.

Since the representation (10) for the future value of I holds and the recurrence relation (5) for debt is given, the problem at hand can be solved using the discrete maximum principle.

Let $H(D_s, a_{s+1}, p_{s+1}, s)$ be the Hamiltonian [7]

$$H(D_s, a_{s+1}, p_{s+1}, s) \equiv$$
$$\equiv \tau_s(\mu, \mu^*) + p_{s+1} [D_s(1 + \delta_s) - a_{s+1} - D_{s+1}],$$

---

[7] See, for example, Whittle, P., Optimization over time, J. Wiley, New York, 1982.

where p_{s+1} is the dynamic multiplier for debt at time $s + 1$, D_s the state variable, a_{s+1} the control.

With the above notation our optimization problem can be stated as:

$$\max_{p,a.D} \sum_{s=0}^{N-1} H(D_s, a_{s+1}, p_{s+1}, s),$$

where p, a and D are the n-dimensional vectors formed by p_{s+1} and a_{s+1}, $s = 0, 1, 2, \ldots, N-1$, D_s, $s = 1, 2, \ldots, N$.

This problem is still subject to the constraint:

$$a^{sm} \leqslant a_s \leqslant a^{sM}.$$

The optimum with respect to the dynamic multipliers gives back the equations of motion that have already been used in defining $\tau_s\ (\mu, \mu^*)$.

As concerns debt at time s, $s = 1, 2, \ldots, N-1$, the stationarity condition of the Hamiltonians with respect to it provides a difference equation in p_s:

$$[\beta_s - (1 + \delta_s(1 - t_s))\,\beta_{s+1}] + p_{s+1}\,(1 + \delta_s) - p_s = 0,$$

with the final condition $p_N = 0$ (so that the borrower can pay back the whole remaining debt).

The equation above is satisfied by

$$(16) \qquad p_s = \sum_{u=s}^{N-1} [\beta_u - (1 + \delta_u(1 - t_{cu}))\,\beta_{u+1}] \prod_{t=s}^{u-1} (1 + \delta_t).$$

Therefore, the shadow value of debt at time s is the future value (at N) of the margin provided by \$1 of debt at time s, as evidenced in (14) [8]. The future value is determined taking into account the fact that \$1 of debt at s becomes $\$(1 + \delta_s)$ at $s + 1$, $\$(1 + \delta_s)\,(1 + \delta_{s+1})$ at $s + 2$, and so on.

Finally, since the Hamiltonian is linear in the control, the most profitable control policy is of the bang-bang type, depending on the sign of the dynamic multipliers, which we know from (16), and on the compound factors for debt. Because of the constraint on the instalments mentioned above, $a^{sm} \leqslant a_{s+1} \leqslant \leqslant a^{sM}$, a_{s+1} is a) a^{sm} if

$$p_{s+1} > (1 - b_{s+1}) \sum_{u=s+1}^{N-1} p_u\, \beta_{u+1},$$

b) a^{sM} in the opposite case.

---

(8) The change in sign is due only to the formulation (12).

This policy perfectly corresponds to our intuition. Note for instance that, if $b_u = 0$, $u = s, s+1, \ldots, N-1$, p_s is negative – and the whole debt is paid back – if in the future the after-tax cost of debt ($\delta_u(1 - t_{cu})$) is "in the average" lower than its after-tax rate of return through I ($\rho_u(1 - t_{cu})$).

With respect to intuition, the discrete maximum principle gives the correct weights for averaging future spreads:

$$\prod_{t=s}^{u-1} (1+\delta_t) \prod_{t=u+1}^{N-1} (1+\rho_t(1-t_t)).$$

Analogous conclusions can be drawn when at least one of the b_s is non null.

3.2. Optimal equity path

The problem studied above can be turned into the opposite: for a given time path of debt and given initial equity, how can the future value of I be maximized by a proper reinvestment policy, i.e. by a proper choice of b_s, $0 \leqslant b_s \leqslant 1$? As in the previous case, the Hamiltonian formulation helps us a lot. Formally, the problem at hand can in fact be stated as

$$\max_{b_1, \ldots, b_N} \Gamma(\mu, \mu^*), \tag{17}$$

subject to (8) and (5) above.

Its Hamiltonian formulation is

$$\max_{q,b,w} \sum_{s=0}^{N-1} M(w_s, b_{s+1}, q_{s+1}, s),$$

where q, b and w are the n-dimensional vectors formed by q_{s+1}, the multipliers for w_s, b_{s+1}, $s = 0, 1, \ldots, N-1$, w_s, $s = 1, 2, \ldots, N$, and

$$M(w_s, b_{s+1}, q_{s+1}, s) \equiv$$

$$\equiv \tau_s(\mu, \mu^*) + q_{s+1}\Big[w_s(1+\rho_s) - f_{s+1} - \sum_{u=1}^{s} (1-b_u)\cdot$$

$$\cdot (f_u - a_u + \Omega_u)\,\rho_s - w_{s+1}\Big].$$

The equation for the dynamic multiplier becomes:

$$k_s + q_{s+1}(1+\rho_s) - q_s = 0,$$

with the final condition $q_N = 0$. Its solution is:

$$q_s = \sum_{u=s}^{N-1} k_u \prod_{t=s}^{u-1} (1 + \rho_t).$$

Therefore, the shadow value of reinvestments is the value at time zero of the margins they create, as pointed out in (10).

Similarly to what happened with debt, these margins take into account the "internal" growth of invested capital: \$ 1 of equity at s becomes \$ $(1 + \rho_s)$ at $s + 1$, \$ $(1 + \rho_s)(1 + \rho_{s+1})$ at $s + 2$, \$

$$\prod_{t=s}^{u-1} (1 + \rho_t)$$

at u, $u > s$.

As concerns optimal controls, the Hamiltonians are still linear in them. It follows that reinvestment is optimal ($b_s = 0$) whenever

$$(f_s - a_s + \Omega_s) \sum_{u=s+1}^{N} q_u \rho_{u-1} + [f_s - a_s + \Omega_s - t_{s-1}(\rho_{s-1} w_{s-1} + \Omega_s + \\ - \delta_{s-1} D_{s-1})] [\mu(s, N) - \mu^* (s, N)],$$

is negative, rerouting ($b_s = 1$) is optimal if the above quantity is positive. As in the debt case, this control policy perfectly corresponds to our intuition.

4. OPTIMAL PORTFOLIO POLICIES: FURTHER SUGGESTIONS

The joint use of the discrete maximum principle and of the proposed intra-period, inter-period decomposition of future value can be extended to portfolio selection in the usual sense.

As a matter of fact, it can be used in order to choose both assets and liabilities, given an initial structure: it is only a matter of combining the optimality conditions given above. But in order to do this, it must be written explicitly with reference to a portfolio. In the previous sections in fact I could be thought of as a portfolio only because its structure was given.

Following Peccati, let us denote with w_{sa} the outstanding capital of asset a, $a = 1, 2, \ldots, A$. Let f_{sa}, a_{sa} and Ω_{sa} be the cash flow components belonging to a at s, $1 - b_{sa}$ the share of net cash flow for shareholders from asset a reinvested (in a) at s and r_a the rate of return which solves [(9)]

[(9)] The hypothesis of a constant rate of return is introduced just in order to simplify notation: the reader can easily generalize it to the case in which this rate or return fluctuates over time.

$$\sum_{s=0}^{N}\left[f_{sa}+\sum_{u=1}^{s-1}(1-b_{ua})(f_{ua}-a_{ua}+\Omega_{ua})r_a\right](1+r_a)^{-s}=0.$$

In addition let ω_{sa} represent the ratio of Ω_{sa} – cash costs and/or revenues referred to asset a – to w_{s-1a} and let θ_{sai} be the ratio of D_{sai} to w_{sa}, where D_{sai} is the amount at s of debt of type i, $i = 1, 2, \ldots, I$, invested in asset a. The cost of D_{si} is δ_{si}. Finally, let $\mu^*_a(s, N)$ be the compound factor corresponding to r_a: $\mu^*_a(s, N) = (1 + r_a)^{N-s}$, and let k_{sa} and β_{sa} be:

$$k_{sa}\equiv b_{s+1a}(1+r_a(1-t_s))-b_{sa}(1+R_s(1-t_s))+$$
$$+(b_{sa}-b_{s+1a})(1+r_a(1-t_s)),$$
$$\beta_{sa}\equiv b_{sa}\,\mu(s,N)+(1-b_{sa})\,\mu_a^*(s,N).$$

Then it can be easily shown that the decomposition (18) of the future value for a portfolio can be rewritten as:

$$\Gamma_a(\mu,\mu^*)=\sum_{a=1}^{A}\sum_{s=0}^{N-1}\tau_{sa}(\mu,\mu^*)\equiv$$

$$\equiv\sum_{a=1}^{A}\sum_{s=0}^{N-1}\left\{w_{sa}\left[\left(1-\sum_{i=1}^{I}\theta_{sai}\right)k_{sa}+\left[\sum_{i=1}^{I}\theta_{sai}(r_a-\delta_{si})(1-t_s)+\right.\right.\right.$$
$$\left.\left.\left.+\,\omega_{sa}(1-t_s)\right]\beta_{s+1a}\right]-\sum_{u=1}^{s}(1-b_{ua})(f_{ua}-a_{ua}+\Omega_{ua})r_a\,\beta_{s+1a}\right\}.$$

This formula proves to be extremely useful in dynamic optimization problems.

Obviously, reinvestment control modifies the composition of the overall portfolio, both assets and liabilites. The approach would allow us to define exactly the most profitable position in each asset, and to put into evidence the role played in its definition by taxes and interest rates. Furthermore, the time path of the asset holdings would easily be derived.

5. SUMMARY AND EXTENSIONS

This paper combines a particular intra-period, inter-period splitting up of the future value of a portfolio with the traditional discrete maximum principle. The results of this union have been partially explored in sections 3 and 4 above.

On the one side, we have defined the optimal time path of debt for given asset policy.

On the other hand, we have solved the opposite problem, that is choosing the optimal asset trajectory for given liabilities.

As suggested in section 4, the corresponding optimality conditions can be solved simultaneously in order to get the usual portfolio selection.

The obvious extension of these portfolio choice criteria is to uncertainty: the descriptive background is in Luciano and Peccati (1990) [10].

Liquidity constraints (stemming from a financial budget) are likely to prove useful extensions too.

APPENDIX

This appendix provides a numerical example of the optimal choice criteria presented in section 3.1.

Let the following investment be given:

$$f_0 = -100, f_1 = f_2 = f_3 = 10, f_4 = 110.$$

A natural choice for the internal financial law of this project is characterized by $\rho_s = .1, s = 0, \ldots, 3$. The corresponding outstanding are $w_0 = w_1 = w_2 = = w_3 = 100, w_4 = 0$.

Let us assume that no cash costs or revenues exist ($\Omega_s = 0, s \geqslant 1$), that the corporate tax rate is constant: $t_s = .4, s = 0, \ldots, 3$, and that the cost of debt is .04 for the whole time span of the investment ($\delta_s = .04, s = 0, \ldots, 3$). Suppose that half of the initial outflow is financed with debt, half with equity, so that $\theta_0 = .5$. Finally, suppose that reinvestment is not allowed ($b_s = 1, s \geqslant 1$), so that retained earnings are invested in the alternative project, with rate of interest R_s. Let this one be constant: $R_s = .05, s = 0, \ldots, 3$.

Under these hypotheses, the problem of section 3.1 has the following Hamiltonian formulation:

$$\max_{p,D,a} \; (50 \cdot .05 \cdot .6 + 50 \cdot .06 \cdot .6)(1 + .05 \cdot .6)^3 +$$

$$+ \sum_{s=1}^{3} 100\{(1 - \theta_s)[.1(1 - .4) - .05(1 - .4)] +$$

$$+ \theta_s (.1 - .04)(1 - .4)\}(1 + .05(1 - .4))^{3-s} +$$

$$+ \sum_{s=0}^{3} p_{s+1}[D_s \cdot (1 + .04) - a_{s+1} - D_{s+1}].$$

The difference equation for the debt multiplier, p_s, has the following solution:

---

(10) See Luciano, E., Peccati, L., The decomposition of random cash flows, paper presented at the 5th FUR Conference, Durham, 1990.

$$p_s = \sum_{u=s}^{3} (1 + .05(1 - .4))^{3-u} (.05 - .04)(1 - .4)(1 + .04)^{u-s},$$

so that

$$p_1 = [(1 + .05(1 - .4))^2 + (1 + .05(1 - .4))(1 + .04) + \\ + (1 + .04)^2](.05 - .04)(1 - .4) = .01928,$$

$$p_2 = (2 + .05(1 - .4) + .04)(.05 - .04)(1 - .4) = .00074,$$

$$p_3 = (.05 - .04)(1 - .4) = .006.$$

These values of p_s are used in order to decide the most profitable control policy.

Suppose that i) there is no lower limit on a_s, but debt cannot be increased, i.e. suppose that $a^{ms} = 0$, and that ii) the upper limit on a_s is given by the compound amount of debt:

$$a^{sM} = 50(1 + .04)^s - \sum_{u=1}^{s-1} a_u (1 + .04)^{s-u}.$$

Under these hypotheses, since:

$$p_1 > 0, p_2 > 0, p_3 > 0,$$

we have $a_1 = a_2 = a_3 = 0$. Due to the fact that $p_4 = 0$, a_4 is free. In our case it must be equal to the compound amount of debt: $a_4 = 50(1 + .04)^4$.

This policy corresponds to our intuition: even if we disregard tax shields, since the cost of debt (.04) is less than the rate of return on the investment (.05) [(11)], and substitution of external financing with the internal one is not allowed, the most profitable financial policy is to pay debt back as late as possible.

All others equal, if we suppose that retained earnings are reinvested in the project ($b_s = 0$ when $s = 0, 1, 2, 3$), we get the following Hamiltonian:

$$100 \cdot .5 \cdot (.1 - .04)(1 - .4)(1 + .1)^3 + [100 \cdot \theta_1 \cdot (.1 - .04)(1 - .4) + \\ - (10 - a_1) .1](1 + .1)^2 + [100 \cdot \theta_2 \cdot (.1 - .04)(1 - .4) + \\ - (20 - a_1 - a_2) \cdot .1](1 + .1) + 100 \cdot \theta_3 \cdot (.1 - .04)(1 - .4) + \\ - (30 - a_1 - a_2 - a_3) \cdot .1.$$

The multipliers become:

(11) Remind that retained earnings are rerouted.

$$p_1 = (1 + .1)^2 \, [(1 + .1) - (1 + .04(1 - .4))] + (1 + .1) \, [(1 + .1) +$$
$$- (1 + .04(1 \; -.4))] \, (1 + .04) + [(1 + .1) - (1 + .04(1 - .4))] \, (1 + .04)^2 = .2611,$$
$$p_2 = (1 + .1) \, [(1 + .1) - (1 + .04 \, (1 - .4))] +$$
$$+ [(1 + .1) - (1 + .04(1 - .4))] \, (1 + .04) = .16264,$$
$$p_3 = (1 + .1) - (1 + .04(1 - .4)) = .076,$$

and satisfy the inequalities:

$$p_1 > .1(1 + .1) + .1 = .21,$$
$$p_2 > .1,$$
$$p_3 > 0.$$

As a consequence, also in this case the instalments paid at time 1, 2 and 3 (a_s, s = 1, 2, 3) must be at their minimum level (zero). The whole debt is paid back at time 4. Once again, this policy is consistent with our intuition: apart from the tax shield, external financing costs .04 and is reivested at .1. As a consequence, it is worth keeping it.

THE SPLITTING UP OF A FINANCIAL PROJECT INTO UNIPERIODIC CONSECUTIVE PROJECTS

PAOLO MANCA
Dipartimento di Statistica e Matematica Applicata all'Economia
Università di Pisa, Italia

The splitting up of a financial project into "uniperiodic" consecutive financial projects, has been discussed for special cases in a rather theoretical context.

The aim of the present paper is to explore this topic within a general framework, illustrating the capability of the proposed approach.

The resulting implication which are specifically pertinent to the valuation of a financial operation will be discussed in a forthcoming paper.

§1. We start with some notations, definitions and a theorem which will be used in the following.

A project whose net cash flows are all zero is a zero-project.

By A we will denote a non zero-project whose (net) cash flows: $a_0, \ldots, a_n$, are not all of the same sign and which take place at the times $t_0 = 0, \ldots, t_n = n$, respectively.

We suppose that for each non zero project we have:

$$a_0 \, a_n \neq 0 \tag{1}$$

Let i, $i \in (-1, +\infty)$, denote the interest rate, $u = 1 + i$ and $v = (1 + i)^{-1}$. $V(i)$ and $W(i)$ stand for the discounted cash flow – or present value – and for the future cash – or amount – of the project A, respectively.

The internal rate of return (irr) of A corresponds to the *unique* value of the rate of return i for which $V(i) = 0$; in the case of a non-unique solution we speak simply of "a root" of the present value.

A simple project is a project of the kind:

a,	b	(cash flows)
p,	q	(times)

A simple project is a simple investment (s.i.) if:

(2) $$a < 0, b > 0, p < q$$

A simple project is a simple financing (s.f.) if:

(3) $$a > 0, b < 0, p < q$$

Let us observe that, according to our definition, the cash flows of a simple project are either both zero or both non-zero.

We call "uniperiodic" a simple project if $q = p + 1$.

THEOREM. If $a_0, \ldots, a_n$ are $n + 1$ real numbers not all of the same sign, with $n \geqslant 1$ and $a_0 a_n \neq 0$, then the system

(*) $$\begin{aligned} & u_k > 0 \qquad\qquad k = 0, 1, \ldots, n-1 \\ & a_n + u_{n-1} P_{n-1} = 0 \end{aligned}$$

where

$$P_0 = a_0$$

$$P_k = \sum_{r=0}^{k-1} a_r \left(\Pi_{s=r}^{k-1} u_s\right) + a_k \qquad k = 1, \ldots, n-1$$

always has solutions.

The very simple proof is omitted.

§2. Given the project A:

$$A = \begin{matrix} a_0, \ldots, a_n \\ 0, \ldots, n \end{matrix}$$

and the simple projects

(4) $$A_k = \begin{matrix} \alpha_k, & \beta_k \\ k, & k+1 \end{matrix} \qquad k = 0, \ldots, n-1$$

we are interested in finding under which conditions

(5) $$A = \sum_{k=0}^{n-1} A_k$$

where ΣA_k is the project whose cash flows are the sum of the cash flows of the A_k's projects.

As a general rule we will not consider zero-projects in presenting our results.

Obviously every splitting up of A into A_k's, according to (5), is obtained as a solution of the linear system of $2n$ unknowns $\alpha_0, \ldots, \alpha_{n-1}, \beta_0, \ldots, \beta_{n-1}$:

$$\begin{aligned} &\alpha_0 = a_0 \\ (6) \qquad &\beta_k + \alpha_{k+1} = a_{k+1} \qquad k = 0, \ldots, n-2 \\ &\beta_{n-1} = a_n \end{aligned}$$

The system has infinitely many solutions, and embodies the general formula for splitting up a project A as a sum of consecutive uniperiodic simple projects.

The requirement that A or the A_k's should satisfy further specific, financially meaningful conditions, determs particular subsets of the infinite set of solutions of (6).

§3. Many articles about Soper's projects (see [1, 2] and ref's therein) or about the evaluation of "investment", fit into the framework of what has been said above in § 1., provided one consider the following system

$$\begin{aligned} &\alpha_0 = a_0 \\ &\beta_k + \alpha_{k+1} = a_{k+1} \qquad k = 0, \ldots, n-2 \\ (7) \qquad &\beta_{n-1} = a_n \\ &\beta_k = -u_k \alpha_k \\ &u_k > 0 \qquad k = 0, \ldots, n-1 \end{aligned}$$

which is obtained from the system (6) with the auxiliary conditions that

α_k e β_k, for $k = 0, \ldots, n-1$,

be of opposite sign, unless $\alpha_k = \beta_k = 0$.

System (7) expresses the general formula for splitting up A into simple projects which are zero-projects, or simple investments, or simple financing: "z.i.f." will stand in the following for the class of the above projects.

The solutions of (7), as function of the parameters $u_0, \ldots, u_{n-1}$, can be immediately obtained recursively either from $\alpha_0 = a_0$, or from $\beta_{n-1} = a_n$.

The solutions of (7) starting from $\alpha_0 = a_0$, are

$$\begin{aligned} (8) \qquad &\alpha_k = P_k \qquad k = 0, \ldots, n-1 \\ &\beta_k = -u_k P_k \qquad k = 0, \ldots, n-1 \end{aligned}$$

where

$$P_0 = a_0$$

(9)
$$P_k = \sum_{r=0}^{k-1} a_r \left(\Pi_{s=r}^{k-1} u_s\right) + a_k \qquad k = 1, \ldots, n-1$$

and where the parameters $u_0, \ldots, u_{n-1}$, are constrained by the conditions:

(8′)
$$u_k > 0 \qquad k = 0, 1, \ldots, n-1$$
$$a_n + u_{n-1} P_{n-1} = 0$$

which are compatible with the theorem proved in § 1.

With the position $i_k = u_k - 1$ for $k = 0, \ldots, n-1$, – which entails $i_k \in \in (-1 + \infty)$ – we can assign to the solution a significant financial interpretation:

In fact P_k represents the retrospective "project balance" of A – to adopt the terms used by Teichroew, Robichek, Montalbano – at time $t = k$, where i_k represents the interest rate in the period $(k, k+1)$ for $k = 0, \ldots, n-1$.

Such interest is to be understood as "red" interest if the simple project

$$\begin{matrix} \alpha_k, & \beta_k \\ k, & k+1 \end{matrix}$$

is a s.f., as "black" interest if it is a s.i., and as insignificant interest if $\alpha_k = \beta_k = 0$.

If all interest rates i_k are equal to the same value i, P_k coincides with W_k, the amount at time $t = k$, and interest rate i, of the project whose net cash flows are $a_1, \ldots, a_k$:

(10)
$$W_k(i) = \sum_{h=0}^{k} a_h u^{k-h} \qquad k = 0, \ldots, n$$

The solution of (7) starting from $\beta_{n-1} = a_n$, where $v_k = 1/u_k$, for $k = 0, \ldots, n-1$, is

(8a)
$$\alpha_k = -Q_k \qquad k = 0, \ldots, n-1$$
$$\beta_k = u_k Q_k \qquad k = 0, \ldots, n-1$$

where

$$Q_{n-1} = v_{n-1} a_n$$

(9 bis)
$$Q_k = v_k \left\{ a_{k+1} + \sum_{r=k+2}^{n} a_r \left(\prod_{t=k+1}^{r-1} v_t \right) \right\} \qquad k = 0, \ldots, n-2$$

and where the parameters $u_0, \ldots, u_{n-1}$, are constrained by the conditions

(8'a)

$$u_k > 0 \qquad k = 0, 1, \ldots, n-1$$

$$a_0 + Q_0 = 0$$

consistently with the theorem in § 1.

With the position $i_k = u_k - 1$ for $k = 0, \ldots, n-1$, – which entails $i_k \in \in (-1 + \infty)$ – we can assign to the solution a significant financial interpretation:

Infact Q_k represents the prospective "project balance" of A at time $t = k$, where i_k represents the interest rate in the period $(k, k+1)$ for $k = 0, \ldots, n-1$. Such interest is to be understood as "red" interest if the simple project

$$\begin{matrix} \alpha_k , & \beta_k \\ k , & k+1 \end{matrix}$$

is a s.f., as "black" interest if it is a s.i., and as insignificant interest if $\alpha_k = \beta_k = 0$.

If all interest rates i_k are equal to the same value i, Q_k coincides with V_k the discounted cash flows at time $t = k$, and interest rate i, of the project whose net cash flows are $a_{k+1}, \ldots, a_n$:

(10 bis) $$V_k(i) = \sum_{r=k+1}^{n} a_r v^{r-k} \qquad k = 0, \ldots, n-1$$

§4. The results of the previous paragraphs open up many interesting possible developements, of a theoretical and an applied character.

For instance a project A which can be expressed as the sum of simple investments (apart from zero-projects), is characterized, according to (8), by:

$$P_k \leqslant 0 \qquad k = 0, \ldots, n-1$$

$$a_n > 0$$

This conditions, because $a_0 a_n \neq 0$, are equivalent to

(11)

$$a_0 < 0$$

$$a_n > 0$$

$$P_k \leqslant 0 \qquad k = 1, \ldots, n-1$$

In an analogous way a project A which can be expressed as the sum of simple financing (apart from zero-projects), is characterized by

(11')

$$a_0 > 0$$

$$a_n < 0$$

$$P_k \geqslant 0 \qquad k = 1, \ldots, n-1$$

Since the interest rate i_k is the irr of A_k (apart from zero-projects), it is interesting, given A, to determine in which case all A_k's have the same irr.

From (8) (8′) (9) (10) one obtains

$$\text{(12)}\qquad \begin{aligned} &\alpha_k = W_k(i) && k = 0, \ldots, n-1 \\ &\beta_k = -(1+i)\, W_k(i) && k = 0, \ldots, n-2 \\ &W(i) = (1+i)\, W_{n-1}(i) + a_n = 0 \end{aligned}$$

Therefore A can be split up into z.i.f. having the same irr i_0 if and only if i_0 is a root of $V(i)$. Moreover there are as many ways of splitting up A into z.i.f. having the same irr as the roots of $V(i)$.

One may also inquire under which conditions A can be split up into s.i. or into s.f. with the same irr, respectively.

From (10), (11), (12) we obtain

$$\text{(13)}\qquad \begin{aligned} &a_0 < 0 \\ &a_n > 0 \\ &W_k(i) \leqslant 0 \qquad k = 1, \ldots, n-1 \\ &W(i) = 0 \end{aligned}$$

which are the well-known conditions characterizing Soper's projects. From (10), (11), (11′) we get

$$\text{(13′)}\qquad \begin{aligned} &a_0 > 0 \\ &a_n < 0 \\ &W_k(i) \geqslant 0 \qquad k = 1, \ldots, n-1 \\ &W(i) = 0 \end{aligned}$$

Moreover, one can investigate under which conditions A can be split up into simple projects A_k which are s.i. or s.f. having the same irr i, except at most the last one.

From (13), (13′), we obtain the conditions introduced by Teichroew-Robichek-Montalbano [6] in order to define the projects that they call "pure investment" and "pure financing", respectively

$$\text{(14)}\qquad \begin{aligned} &W_k(i) \leqslant 0 \qquad k = 0, \ldots, n-1 \\ &a_0 < 0 \end{aligned}$$

$$\text{(14′)}\qquad \begin{aligned} &W_k(i) \geqslant 0 \qquad k = 0, \ldots, n-1 \\ &a_0 > 0 \end{aligned}$$

§5. The reasoning of the preceeding paragraph can be repeated using relations (8a), (8;a), (9a).

In particular, the conditions corresponding to (14) and (14') are

(14a) $$V_k(i) \geqslant 0 \qquad k = 0, \ldots, n-1$$
$$a_n < 0$$

(14'a) $$V_k(i) \leqslant 0 \qquad k = 0, \ldots, n-1$$
$$a_n > 0$$

These conditions define the project we will call *prospective* pure investiments and financing respectively (In these sense the projects defined by (14) and (14') should be most properly called retrospective).

As is well known (see [6]), the set of solutions of (14) has been shown to coincide with a half-line whose lower bound we denote by i^-:

$$i \in (i^-, +\infty).$$

As we have demostrated in [2], the set of the solution of (14a) coincides with a right neighborhood of $i = -1$, and we denote by i^+ its upper bound:

$$i \in (-1, i^+).$$

For a project to be at the same time a pure investment both retrospective and prospective, i.e. satisfying (14) and (14a), it is necessary and sufficient that: $i^+ \geqslant i^-$.

As we have already proved in [2], this last condition characterizes Soper's projects, and it is easy to demonstrate that

$$i^+ \geqslant i_0 \geqslant i^-$$

where i_0 is the irr of the project.

Then it is possible to demonstrate as a consequence that:

a project A can be expressed as the sum of s.i. all with the same irr

if and only if: $W_A\ (i^+) \geqslant 0$

if and only if: $W_A\ (i^-) \leqslant 0$

Corresponding results can be obtained by using analogous considerations applied to systems (14') and (14'a) so as to characterized the project A which can be split up into s.f. all with the same irr.

§6. If A is a project that cannot be split up into simple projects which are all s.i. or all s.f. with the same irr, then the irr of A, if it exists, has a contradictory financial meaning.

To overcome this "impasse", we must deal with the topic of how to split up a project within a broader framework.

Let us briefly recall that $W_k(i)$ is the retrospective balance project at interest rate i of A at time k, and that $-V_k(i)$ is the prospective balance project of A at time k and at interest rate i:

$$-V_k(i) = -\sum_{r=k+1}^{n} a_r v^{r-k} \qquad k = 0, \ldots, n-1 \tag{15}$$

Moreover:

$$u^k V(i) = W_k(i) + V_k(i) \tag{16}$$

because

$$u^k V(i) = u^k(a_0 + a_1 v + \ldots + a_n v^n)$$
$$= [a_0 u^k + a_1 u^{k-1} + \ldots + a_k] + [a_{k+1} v + \ldots + a_n v^{n-k}]$$

If i_0 is a root of $V(i)$, it hence follows that

$$W_k(i_0) = -V_k(i_0) \tag{17}$$

Therefore, for each root of $V(i)$, we can split up A into the sum of A_k's of the form

$$A_k = \begin{matrix} W_k(i_0) & , & -(1+i_0) V_k(i_0) \\ k & , & k+1 \end{matrix} \tag{18}$$

(It may be noted that (18) could have been proved by starting from (7) and considering (10) and (10a)).

By examining the last formula (18), it can be clearly seen a well known result: the irr is a "good" utility function for the projects which can be expressed as the sum of all s.i. or all s.f., and the irr is a contradictory parameter for evaluating any other project.

In order to reach a more general system in splitting up a project A into simple projects, we have to pointed out the results obtained by Teichroew-Robicheck-Montalbano [6], considering also some recent results reached by L. Peccati [3] (see also [4, 5]): so we can satisfy both financial rules and accounting requirements in periodically assigning items to the balance sheet.

If in each period $(k, k+1)$ for $k = 0, \ldots, n-1$, the "red" interest rate c_k and the "black" interest rate r_k are constant, then the retrospective and prospective balance project of A at time $t = k$ are

$$W_k = \begin{cases} (1 + r_{k-1}) W_{k-1} + a_k & \text{if } W_{k-1} > 0 \\ (1 + c_{r-1}) W_{k-1} + a_k & \text{if } W_{k-1} \leqslant 0 \end{cases}$$

$$k = 1, 2, \ldots, n$$

or

$$W_0 = a_0$$

$$V_k = \begin{cases} (1 + r_k)^{-1} V_{k+1} + a_k & \text{if } V_{k+1} > 0 \\ (1 + c_k)^{-1} V_{k+1} + a_k & \text{if } V_{k+1} \leqslant 0 \end{cases}$$

$$k = 0, 1, \ldots, n-1$$

$$V_n = a_n$$

Where c_k and r_k can represent a priori or a posteriori values, and where W_k and V_k can be evaluated recursively starting with from W_0 and V_n, respectively.

With the premises and the notations adopted above, we can consider two possible ways of splitting up a project A which can be optained by (6) adding some constraints whose financial meanings is clear:

(19)

$$\alpha_0 = a_0$$

$$\beta_k + \alpha_{k+1} = a_{k+1} \qquad k = 0, 1, \ldots, n-2$$

$$\beta_{n-1} = a_n$$

$$\beta_k = \begin{cases} -(1 + r_k)\,\alpha_k & \text{if } \alpha_k > 0 \\ -(1 + c_k)\,\alpha_k & \text{if } \alpha_k \leqslant 0 \end{cases} \qquad k = 0, 1, \ldots, n-2$$

(20)

$$\alpha_0 = a_0$$

$$\beta_k + \alpha_{k+1} = a_{k+1}$$

$$\beta_{n-1} = a_n$$

$$\alpha_k = \begin{cases} -(1 + r_k)^{-1} \beta_k & \text{if } \beta_k > 0 \\ -(1 + c_k)^{-1} \beta_k & \text{if } \beta_k \leqslant 0 \end{cases} \qquad k = 0, 1, \ldots, n-2$$

The solutions of the system (19) – or (20) – allow us to express A as a sum of A_k's as follows

$$A_k = \begin{matrix} W_k\,, & -(1 + x)\,W_k \\ k\,, & k+1 \end{matrix}$$

or

$$A_k = \begin{matrix} -V_k\,, & (1 + x)\,V_k \\ k, & k+1 \end{matrix}$$

where x stands for c_k or for r_k.

By splitting up a project A in this way, we display – both a priori and a posteriori – the periodical allocations of profits and losses we can attribute to A if we adopt a financial policy of indebtedness, or of discount, of future items, respectively.

Of the various possible applications of (19) and (20), it seems worth mentioning two:

I – Under stable conditions it seems reasonable to admit that both "red" and "black" interest rates are constant throghout the period of the project, In this case we obtain on one hand the splitting up of A from a retrospective point of view, and on the other, an analogous splitting up from a prospective point of view.

II – Once we suppose that for each period the liability interest rates $c_0, \ldots, c_{n-1}$, are known, we note

$$W_k = \begin{cases} (1+i)\, W_{k-1} + a_k & \text{if } W_{k-1} > 0 \\ (1 + c_{k-1})\, W_{k-1} + a_k & \text{if } W_{k-1} \leqslant 0 \end{cases}$$

If i_0 is a root of $W_n(i) = 0$,
then the system:

$$\alpha_0 = a_0$$

$$\beta_k + \alpha_{k+1} = a_{k+1}$$

$$\beta_{n-1} = a_n$$

$$\beta_k = \begin{cases} -(1+i_0)\,\alpha_k & \text{if } \alpha_k > 0 \\ -(1+c_k)\,\alpha_k & \text{if } \alpha_k \leqslant 0 \end{cases}$$

splits up A by allocating the periodic profits and losses when $c_0, \ldots, c_{n-1}$ are the predetermined "red" interest rates and i_0 is the resulting "average black interest rate".

Analogous splitting operations are obtained when we consider that the "black" interest rates are known, and we determine an "average red interest rate".

Analogous and corresponding splitting up can be obtained by considering the prospective point of view.

REFERENCES

[1] GRONCHI S., *Tasso interno di rendimento e valutazione dei progetti: un'analisi teorica.* Collana Istituto di Economia, Siena, 1984.

[2] MANCA P., *Operazioni finanziarie di Soper e operazioni di puro investimento secondo Teichroew-Robichek-Montalbano.* Atti del XII Convegno Amases, 1988.

[3] PECCATI L., *DCF e risultati di periodo.* Atti dell'XI Convegno Amases, 1987.

[4] PECCATI L., *La valutazione di attività finanziarie singole e in portafoglio.* Atti del Convegno "Metodi quantitativi per le applicazioni finanziarie", 1987.

[5] PECCATI L., *Rendimento di attività finanziarie ed effetto di leva"* Torino, 1988.

[6] TEICHROEW D., ROBICHEK A., MONTALBANO M., *Mathematical analysis of rates of return under certainty. An analysis of criteria for investment and financing under certainty.* Management Science, Vol. 11 e Vol. 12, 1965.

MODELLING STOCK PRICE BEHAVIOUR BY FINANCIAL RATIOS (*)

TEPPO MARTIKAINEN
School of Business Studies
University of Vaasa
P.O. Box 297 SF-65101 Vaasa, Finland
e-mail tlmEchyde.uwasa.fi

The main purpose of this study is to find out which economic dimensions of the firm are reflected in stock price behaviour in the Finnish stock market. Based on the previous theoretical articles, four economic dimensions are chosen: profitability, financial leverage, operating leverage and corporate growth. Twelve (12) financial ratios are then selected to represent these four dimensions. All the Finnish firms common series listed for the whole 1974-1986 period are included in the empirical analysis.

All of the four expected dimensions above are found in the empirical classification pattern of ratios. On the cross-sectional level, profitability and financial leverate are reported as determinants of stock price behaviour. Corporation growth is merely connected to the risk of the common stock. Somewhat weaker results concerning the association between stock price behaviour and operating leverage factor may be due to difficulties measuring operating leverage on an empirical level.

When studying the intra-year explanatory power of financial ratios, it is reported that the explanatory power of financial ratios tends to increase when the reporting day approaches, and starts to decrease after that releasing day of financial statement numbers. Empirical evidence strongly indicates that financial ratios represent pricing relationships in a substantive manner.

1. Introduction

There exists strong empirical evidence on the connection between accounting earnings and stock prices (see e.g. Ball & Brown 1968, Foster & Ohlsen & Shevlin 1984 and Dyckman & Morse 1986 and the literature cited there). However, other financial statement numbers have received relatively little attention. The main interest of this paper is to find out which economic dimension of the firms are reflected in stock price behaviour in the Finnish stock market. The economic dimensions are measured using financial ratios of the companies. With stock

---

(*) The financial support by the Academy of Finland as well as the helpful comments and suggestions of an anonymous referee are gratefully acknowledged.

price behaviour one refers to stock prices, stock returns, as well as risk of the common stock.

In this paper we concentrate on solely those dimensions which can be regarded as theoretical determinants of common stock systematic risk. These determinants are profitability, capital structure, growth and operating leverage. The theoretical connection between these dimensions and stock price behaviour has been considered by e.g. Ball & Brown (1969), Bowman (1979), Lev (1974), Fewings (1975), Hamadå (1969, 1972) and Martikainen (1989).

In previous empirical studies concerning the association between stock prices and financial ratios, financial statement data has typically been studied on a single ratio level.

However, it should be taken into account that a single ratio may measure somewhat different things for different firms. That is why economic dimensions will be created in this paper. This is carried out applying factor analysis. The stability of the results will also be tested studying how he explanatory power of financial ratios on stock prices behaves over time.

2. Data and statistical methods

2.1. The data

The data consists of numbers collected from two information sources: annual financial statements of the firms and monthly stock prices in the Helsinki Stock Exchange. The financial statement data is bases on multivariate cross-sectional data. The data consists of firms common share listed for the whole 1974-1986-period. Financial firms are excluded. The data thus consists of 26 firms.

The basic properties of the average values (averaged over years) of the ratios across firms are reported in Table 1. About the definitions of the ratios see also Yli-Olli (1983) and The Credit Analysis Commission (1983). The ratios are collected from the Tilpana data base constructed in the University of Vaasa (see Laakkonen 1982). When computing the ratios, the maximum depreciations allowed by the Finnish government are used (see e.g. Martikainen & Ankelo 1989). The normality test in Table 1 is carried out using the Shapiro-Wilk W-statistic. This test ratio is the best estimator of the variance (based on the square of a linear combination of the order statistics) to the usual corrected sum of squares estimator of the variance (Shapiro & Wilk 1965). Testing the normality assumption of ratio distributions is crucial due to the assumptions of statistical method used in this paper. To be precise, the parametric significance tests following are based on the normality of the variables. Thus, the Shapiro-Wilk test for normality in Table 1 indicates that especially the empirical results concerning the Debt to Equity and the Wages to Operating Margin ratios must be interpreted

Table 1. Test of normality in average financial ratios of firms.

S-W H0: ratios are normally distributed

* H0 is rejected at 0.05 significance level
** H0 is rejected at 0.01 significance level

kurtosis = skewness = 0 for normal distribution

	mean	skewness	kurtosis	S-W
Net Income Margin	0.857	-0.701	0.178	0.928
Return on Invested Capital	6.746	0.383	0.583	0.947
Return on Investment	8.777	0.380	0.307	0.962
Equity to Capital	0.403	-1.178	1.337	0.896 *
Debt to Sales	0.691	0.199	-0.664	0.959
Debt to Equity	5.863	3.157	9.227	0.446 **
Growth on Revenue Finance	15.573	1.984	7.097	0.837 **
Growth on Capital Investment	15.347	-0.007	-0.412	0.987
Growth on Sales	11.834	-0.383	0.902	0.955
Wages to Operating Margin	7.766	5.082	25.884	0.237**
Fixed to Variable Costs	0.264	0.511	0.653	0.969
Wages to Fixed Assets	0.648	0.743	0.120	0.935

with a moderate level of caution.

In this context it is relevant to emphasize that the informational value of financial ratios may decrease due to several aspects. Typically, financial statements do not make any effort to report changes in the value of the assets held by the corporation. The earnings in accounting reports thus differ from the economic earnings of the company determined in terms of changes in value. In addition, accounting earnings are based on realization and matching and different allocation and accounting methods are used (see e.g. Bernstein 1978, Tamari 1978 and Dyckman & Morse 1986).

The basic assumption when using the ratio form is the strict proportionality between the numerator and the denominator of the ratio, i.e. the relationship between these two items is linear and the constant is zero. This basic assumption of financial ratio analysis has been considered by e.g. McDonald & Morris (1984) and Barnes (1986). The empirical evidence obtained by Perttunen & Martikainen (1989) indicates that this basic assumption of financial ratios typically holds true on Finnish data.

The stock market data used in the empirical analysis consists of average monthly prices from the beginning of January 1974 through December 1986. Average monthly prices are computed from daily stock indexes. The prices are corrected for dividends, splits and new issues. The returns are determined as changes in logarithmic indexes including dividend, issues and splits, i.e.

$$R_{it} = \log(P_{it}) - \log(P_{it-1}),$$

where

R_{it} = return for stock i in month t

P_{it} = stock price index in month t for firm i

The natural logarithm will be used throughout this study. It thus means that the function «log» is to the base e.

2.2. Statistical methods

Three main statistical techniques will be applied in this study: regression analysis, factor analysis and transformation analysis. Regression and factor analysis are very commonly used methods in financial literature (for an illustration of these methods see e.g. Green 1978). However, transformation analysis has not been applied as often. Thus, a short description of this method is included in this paper.

One of the most crucial aspects of the results in factor analysis is the degree of stability in factor patterns. Paying no attention to this stability, factor analysis can become a method of brute empiricism (see e.g. Foster 1986, Lovell 1983). Traditionally, this stability has been measured by simple correlation and congruency coefficients. These two methods are, however, unable to characterise the reason for the non-invariant part prêvailing in these factor solutions (Yli-Olli & Virtanen 1989a).

In the context of the explanation ability of the dissimilar part of the comparable factor solutions, transformation analysis offers a more efficient method to study the stability of factor patterns over time or even across different samples. This method was originally presented by Ahmavaara (1954). Compared with the simple correlation and congruency coefficients, it offers a regression type model shifting of variables from one factor to another (normal transformation). This normal transformation can be seen from the non-zero elements in the transformation matrix. Using transformation analysis we can also via large elements in the residual matrix see if the contents of the corresponding variables has changed (abnormal transformation). A deeper presentation of transformation analysis can be found e.g. in articles by Yli-Olli & Virtanen 1989a, 1990).

Transformation analysis has been mainly applied in Finnish sociological studies. In financial literature transformation analysis was first applied by Yli-Olli (1983) in order to study the degree and nature of medium-term stability exhibited by the factor patterns of financial ratios. In classification of financial ratios this method was further deepened by Yli-Olli & Virtanen (1990) who applied it into cross-sectional samples over different countries. They (Yli-Olli & Virtanen 1989b) also applied it in order to study the long-term stability of factor patterns in the Arbitrage Pricing Theory on stock returns.

3. Long-term association between stock prices and financial ratios

3.1. Classification pattern of financial ratios

The financial statement based variables used in this study are the average values of the financial ratios shown in Table 1. The three-factor solution based on these ratios found by principal component factor analysis method (see Green 1978; 341-379) and varimax rotation thereafter is presented in Table 2 (solely the loadings over 0.25 and below – 0.25 are introduced, the strongest loading for each ratio in bold text). The factor analysis is based on the covariance matrix of the ratios averaged over the period 1974 - 1986. When using the eigenvalue criterion, the four-factor solution would have been chosen. As the interpretation of three-factor solution is much clearer and the so called Cattel's scree-test was in favour of two or three factors, the three-factor solution will be introduced as the main alternative.

Table 2. The varimax-rotated 3-factor solution.

	FACT1	FACT2	FACT3	COMMUNALITY
Net Income Margin	**0.91**			0.87
Return on Invested Capital	**0.89**			0.82
Equity to Capital	**0.88**			0.82
Return on Investment	**0.88**			0.79
Wages to Fixed Assets	**0.73**			0.56
Debt to Sales	**-0.84**			0.79
Growth on Cap.Investments		**0.92**		0.83
Growth on Revenue Finance		**-0.85**		0.73
Debt to Equity	-0.26	**0.45**		0.27
Growth on Sales		0.40	**0.74**	0.73
Fixed to Variable Costs		0.44	**0.52**	0.52
Wages to Operating Margin			**-0.74**	0.60
VARIANCE EXPLAINED	4.59	1.98	1.58	8.15
RATE OF DETERMINATION	0.38	0.17	0.13	cumulative 0.68

As one can notice from the classification pattern above, only all of the a priori profitability ratios had their strongest loading on the same empirical factor. Debt to Equity, Growth on Sales and Wages to Fixed Assets have their loadings on unexpected dimensions above. However, it should be emphasized that the loadings of these ratios (excluding Wages to Fixed Assets) on their a priori expected factors were quite high (Debt to Equity – 0.26 on the 1st factor and Growth on Sales 0.40 on the 2nd factor).

The interpretation of the three empirical factors above can now be presented as follows:

Factor 1 : profitability and capital structure
Factor 2 : growth
Factor 3 : operating leverage

It is quite interesting that the dimensions of profitability and capital structure are so engaged with each other. Even with four – and five – factor solutions they loaded to the same factor. In previous studies the ratios of these dimensions have also had high correlations, but usually they had their strongest loadings on separate empirical factors.

To obtain more information concerning the empirical classification of financial ratios, factor analysis was also carried out based on the first differences of the ratios (the growth rates are used as absolute values also in this analysis). This kind of approach removes the possible problems relating to some trend movements causing from e.g. firm size or time in financial ratio series (see Yli-Olli & Virtanen 1985). Using first-differences also enables us to study the sensitivity of factor patterns to different methods determining the economic dimensions of the firm. The interpretation of the factors in the context of first-diffe-

Table 3. Varimax-rotated three-factor solution based on the first differences of the ratios (growth measured as absolute growth rates).

	FACT1	FACT2	FACT3	COMMUNALITY
Return on Investment	**0.95**			0.91
Return on Invested Capital	**0.95**			0.92
Net Income Margin	**0.93**			0.91
Debt to Equity	**-0.62**	0.42		0.57
Debt to Sales		**0.82**		0.79
Fixed to Variable Costs		**0.76**		0.64
Equity to Capital		**-0.80**		0.65
Growth on Cap. Investments			**0.87**	0.81
Growth on Revenue Finance		0.25	**0.75**	0.82
Growth on Sales			**0.61**	0.38
Wages to Operating.Margin.			**0.32**	0.23
Wages to Fixed Assets			**-0.52**	0.48
VARIANCE EXPLAINED	3.66	2.73	2.14	8.53
RATE OF DETERMINATION	0.31	0.23	0.18	cumulative 0.71

rences will now be the change of economic dimensions of the firms. The three-factor solution after varimax-rotation based on the first differences of the ratios is now presented in Table 3 (again, solely the loadings over 0.25 and below – 0.25 are introduced, the strongest loading for each ratio in bold text).

Compared with the previous classification pattern based on absolute averages of the ratios, some remarkable changes can be noticed. The ratios measuring operating leverage (Wages to Operating Marging and Wages to Fixed Assets) have now their strongest loadings on the same factor with variables measuring corporate growth. The interpretation of these factors is not at all as clear than in the context of the previous classification pattern which was based on levels of the ratio series.

To test the differences between these two three-factor solutions (first differences vs. absolute values of the ratios) transformation analysis was performed. The transformation matrix is presented in Table 4.

Table 4. Transformation matrix of financial ratios from absolute values to first differences.

		First differences		
	Factor	1	2	3
Absolute values	1	**0.858**	-0.512	0.042
	2	-0.192	-0.245	**0.950**
	3	0.476	**0.823**	0.309

The normal transformation between the factor patterns in transformation analysis can be seen from the large non-zero elements in the transformation matrix. The interpretation of the highest non-zero values in the transformation matrix can be viewed to reflect that the second and the third empirical factor changed their positions when first differences of the ratios instead of the absolute values of the ratios were used. To see the changes in a single ratio level, the residual matrix between these factor patterns is now introduced (see Table 5).

In the residual matrix via large non-zero elements we can see if the contents of the corresponding ratios have changed. The highest abnormal transformation occurred with the ratio measuring Wages to Fixed Assets. Other measures of operating leverage and profitability were not significantly abnormally transformed. The low level of abnormal transformation with the growth rates was expected since these ratios were measured in the same way on level as well as on first difference form.

3.2. Classification pattern and stock market

To obtain information on the connection between the stock market variables

Table 5. Residual matrix and abnormal transformation for first differences of the financial ratios studied.

Ratio / Factor	1	2	3	abnormal transformation
Net Income Margin	-0.046	-0.065	0.116	0.020
Return on Investment	-0.136	-0.337	0.083	0.083
Return on Invested Capital	-0.121	-0.254	0.211	0.124
Equity to Capital	0.534	0.167	0.078	0.319
Debt to Equity	0.275	0.423	0.331	0.364
Debt to Sales	-0.300	-0.137	0.234	0.163
Fixed to Variable Costs	0.045	-0.322	0.107	0.117
Wages to Oper. Margin	-0.196	-0.442	-0.465	0.450
Wages to Fixed Assets	1.074	-0.322	0.380	1.403
Growth on Revenue Finance	0.356	-0.153	0.069	0.155
Growth on Cap. Investments	-0.127	-0.119	0.006	0.030
Growth on Sales	0.576	0.361	-0.002	0.462
abnormal transformation	2.155	0.979	0.612	3.746

and economic dimensions of the firms on cross-sectional level the correlation coefficients between empirical factors and average stock prices, average returns and variances in stock returns (i.e. measure of the common stock risk) were computed. Thus, the riskiness of the stock in this paper empirically approached by measuring variance in stock returns. Using this measure for stock risk one aims to exclude the problems measuring systematic risk on a thin security market (on these problems see e.g. Berglund & Liljeblom & Löflund 1989). Variance as a risk measure for thin security markets has been suggested by e.g. Levy (1978). The price variable used in the following tables is measured using the price index described earlier in Section 2.1. Thus, the interpretation of this variable is close to a measure of cumulative stock return. The correlations between estimated factor scores and stock market variables are reported in Table 6.

Table 6. Correlation coefficients between varimax-rotated three-factor solution and stock market variables.

Factor 1 = Profitability and Capital Structure
Factor 2 = Growth
Factor 3 = Operating Leverage

	stock prices	stock returns	stock risk
Factor 1	0.64 ***	0.56 **	-0.43 *
Factor 2	-0.24	-0.07	0.40 *
Factor 3	-0.12	-0.19	-0.09

* significant at 0.05 level of significance *** significant at 0.001 level of significance

** significant at 0.01 level of significance

As one can see, the correlations between the first factor and stock market variables were quite high. Firms with high level of profitability and low level of financial leverage tend to have had high returns and low risk. Firms which have been growing fast have had high level of risk connected in their stock returns during the research period.

The connection between capital structure and firm value is especially interesting. The traditional Modigliani & Miller (1958, 1963) theory shows that in perfect capital markets (no taxes occur) there is no connection between stock prices and capital structure of the firm. They also showed that when corporate taxes are included, the firm gains from the financial leverage because of the tax benefit it will obtain.

In recent years the existence of the optimal capital structure has been studied extensively. Miller (1977) showed in his study that under certain conditions the tax advantage of debt financing is exactly offset by the disadvangate of debt at the personal level. In more recent studies (for a review see e.g. DeAngelo & Masulis 1980, Modigliani 1982) certain leverage-related costs (bankruptcy costs, agency costs) have interpreted to cause the possible existence of the optimal capital structure. The empirical results in this study indicated that high leverage have caused lower returns in cross-sectional level in the sample used in the paper. This means that firms in average have not gained from the leverage in terms of the market value of the firm in Finland during the research period.

Table 7. Correlations between financial ratios and stock market variables on cross-sectional level.

	PRICE	RETURN	RISK
1. Profitability			
Return on Investment	0.52 **	0.41 *	-0.39 *
Net Income Margin	0.50 **	0.50 **	-0.48 **
Return On Invested Capital	0.66 ***	0.62 ***	-0.39 *
2. Financial Leverage			
Equity to Invested Capital	0.48 **	0.43 *	-0.44 *
Debt to Equity	-0.43 *	-0.05	-0.01
Debt to Sales	-0.59 **	-0.50 **	0.32
3. Operating Leverage			
Fixed Costs to Var. Costs	0.11	0.28	-0.04
Wages to Operating Margin	0.43 *	0.54 **	-0.04
Wages to Fixed Assets	0.43 *	0.33	-0.25
4. Growth			
Growth on Revenue Finance	-0.18	-0.20	0.62 ***
Growth on Capital Investments	-0.14	0.09	0.30
Growth on Sales	0.08	-0.05	-0.14

* significant at 0.05 level of significance *** significant at 0.001 level of significance

** significant at 0.01 level of significance

As one can expect from the results presented in Table 6, most of the significant correlations between the stock market variables and single financial ratios were found in the ratios belonging to the first empirical factor. Some statistically significant correlations between stock market variables and the other dimensions were also reported (see Table 7).

After the correlation analysis was carried out, factor analysis was run again. At this time the stock market variables were also included in the factor pattern in order to study in which dimensions the stock market variables are connected. The varimax-rotated three-factor pattern based on financial ratio averages is reported in Table 8 (again solely the factor loadings over 0.25 and below – 0.25 included).

It can be seen that prices and returns were closely connected to the profitability and capital structure of the firm. The risk of the common stocks then tends to be merely dependent on the growth rate of the firm. However, as one can notice from the correlation analysis in Table 7, common stock risk is not independent of the other economic dimensions either.

Finally, the association with the classification pattern based on first differences of the financial ratios and stock market variables was studied. These correlations are reported in Table 9. The results based on first-differences of the ratios are quite similar to the results obtained with absolute ratios. However, the connection between stock prices and ratios decreased.

Table 8. Three-factor varimax-rotated factor solution including stock market variables.

	FACT1	FACT2	FACT3	COMMUNALITY
Return on Invested Capital	**0.90**			0.83
Net Income Margin	**0.88**			0.87
Equity to Capital	**0.86**			0.73
Return on Investment	**0.84**			0.77
PRICE	**0.72**	0.25		0.67
Wages to Fixed Assets	**0.68**			0.48
RETURN	**0.68**	0.26		0.65
Debt to Sales	**-0.83**			0.72
Growth on Revenue Finance		**0.92**		0.85
Growth on Investments		**0.88**		0.82
RISK	-0.27	**0.63**		0.61
Debt to Equity		**0.32**		0.15
Wages to Oper.Marg.			**0.86**	0.85
Growth on Sales			**-0.75**	0.67
Fixed to Variable Costs				0.03
VARIANCE EXPLAINED	5.64	2.32	1.76	9.71
RATE OF DETERMINATION	0.38	0.15	0.12	cumulative 0.65

Table 9. Correlation coefficients between varimax-rotated three-factor solution based on the first differences of the ratios and stock market variables.

Factor 1 = Profitability
Factor 2 = Capital Structure
Factor 3 = Growth and Operating Leverage

	stock prices	stock returns	stock risk
Factor 1	0.04	0.46 *	-0.41 *
Factor 2	0.28	-0.10	0.16
Factor 3	-0.11	0.04	0.31

* significant at 0.05 level of significance *** significant at 0.001 level of significance
** significant at 0.01 level of significance

4. Intra-year explanatory power of financial ratios

The main interest in this part of the study is to find evidence on the intra-year explanatory power of financial ratios in the Finnish stock market. This part of the study is important in two levels. First, it will show the validity of financial ratios as independent variables in the Finnish stok market. If financial ratios are valid explanatory variables of stock prices, one could assume them to represent pricing relationships in a substantive manner. Secondly, we will consider at which time of the year the highest level of association between financial ratios and stock prices exists. In the context of the previous Chapter 3, this chapter is important because the stability of association between stock prices and financial ratios will be considered.

The research hypothesis in this chapter can be stated as follows. The explanatory power of financial ratios increases as the day when annual income numbers are reported approaches. This kind of increase is expected in two reasons:

– investors use accounting data when it is current

– investors' knowledge about the relevant accounting numbers is at its highest when they are released.

After the numbers have been published, one could assume that the explanatory power of financial ratios begins to decrease instantaneously or with a lag depending on the level of stock market efficiency.

The methodology used in this study is quite close to Tse (1986). He studied two formulations of the valuation model created by Litzenberger & Rao (1971) on Wall Street data. His results indicated certain trend movements of the explanatory power of this valuation model. However, no direct information about the explanatory power of financial ratios was obtained.

Three financial ratios are selected in this chapter. Net Income Margin, Wages to Fixed Assets and Equity to Capital. The selection of these ratios is based on factor analysis and normality test in previous chapters. The growth dimension is excluded in this chapter since we are now studying differences on a year level and growth is defined only as a long-term variable for the whole period of 13 years.

The stock prices are determined with the aid of logarithmic price index 1970 as a basic year. Closing prices for each month are calculated. When no trade, the real price is proxied by bid quotation. One company, Lohja, is excluded in this chapter since its fiscal year does not end in December 31st. Thus, the total number of firms in the analysis, i.e. number of observations, is now 25.

4.1. Pre-report explanatory power of financial ratios

The estimation period is divided into 12 two-year subperiods: 1974-1975, 1975-1976, 1976-1977, 1977-1978 . . . 1985-1986. For each period a month index from 1 to 20 is created. 20 first months in each of the 12 periods are thus studied. Using the month index one aims to find out how the explanatory poter of financial ratios on stock prices behaves over time. This is carried out studying how the explanatory power of financial ratios on stock returns behaves over the period of 12 month before and 8 months after the balance sheet date.

Firstly, the first subperiod prices will be explained cross-sectionally by the financial ratios from the year 1974 separately for each month during the research period from January 1974 to August 1975. Thus, 20 cross-sectional regressions are run in this phase. In the second phase, the second subperiod prices are then explained by 1975 financial ratios and so on. Thus, for each subperiod 20 cross-sectional regressions will be run. The regression equation for each month is:

$$\begin{aligned} P_i = \alpha + \beta_1 \; & NetIncomeMargin_t \; + \\ \beta_2 \; & Wages\ to\ Fixed\ Assets_i \; + \\ \beta_3 \; & Equity\ to\ Capital_i + \epsilon_i, \end{aligned} \qquad (4.1)$$

where P_i = stock price index for firm i and $i = 1 \ldots 25$.

The summary of the unadjusted R-squares from the OLS-regressions in reported in Table 10.

According to the research hypothesis stated in the beginning of this chapter, one could assume that the rate of determinations of our regression equations increase until month 15, i.e. until the month financial statement numbers are released. In order to study if the hypothesis is supported by the data, the Spearman rank correlations between the month index from the months (1-15) and the rate of determinations of the 15 regression equations for each subperiod are reported in Table 11.

If the model based on financial ratios represents pricing relationships in an intuitive manner, the Spearman rank correlation coefficients should be positive by sign. As one can notice, in 9 cases of total 12 correlations, the Spearman rank correlation had a positive sign. In three cases (2 significant on 0.05 level of significance) the correlation coefficient was negative by sign.

To estimate the trends in explanatory power, regression analysis will now be run with unadjusted R-square as the dependent variable and month index

Table 10. Explanatory power of financial ratios on stock prices (unadjusted R-squares for each month from model 4.1).

	MONTH INDEX	1974	1975	1976	1977	1978	1979
JAN	1	0.1863	0.0511	0.0584	0.1075	0.1600	0.2801
FEB	2	0.1483	0.0459	0.0590	0.1129	0.1709	0.2801
MAR	3	0.1388	0.0461	0.0615	0.1207	0.1872	0.3232
APR	4	0.1648	0.0633	0.0828	0.1242	0.1848	0.3638
MAY	5	0.1934	0.0708	0.0641	0.1387	0.2137	0.3940
JUN	6	0.2011	0.0481	0.0740	0.1563	0.2054	0.3969
JUL	7	0.1988	0.0645	0.0752	0.1434	0.2098	0.3812
AUG	8	0.1902	0.0713	0.0784	0.1475	0.1977	0.3883
SEP	9	0.2063	0.0707	0.0720	0.1541	0.1889	0.3950
OKT	10	0.2018	0.0722	0.0696	0.1551	0.2047	0.4080
NOV	11	0.1879	0.0616	0.0969	0.1862	0.2054	0.4030
DEC	12	0.2003	0.0630	0.0866	0.1659	0.2556	0.4050
JAN	13	0.2364	0.0581	0.0876	0.1800	0.2349	0.3935
FEB	14	0.2573	0.0529	0.0943	0.1907	0.2349	0.3867
MAR	15	0.2264	0.0583	0.0997	0.2023	0.2599	0.3826
APR	16	0.1753	0.0892	0.1107	0.1934	0.3024	0.3968
MAY	17	0.1781	0.0861	0.1365	0.2099	0.3205	0.3697
JUN	18	0.2334	0.0947	0.1494	0.2035	0.3056	0.3802
JUL	19	0.2095	0.0973	0.1380	0.2082	0.2921	0.3882
AUG	20	0.1926	0.1057	0.1439	0.1965	0.2905	0.3686

	MONTH INDEX	1980	1981	1982	1983	1984	1985
JAN	1	0.3261	0.3005	0.2625	0.3545	0.4069	0.4028
FEB	2	0.3125	0.2941	0.2519	0.3841	0.4187	0.4023
MAR	3	0.3125	0.2998	0.2689	0.3787	0.4378	0.4036
APR	4	0.3245	0.2754	0.2725	0.3943	0.4304	0.4074
MAY	5	0.2982	0.2804	0.2787	0.3940	0.4213	0.4018
JUN	6	0.3065	0.2770	0.2679	0.3914	0.4181	0.3829
JUL	7	0.3126	0.2699	0.2733	0.4057	0.4216	0.3855
AUG	8	0.3071	0.2612	0.2798	0.4056	0.4239	0.3778
SEP	9	0.3123	0.2483	0.2679	0.4091	0.4232	0.3932
OKT	10	0.2992	0.2501	0.3088	0.4138	0.4196	0.3965
NOV	11	0.2900	0.2497	0.3180	0.4310	0.4235	0.3883
DEC	12	0.3046	0.2614	0.3213	0.4336	0.4235	0.3995
JAN	13	0.3018	0.2744	0.3417	0.4284	0.4418	0.3999
FEB	14	0.2974	0.2697	0.3632	0.4304	0.4432	0.3887
MAR	15	0.3063	0.2763	0.3578	0.4625	0.4474	0.3901
APR	16	0.2930	0.2885	0.3650	0.4632	0.4518	0.4247
MAY	17	0.3003	0.2894	0.3602	0.4528	0.4457	0.4254
JUN	18	0.3032	0.2773	0.3740	0.4545	0.4346	0.4139
JUL	19	0.3007	0.2842	0.3921	0.4504	0.4366	0.4100
AUG	20	0.2884	0.2896	0.3955	0.4406	0.4334	0.3695

Table 11. Spearman rank correlation coefficients between unadjusted R^2 and month index in months 1-15.

Fiscal Year	Correlation Coefficient
1974	0.82 ***
1975	0.25
1976	0.85 ***
1977	0.95 ***
1978	0.83 ***
1979	0.56 *
1980	-0.69 **
1981	-0.63 *
1982	0.90 ***
1983	0.95 ***
1984	0.62 *
1985	-0.50

* significant at 0.05 level of significance
** significant at 0.01 level of significance
*** significant at 0.001 level of significance

as independent variable. Since is assumed that the rate of determination is not normally distributed, the following kind of transformation for the rate of determination will be carried out (Harnett 1975, Tse 1986):

$$z = \log((1 + R) / (1 - R))$$

Table 12. Estimates of regression analysis transformed R-squares as dependent variables.

Fiscal Year	Coefficient of Time	t-statistic
1974	0.016	4.930 ***
1975	0.003	1.216
1976	0.010	6.027 ***
1977	0.019	12.988 ***
1978	0.015	6.262 ***
1979	0.018	3.797 **
1980	-0.004	-3.130 **
1981	-0.006	-2.925 *
1982	0.019	8.047 ***
1983	0.015	11.172 ***
1984	0.004	2.861 *
1985	-0.002	-1.633

* significant at 0.05 level of significance
** significant at 0.01 level of significance
*** significant at 0.001 level of significance

The transformation above typically made the R-squares to approximately follow the normal distribution. Also the regression analysis estimates show that there are three years (1980, 1981 and 1985) which do not follow the research hypothesis stated in the beginning of this chapter. Let us now consider some possible reasons for these negative Spearman rank correlation coefficients.

The first two years of the three exceptional years (1980 and 1981) can be viewed to represent some kind of turning point in the Finnish economy. The slack of the 1970's was over. Firms' economic well being had increased. However, stock prices did not follow this increase in companies' earnings. The third exceptional year was thus 1985. The reason for the unexpected change in the explanatory power of financial ratios can now be viewed to be opposite to the reason above. Drastic changes in the Finnish stock market now possibly led to overreaction and overvaluation of stocks, which is also reflected in the explanatory power of financial ratios.

4.2. The highest intra-year level of explanatory power

The approach in Section 4.1 did not give any direct answer on the highest intra-year level of association between financial ratios and stock prices. It was solely reported that the explanatory power of financial ratios increases when the annual reporting day approaches.

In this subchapter the highest point of association between stock prices and financial ratios will be considered. In order to obtain this kind of information, the 12 years studied were divided into three non-overlapping subperiods. From these subperiods average coefficients of determinations were calculated. These arithmetic averages are now reported graphically in Appendices 1, 2 and 3.

As one can see, the highest level of association in the third and second subperiods was obtained in April. In the first subperiod the highest point was in June. After these points the explanatory power of financial ratios tends to fall again. The fall, however, is not especially stable through years. In addition, a systematic increase in the explanatory power over time in the three subperiods is also evident.

The results give support to at least three observations. First, the explanatory power of financial ratios increases when the reporting day approaches. Secondly, financial ratios tend to be reflected in stock prices with a time lag from the fiscal year ending day. A remarkable increase during the first months after the end of the fiscal year was reported. Thirdly, a slight decrease in the explanatory power of financial ratios after the publishing day can also be reported.

5. Summary and conclusions

Based on the previous studies four theoretical dimensions were chosen: profitability, capital structure, growth and operating leverage. These dimensions seemed to be close to the dimensions found in the empirical analysis. When average financial ratios were studied the dimensions of capital structure and profitability were connected. When factor analysis was run on first differences of the ratios, the dimensions of operating leverage and growth moved together.

The connection between the created empirical dimensions and stock market variables (stock prices, returns and risk) was then studied. It was evident that stock returns and prices were closely connected to the long-term profitability and capital structure of the firm on cross-sectional level. Higher prifitability and lower financial leverage tended to lead to a higher market value of the firm. Evidence on the connection between these variables and operating leverage was also found to some extent. However, no empirical connection between the growth rate of the firm and stock returns and prices was found.

The measure of common stock total risk, variance in stock returns, was found to be connected to the profitability of the firm. A significant correlation between stock risk and the dimension of growth was also reported. From the ratios measuring capital structure, equity to capital and debt to sales were correlated with the level of variance in stock returns. The empirical connection between operating leverage and variance was not extremely strong.

Using first differences of the ratios, the results were quite similar to the results on absolute values of the ratios. However, the empirical connection between stock prices and first differences of the ratios was diminished.

When studying the stability of the results over time, the results gave support to at least three observations. Firstly, the explanatory power of financial ratios increased when the reporting day approached. Secondly, financial ratios tended to be reflected in stock prices with a lag from the fiscal year ending day. A remarkable increase during the first months after the end of the fiscal year was reported. Thirdly, the explanatory power of financial ratios tended to decrease after the publishing day.

REFERENCES

Y. AHMAVAARA (1954). *Transformation analysis of factorial data* Acta Academiae Scientiarum Fennicae. Ser B 88,2.

R. BALL, P. BROWN (1968). *An empirical evaluation of accounting income numbers*. Journal of Accounting Research 6 2, 159-178.

R. BALL, P. BROWN (1969). *Portfolio theory and accounting*. Journal of Accounting Research 7 2, 300-323.

P. BARNES (1986). *The statistical validity of the ratio method in financal analysis. An empirical examination. A comment*. Journal of Business Finance and Accounting 13:4, 627-632.

T. BERGLUND, E. LILJEBLOM, A. LOFLUND (1989). *Estimating betas on daily data for a small stock market.* Journal of Banking & Finance 13:1, 41-64.

L.A. BERNSTEIN (1978). *Financial statement analysis.* Homewood, Ill: Richard D. Irwin Inc.

R.G. BOWMAN (1979). *The theoretical relationship between systematic risk and financial (accounting) variables.* Journal of Finance 34:3, 617-630.

Credit Analysis Commission (1983). *Financial ratio analysis in Finland.* (in Finnish).

H. DEANGELO, R.W. MASULIS (1980). *Optimal capital structure under corporate personal taxation.* Journal of Financial Economics 11:1, 3-29.

T.R. DYCKMAN, D. MORSE (1986). *Efficient capital markets and accounting a critical analysis* Englewood Cliffs, N.J.: Prentice-Hall Inc.

D.R. FEWINGS (1975). *The impact of corporate growth on the risk of common stocks.* Journal of Finance 30:2, 525-531.

G. FOSTER, C. OHLSEN. T. SHEVLIN (1984). *Earnings releases, anomalies and the behaviour of security returns.* Accounting Review 59:4, 574-603.

G. FOSTER (1986). *Financial statement analysis.* Englewood Cliffs, N.J.: Prentice-Hall Inc.

P.E. GREEN (1978). *Analyzing multivariate data.* Hindsdale, Ill: The Dryden Press.

R.S. HAMADA (1969). *Portfolio analysis, market equilibrium and corporate finance.* Journal of Finance 24:1, 13-32.

R.S. HAMADA (1972). *The effect of the firm's capital structure on the systematic risk of common stock.* Journal of Finance 26:2, 435-452.

D. HARNETT (1975). *Introduction to Statistics.* New York: Addison-Wesley.

A. LAAKKONEN (1982). *A computer application for analyzing corporate growth, profitability and finance.* Proceedings of the University of Vaasa. Research Papers 87. (In Finnish).

B. LEV (1974). *On the association between operating leverage and risk.* Journal of Financial and Quantitative Analysis. September, 627-641.

H. LEVY (1978). *Equilibrium in an imperfect market: a constraint on the number of securities in the portfolio.* American Economic Review, Sept., 245-266.

R. LITZENBERGER, C. RAO (1971). *Estimates of the marginal rate of time preference and average risk aversion of investors in electric utility shares 1960-1966.* Bell Journal of Economics and Management Science. Spring, 265-277.

M.C. LOVELL (1983). *Data mining.* Review of Economics and Statistics 65:1, 1-12.

T. MARTIKAINEN (1989). *Stock price behaviour and economic operations of the firm.* Proceedings of the University of Vaasa. Research Papers 135.

T. MARTIKAINEN, T. ANKELO (1989). *On the association between stock returns and corporate earnings adjusted for four alternative depreciation methods.* Empirical evidence on Finnish data. Proceedings of the University of Vaasa. Discussion Papers 98.

B. MCDONALD, M.H. MORRIS (1984). *The statistical validity of the ratio method in financial analysis :an empirical investigation.* Journal of Business Finance and Accounting 11:1, 89-98.

M.H. MILLER (1977). *Debt and Taxes.* Journal of Finance. May, 261-275.

F. MODIGLIANI, M. MILLER (1958). *The cost of capital, corporation finance and the theory of investment.* American Economic Review 48, 261-297.

F. MODIGLIANI, M. MILLER (1963). *Taxes and the cost of capital: A correction.* American

Economic Review 53, 433-443.

F. MODIGLIANI (1982). *Debt, dividend policy, taxes, inflation and market valuation.* Journal of Finance 37:2, 255-273.

J PERTTUNEN, T. MARTIKAINEN (1989). *On the proportionality assumption of financial ratios.* Finnish Journal of Business Economics 38: 4, 343-359.

S.S. SHAPIRO, M.B. WILK (1965). *An analysis of variance test for normality* (complete samples). Biometrika 65:3-4, 591-611.

M. TAMARI (1978). *Financial ratio analysis.* Analysis and prediction, London: Pitman Press.

S. TSE (1986). *Intra-Year trends in the degree of association between accounting numbers and security prices'* Accounting Review 61:3, 475-497.

P. YLI-OLLI (1983). *The empirical classification of financial ratios and the stability of the classification.* (In Finnish, Summary in English). Proceedings of the University of Vaasa. Research Papers 95.

P. YLI-OLLI, I. VIRTANEN (1985). *Modelling a financial ratio system on the economy-wide level.* Proceedings of the University of Vaasa. Acta Wasaensia 21.

P. YLI-OLLI, I. VIRTANEN (1989a) *On the long-term stability and cross-country invariance of financial ratio patterns.* European Journal of Operational Research 39, 40-53.

P. YLI-OLLI, I. VIRTANEN (1989b). *Arbitrage pricing theory and its empirical applicability for the Helsinki Stock Exchange.* Working Paper 89-7. European Institute for Advanced Studies in Management. Brussels, Belgium.

P. YLI-OLLI, I. VIRTANEN (1990). *Transformation analysis applied to long-term stability and structural invariance of financial ratio patterns: U.S. versus Finnish firms.* American Journal of Mathematical and Management Studies (Forthcoming).

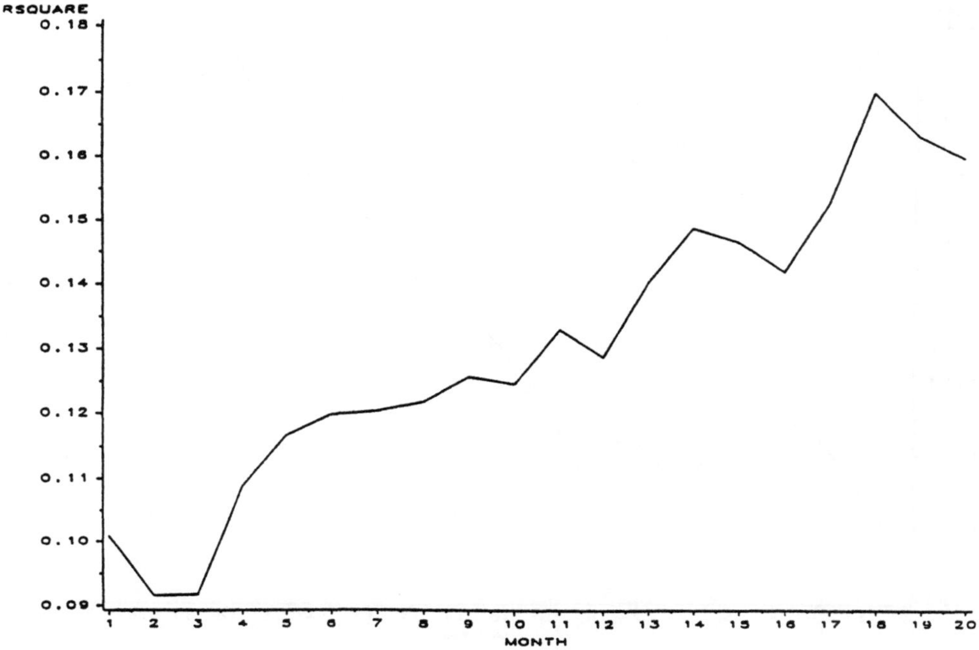

Appendix 1 The arithmetic average of explanatory power in 1974-1977

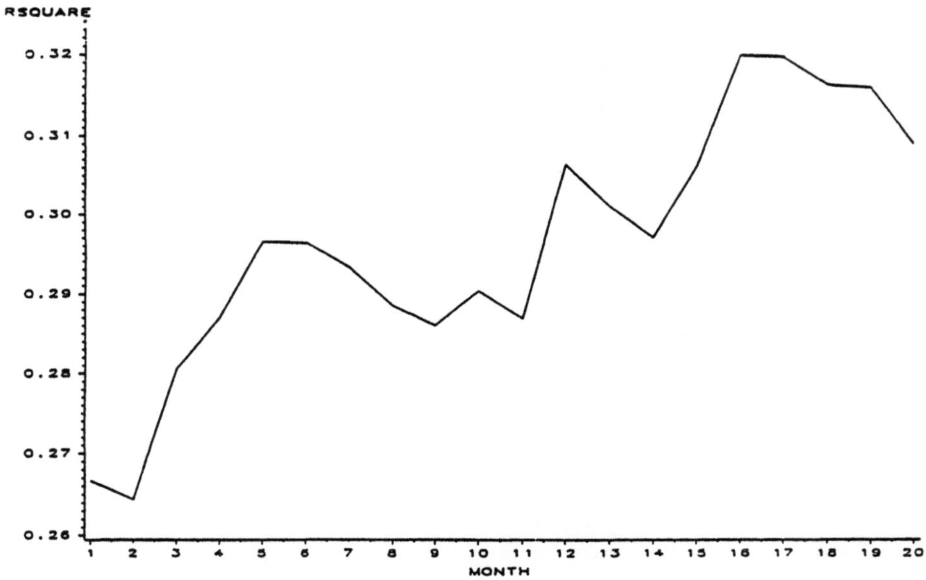

Appendix 2 The arithmetic average of explanatory power in 1978-1981

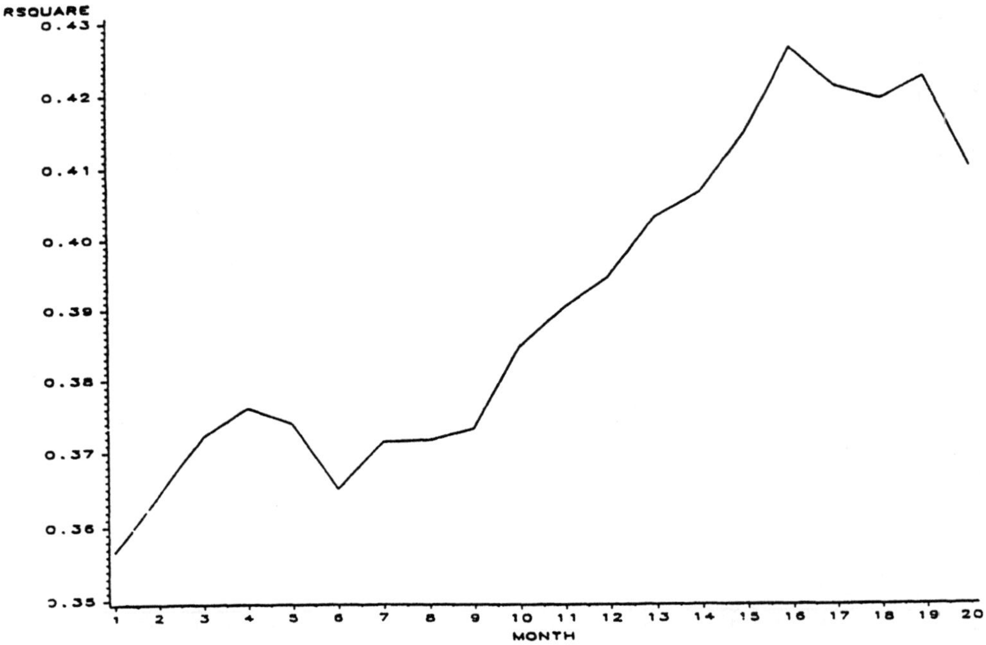

Appendix 3 The arithmetic average of explanatory power in 1982-1985

AN ACTUARIAL AND FINANCIAL ANALYSIS FOR ECU INSURANCE CONTRACTS (*)

PIERA MAZZOLENI
University of Verona, Italy

The aim of this paper is to analyse the Italian ECU linked policy "Europea". We will show that the adjustment of premium and capital as well as the investment policy have to take into account targets of purchasing power and stability. In our approach a recursive improvement is allowed according to the market conditions. A game model is described and qualitative aspects are introduced through fuzzy elements, showing that the Company's behavior has to be more flexible towards a truly dynamic contract, which is also adjusted through the implementation clauses for premium and capital.

1. Introduction

The evolution of life insurance is strictly linked to the development of new financial instruments.

Indeed when insurance contracts were dependent only on interest policies and inflation was reaching very high levels, insurance portfolios faced a substantial decrease with negative effects on the profitability of the Companies.

The introduction of indexed life contracts, which attempt to maintain the purchasing power, gave a new development to this sector.

Special financial funds were managed separately and indexation simply linked to inflation was replaced by a share of the total return on the business management.

The marketability of the new contracts increased considerably: for instance, in Italy insurance premia amounted to 32.000 milliard lira, in spite of 45.000 milliard lira collected by banks with a ratio between the two sectors equal to 1.406 on behalf of the banking sector during 1987. This ratio was 8 in 1978.

(*) The research has been partially supported by the Italian Ministry of Education and the National Research Council.

As a further development the fundamental principle of the risk theory, which leads to the diversification of the portfolio, and the development of international exchanges have promoted the definition of new life contracts to open the European market to free currency insurances.

In this framework it is no longer sufficient to analyse the Company's portfolio of insurance contracts. We also have to pay our attention to its portfolio of assets.

The financial features of an insurance contract are typically time and production cycle between premium and payment.

Therefore insurance aspects cannot be treated separately and the financial problems are even more important in an unstable framework for prices and exchange rates than for other financial institutions.

The opening of the international markets and the construction of international insurance portfolios is continuously threatened by the instability of the exchange rates, while the reinsurance mechanism is too cumbersome to be adjusted to fluctuations. Therefore it is natural to turn one's attention to the ECU basket which promises stability guarantees. For instance during the period 1980-85 the Italian Lira has floated 34% against the English Pound, 36% against the Deutch Mark, 2% against the French Franc, while it has floated 20% against the ECU basket; in the Paris market the Deutch Mark has floated 33% while the ECU basket only 18.8% (DESIATA (1985)).

Moreover the interest rates on ECU transactions are very profitable both for weak borrower countries and strong lender countries.

The unquestionable importance of the ECU basket has not yet reached the insurance sector and Italy has been the first European Country to introduce an insurance contract linked to the ECU basket.

The aim of this insurance policy is to protect the insured from the national inflation as long as such inflation produces national currency devaluation against the other currencies forcing the ECU upward. The development of the ECU market will promote a larger and larger geographical expansion of insurance portfolios to European Countries towards a deeper cooperation.

Section 2 briefly review the classical theory of indexation and shows that an ECU based indexation should improve the protection of the purchasing power.

In section 3 we will show that there is a feedback of the levels of collected policies on premia and capital adjustment in order to minimize the variability of the contracts.

But what is even more important is that we have to take into account the different expectations on premia to be collected from the Company and on the Company's performance to be offered to the insured. The option pricing approach links the premium evaluation to a preassigned benefit at the end of the policy-holder's horizon. (BRENNAN and SCHWARTZ (1976)).

In our approach the clauses are adjusted according to the market conditions. JACQUE and TAPIERO (1987) pay attention to payment of premia in a foreign currency without any reference to the point of view of the national purchasing power for the insured. Indeed «when the exchange rate dynamic process becomes more unstable, the rate of indexation will increase the firm utility», but we have to balance the gain for the firm and the transfer of benefit to the clients. Therefore in section 4 we apply game theory to model this bargain but we also have to take into account the different exchange of information between the Company and the insured so that the fuzzy elements are suitably added to represent the possible interval of values for the chosen loading factor.

2. Indexed and revalued policies

Starting from the first adjusting insurance contracts we now face sophisticated mechanisms linking the excess return on investments and the law of premium and capital.

The classical equilibrium law requires that the mathematical reserve V_t at time t satisfies equation

$$\begin{aligned} &V_t + \text{expected average value of the future premia} = \\ &= \text{expected average value of the Company's services} \end{aligned} \tag{1}$$

The adjustment of the contract terms is done recursively usually every year and its amount is fixed within the contract clauses.

Denote s the rate of inflation of the year $t-1$ for the adjustment at time t, and denote r the rate of return on the Company's investments or a fixed ratio of them.

Then if we denote $j^{(1)}$, $j^{(2)}$, $j^{(3)}$, the rate of adjustment for capital, reserve and premium, respectively, we face several choices linking these indexes to r and s.

One of the most common kinds of life policies transfers a ratio of the investment returns to the insured and requires an adjustment of the premium in the same amount: this is the behavior of the Italian policies called «revaluable». Particular attention has to be paid to the rate of adjustment, which is linked to the financial management of the Company, but in different forms: indeed the financial activities might be related to mutual funds' market indexes and assets portfolios. The rule is better, the higher the correlation between r and s, that is between the Company's return and inflation.

This demonstrates that we have to make the scheme

$$j^{(1)} = f(r, s) \quad j^{(2)} = r \quad j^{(3)} = s \tag{2}$$

more precise (PITACCO (1988)).

The study, directed to the Italian policy «Europea», introduced in the market by Assicurazioni Generali in 1986 and then followed by the «Europolizza» by Ras in 1987, strengthens the importance of analysing the relationship between the loading rate for premia and the rate of return on assets. The main aim of this kind of contract is to protect the insured from devaluation, to promote gains on the Lira-ECU exchange rate differences and, what is more relevant, to prepare Italy for the opening of the European markets.

Indeed the Lira-ECU difference might also have some drawbacks due to the instability of the policy behavior.

The policy «Europea» is a mixed life-insurance policy both with unique and annual premia, adjusted according to the return on a special ECU investment fund, mainly CTE up to now, called «GECU».

The Company guarantees to implement premium and capital according to a suitable percentage of the financial return. We will not enter here into the technical details.

Moreover premium and capital are expressed in ECU and then converted into Italian Lira, by simply multiplying by the exchange rate.

The numerical example compares the financial result of the «Europea» with a simpler and older policy which is only adjusted on parameters of the internal Italian market, the so called «GESAV».

Assume the insured's age is $x = 40$ and the contract life equal to 10 years. If we consider the «Europea» policy and use the return obtained by «Generali» during 1987, that is 9.69%, then the revaluation rate can be set equal to 4.14%.

The after tax discount rate of return of the policy is 8.32%. According to the different values of the ECU-Lira revaluation

2.5% 3.5% 5% (3)

we observe a corresponding rate of return for the «Europea» policy

12.80% 14.34% 17.25% (4)

with a wider variability than the one estimated for the exchange rate.

3.5% is the mean value observed during period 1980-1987. Only in this case the profitability of the «Europea» is comparable with the «GESAV» policy which gives a rate of return equal to 13.00% for a revaluation rate 6.80% equal to the mean rate of return on Italian Treasury Bills and bonds.

The corresponding values for a life contract equal to 15 years become, according to the different values of the ECU-Lira revaluation (3).

11.25% 12.39% 15.75% (5)

with respect to the rate of return 11.40% for the «GESAV» policy.

The simple example (CECCHINI (1989)) shows that the «pure» profitability of the ECU linked policy is lower and more unstable than the corresponding «GESAV» values and that it is mainly based on the exchange rate, which does not always represent the national situation completely.

Moreover the ECU basket is mainly related with the Deutch Mark and the German currency affects the Lira in an opposite direction with respect to the ECU basket.

The figures in the Appendix show the mutual behavior of the exchange rates Lira-ECU and Deutch Mark-ECU during the period 1980-1988.

Indeed during years 1981, 1982 and the second half of 1985 the ECU-Lira exchange rate is substantially increasing, while the Deutch Mark-ECU exchange rate is decreasing.

Alternatively, a common increasing trend is shown in 1980 and 1988, a decreasing one in 1986; for the remaining years 1983, 1984, 1987 the behavior is very unstable.

This example shows that, even if Lira and Deutch Mark often present an opposite trend towards the ECU, nevertheless the stability is not guaranteed. Therefore it is worth taking both internal and foreign parameters simultaneously into account.

3. A system theory approach to the insurance firm management

A system approach framework can be used with control concepts in formalizing insurance firm problems and in obtaining a deeper insight into managing the different kinds of risks.

We draw the concise picture showing the behavior of an insurance company, according to the system theory. Within the brackets we denote the corresponding quantity for an inventory and dams management (TAPIERO (1987)).

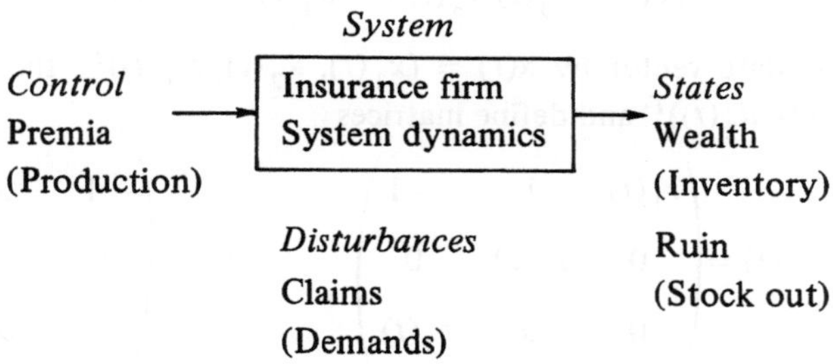

The state-space representation allows one to relate the current state with past states and period disturbances.

At this point we recognize that the maintenance over time of liquidity to meet claims (solvancy) and earning capacity of the asset portfolio are prime goals.

Then, according to TAPIERO (1987), the operating instruments to reach these goals are: the choice of investments; the learning mechanism (expert systems); the selection of risk sharing approaches such as indexed and linked premium formulae which are far more flexible than the classical co-insurance and re-insurance procedures.

Let us now describe a very simple control model to emphasize the importance of a suitable choice for the adjustment rules.

Denote $x_1(t)$ the mathematical reserve at time t, $x_2(t)$ the expected average premium, $x_3(t)$ the expected average capital.

We can analyze the return on the reserve invested on the European market.

$$x_1'(t) = r_1(t)\, x_1(t) + x_2(t) - x_3(t) - d_1(t) \tag{6}$$

where $r_1(t)$ is the increase (or decrease) in the value of the reserve invested in suitable assets and $d_1(t)$ the change on the chosen foreign currency, taken into consideration as a control variable. A part of the premium's evolution $r_2(t)$ $x_2(t)$ is due to the actuarial rules, but the main part depends on the fluctuations of the national currency, which are taken explicitly into account through the control variable $d_2(t)$

$$x_2'(t) = r_2(t)\, x_2(t) - d_2(t) \tag{7}$$

The corresponding effect on the insured capital is represented by a quota a of $d_1(t)$ and b of $d_2(t)$ which transfer the evolution effect of reserve and premium evolution, in order to show that both the internal and the external markets have to be taken explicitly into account to defend the purchasing power of the insured capital. We simply include the actuarial rule of capital adjustment in coefficient $r_3(t)$

$$x_3'(t) = r_3(t)\, x_3(t) + a\, d_1(t) + b\, d_2(t) \tag{8}$$

Denote the state vector by $\mathbf{x}(t) = (x_1(t), x_2(t), x_3(t))^T$, the control vector by $\mathbf{d}(t) = (d_1(t), d_2(t))^T$ and define matrices

$$A_x(t) = \begin{pmatrix} r_1(t) & 1 & -1 \\ 0 & r_2(t) & 0 \\ 0 & 0 & r_3(t) \end{pmatrix} \qquad A_d = \begin{pmatrix} -1 & 0 \\ 0 & -1 \\ a & b \end{pmatrix} \tag{9}$$

Then the system is

$$\mathbf{x}'(t) = A_x(t)\, \mathbf{x}(t) + A_d\, \mathbf{d}(t) \tag{10}$$

where the feedback term is no longer linked with the management return for the Insurance Company but with the mutual relationship between Lira and ECU.

The cost function penalizes deviations of control variables from zero through matrix $Q_d(t)$.

Moreover it is desired that $x_j(t)$ should follow the path $x_j^*(t)$ and we set $\overline{x}_j(t) = x_j(t) - x_j^*(t)$.

In correspondence the cost function penalizes deviations of state $\mathbf{x}(t)$ from target $\mathbf{x}^*(t)$, through matrix $Q_x(t)$.

Therefore we take the minimization of the insurance contract instability over time period $[t_0, t_1]$ as our goal:

$$\min \frac{1}{2} \int_{t_0}^{t_1} (\overline{\mathbf{x}}(t)^T Q_x(t)\, \overline{\mathbf{x}}(t) + \mathbf{d}(t)^T Q_d(t)\, \mathbf{d}(t))\, dt \tag{11}$$

and we have defined a linear-quadratic control model.

If $B(t)$ denotes the solution matrix to the usual Riccati matrix equation (SAGE-WHITE (1977))

$$B(t)' = -B(t)A_x(t) - A_x^{\,T}(t)B(t) + B(t)\,A_d\, Q_d^{-1}(t)\, A_d^{\,T}B(t) - Q_x(t) \tag{12}$$

the explicit solution for the control model

$$\mathbf{d}(t) = -Q_d^{-1}(t)\, A_d^{\,T}[B(t)\,\mathbf{x}(t) - \boldsymbol{\xi}(t)] \tag{13}$$

contains a feedback element given by $-Q_d^{-1}(t)\, A_d^{\,T}B(t)\,\mathbf{x}(t)$, and a feedforward element given by $Q_d^{-1}(t)\, A_d^{\,T}\, \boldsymbol{\xi}(t)$ which depends on the target values.

The perturbation on the optimal control trajectory depends on $\mathbf{x}^*(t)$ through equation

$$\boldsymbol{\xi}'(t) = -[A_x(t) - A_d^{-1}\, Q_d(t)\, A_d\, B(t)]^T\, \boldsymbol{\xi}(t) - Q_x(t)\, \mathbf{x}^*(t) \tag{14}$$

under the suitable boundary conditions.

Therefore it is no longer possible to keep the revaluation parameters for premia and mathematical reserve independent from the level of the corresponding state variables, that is, from their «real» rather than «nominal» value.

Only in this way is it possible to combine external and internal determinants such as inflation, and exchange rates on the one hand, and financial return on the other hand.

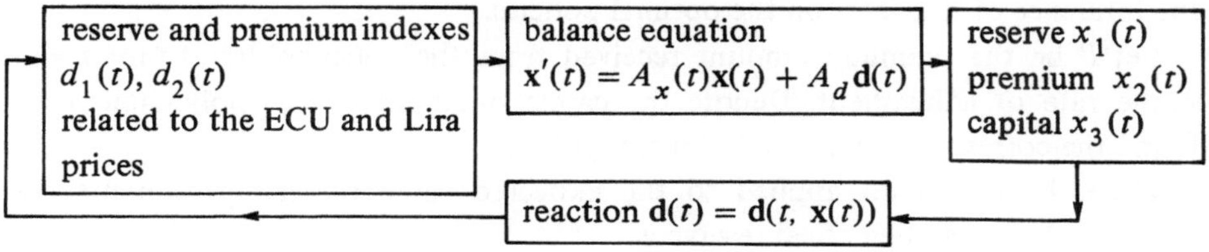

The adjustment parameters $d_1(t)$, $d_2(t)$ for the reserve and premium also depend on the level of capital $x_3(t)$ and through it the fluctuations of the purchasing power also affect the choices on the international transactions.

4. A fuzzy model for insurance policies

The study of the term structure of the interest rates as stochastic processes (BEEKMAN (1987)) has shown the need to compare the evolution with a reference level Γ in order to analyse the deviations from Γ.

Correspondingly BEEKMAN has studied the probability that the process exceeds preassigned bounds during various time intervals. This procedure was already adopted to study the behavior of the EMS currencies and in particular of the ECU basket (MAZZOLENI (1981)).

We then face both the inflation rate and the ECU basket as suitable intervals.

The properties described by CASTAGNOLI and MAZZOLENI (1988) show that such an interval for the ECU basket is in fact a fuzzy interval, so that the bounds can be stated by taking into account the policy instruments to modify the exchange rates and the qualitative opinions on the different mutual relation between the exchange rates and inflation.

Let us also consider the inflation rate as fuzzy interval, where the bounds are no longer stated a priori, but they are calculated in terms of several economic factors, such as the balance of payments, national consumption, production functions and many others.

The equilibrium conditions between the mathematical reserve and the premia on one hand and the capital on the other hand become more complex and require the matching of fuzzy elements.

In this way we are led to a more flexible definition of the insurance product «ECU linked policy». Indeed the weights can be truly adjusted to the interval inflation and to the international instability and contribute towards a greater stability of the insurance contract.

In this paper we do not take into account the tradeoff between extra-profit for the Company and capital adjustment, introducing a simple inequality for liabilities and performances.

First of all, we develop a simple optimization model to give adjustment policies for both premium and capital in a nonfuzzy environment and then we show the influence of fuzziness on the optimal policies.

Let P be the premium amount received from the policyholder, at time t and x the rate of adjustment. Denote the capital required by the policyholder by C and the corresponding rate of adjustment by y.

Then the constraint applied to the expected value of the investments obtained with the mathematical reserve is

$$E(V) + (1 + x)\,P \geqslant (1 + y)C \tag{15}$$

In MAZZOLENI (1981) the optimal intervention policy is modelled as a «barrier» strategy.

Assume now that the loading rate for the premium x has to belong to interval $[0, X]$ and the loading rate for the capital y has to belong to interval $[0, Y]$. The bounds for these loading rates are influenced by the mutual relationship of the return on investments, that is the ECU, and on the national purchasing power, that is the inflation.

Denote by $X - x$ the perception of the ECU fluctuations by the Insurance Company to be transferred to the premium and $Y - y$ the perception of the inflation fluctuations by the insured to be transferred to the capital.

Let z be the random component on the European market with distribution function $F_1(z)$ and w the random component on the internal market with distribution function $F_2(w)$. Then we face problem

$$\max \{U_2(y + \int E_v(Y - y - w)\,\mathrm{d}F_2(w)) - \tag{16}$$

$$- U_1(x + \int E_v\,(X - x - z)\,\mathrm{d}F_1(z)) = U(x, y)\}$$

where E_v is the expected discounted value of the adjustment in the whole period under examination and v the discount factor.

The decision target for the insured U_2 is to maximize the utility and for the Insurance Company U_1 is to minimize the insolvency. Together with the obvious constraints

$$D: 0 \leqslant x \leqslant X \tag{17}$$

$$0 \leqslant y \leqslant Y \tag{18}$$

we have the balance constraint

$$E(V) + (1 + x)P - (1 + y)C = h(x, y) \geqslant 0 \tag{19}$$

Let us now set $U_1' = \partial U/\partial x$, $U_2' = \partial U/\partial y$, $\partial E_v(\xi)/\partial \xi = E_v'$, ξ being the corresponding argument of function E_v, that is alternatively $\xi = X - x - z$, $\xi = Y - y - w$ and write the classical Lagrangian function with respect to constraint (19).

Then the first order conditions are

$$U_2'[1 - \int E_v'\,\mathrm{d}F_2(w)] - \lambda C = 0 \tag{20}$$

$$- U_1'\,[1 - \int E_v'\,\mathrm{d}F_1(z)] + \lambda P = 0 \tag{21}$$

together with the usual complementarity condition $\lambda h(x, y) = 0$. Assume the constraint (19) is satisfied as a strict inequality and $\lambda = 0$. Then we apply the «barrier» strategy both to x and y (BORCH (1974)). Denote Z and W the solution whenever existing, to equations

$$1 - \int E'_v \, dF_1(z) = 0 \tag{22}$$

$$1 - \int E'_v \, dF_2(w) = 0 \tag{23}$$

and set $X - x = Z$, $Y - y = W$. Then the «barrier» strategy is

$$x = \begin{cases} X - Z & \text{if } X > Z \\ 0 & \text{if } X \leqslant Z \end{cases} \qquad y = \begin{cases} Y - W & \text{if } Y > W \\ 0 & \text{if } Y \leqslant W \end{cases} \tag{24}$$

If we now consider case $\lambda > 0$, the third constraint becomes active so that we have to solve equations

$$CU'_1 \, [1 - \int E'_v \, dF_1(z)] = PU'_2 \, [1 - \int E'_v \, dF_2(w)] \tag{25}$$

$$y\,C = E(V) + xP + (P - C) \tag{26}$$

Let us write $y = g(x)$ for the second equation and denote by s^* a possible solution for the first equation

$$X - x = s^* \tag{27}$$

Then a joint «barrier» policy is given by

$$x = \begin{cases} X - s^* & \text{if } X > s^* \\ 0 & \text{if } X \leqslant s^* \end{cases} \qquad y = g(x) \tag{28}$$

Let us denote the bounding interval for the perceived ECU basket fluctuations by $[X_1, X_2] = \{X(a) = aX_1 + \bar{a}X_2 : a \in [0, 1]\}$ and the bounding interval for the perceived inflation fluctuations by $[Y_1, Y_2] = \{Y(b) = bY_1 + \bar{b}Y_2 : b \in [0, 1]\}$.

The upper bar denotes the complement to one, for instance $a = 1 - a$. Therefore for each pair (a, b) we can solve the corresponding problem

$$\begin{aligned} \max \{U_2 \, (y + \int E_v(Y(b) - y - w) \, dF_2(w)) - \\ - U_1 \, (x + \int E_v \, (X(a) - x - z) \, dF_1 \, (z))\} \end{aligned} \tag{29}$$

under the constraints $D(a, b) = \{0 \leqslant x \leqslant X(a), 0 \leqslant y \leqslant Y(b)\}$.

If a solution exists for any pair (a, b), the pure barrier strategy finds a «thick» barrier

$$\begin{aligned} x(a) &= \begin{cases} X(a) - Z & \text{if } X(a) > Z \\ 0 & \text{if } X(a) \leqslant Z \end{cases} \\ y(b) &= \begin{cases} Y(b) - W & \text{if } Y(b) > W \\ 0 & \text{if } Y(b) \leqslant W \end{cases} \end{aligned} \tag{30}$$

for $a \in [0, 1]$, $b \in [0, 1]$

The corresponding balance constraint (19) becomes parametric

$$E(V) + (1 + x)\,P(a) \geqslant (1 + y)\,C(b) \tag{31}$$

and assuming it is active we can find an explicit value for y, $y = g(x; a, b)$ and its relative barrier

$$X(a) - x = s(a, b) \tag{32}$$

$$x(a, b) = \begin{cases} X(a) - s(a, b) & \text{if } X(a) > s(a, b) \\ 0 & \text{if } X(a) \leqslant s(a, b) \end{cases} \tag{33}$$

If a solution (Z, W) exists for any pair (a, b) and U_2 is increasing in y, U_1 decreasing in x, it is natural to take into account only the pure solution which corresponds to the largest feasible region.

It is worth noticing that, when we refer to the perception of the relevant fluctuations for both the national currency and the ECU, we can only use a qualitative appraisal of them and model them as fuzzy variables (CASTAGNOLI-MAZZOLENI (1988)).

Denote the joint membership function for $\tilde{X}$ and $\tilde{Y}$ as fuzzy variables by $\mu_{\tilde{X},\tilde{Y}}(a, b)$ and define the parametric feasible region for each α-level set (ZIMMERMANN (1984))

$$D(\alpha) = \{(a, b) : \mu_{\tilde{X},\tilde{Y}}\,(a, b) \geqslant \alpha\} \tag{34}$$

The fuzzy «barrier» policy is obtained by finding the solution, when existing, for the subproblem

$$N(\alpha) = \{(x^*, y^*) : U^*(x^*, y^*) =$$
$$= \max_{(a,b) \in D(a,b)} U(x, y), (a, b) \in D(\alpha)\} \tag{35}$$

with a membership function

$$\mu_{opt}(x^*, y^*) = \begin{cases} \sup\limits_{(x^*,y^*) \in N(\alpha)} \alpha & \text{if } (x^*, y^*) \in \bigcup\limits_{\alpha > 0} N(\alpha) \\ 0 & \text{else} \end{cases} \tag{36}$$

and a fuzzy «barrier» policy

$$\tilde{x} = \begin{cases} X - x^* & \text{if } X > x^* \\ 0 & \text{if } X \leqslant x^* \end{cases} \qquad \tilde{y} = \begin{cases} Y - y^* & \text{if } Y > y^* \\ 0 & \text{if } Y \leqslant y^* \end{cases} \tag{37}$$

The mixed «barrier» type solution is easily found with respect to the balance constraint

$$E(V) + (1 + \tilde{x})\,P(a) \geqslant (1 + \tilde{y})\,C(b) \tag{38}$$

The practical implementation of the joint membership function $\mu_{\tilde{X},\tilde{Y}}$ for the feasibility intervals of the adjustment rates x and y will emphasize the importance of a stronger cooperation within the EMS.

Moreover a suitable expert system should be formalized to dynamically add the information on the insured's tastes with respect to the different kinds of indexation and revaluation for both premium and capital.

Our aim has been to promote a deeper insight to the internal as well as the external markets in order to defend the purchasing power of an insured capital.

Therefore it is worth taking into account a wider set of parameters to adjust the policy's elements.

Moreover, the paper has shown how the fuzzy set theory can contribute to the development of flexible contrasts for the life insurance policies introduced onto the international market. It is a further example of the cautions that are required, when considering harmonization within the EMS market.

REFERENCES

[1] J.A. BEEKMAN (1987) "Ornsstein-Uhlenbeck stochastic processes applied to immunization" in [10].

[2] K.H. BORCH (1974) *The mathematical theory of insurance,* Lexington.

[3] M.J. BRENNAN, E.S. SCHWARTZ (1986) "The pricing of equity-linked life insurance policies with an asset value guarantee" J. of Financial Economics, vol. 3 pp. 195-213.

[4] U. CARRARO, D. SARTORE eds. (1987) *Developments of control theory for economic analysis,* M.Nijhoff Publ.

[5] E. CASTAGNOLI, P. MAZZOLENI (1988) "From an oriental market to the EMS: some fuzzy-sets-related ideas" in [9].

[6] M. CECCHINI FANT (1989) "Analisi attuariale e finanziaria di una polizza vita in ECU" tesi di laurea, Univ. Venezia, Italia.

[7] A. DESIATA (1983) "The European currency unit and the insurance sector" The Geneva Papers on risk and Insurance, vol. 10, n. 5, pp. 112-119.

[8] L.L. JACQUE, C.S. TAPIERO (1987) "Premium valuation in international insurance" Scand. Actuarial J. pp. 50-61.

[9] J. KACPRZYK, M. FEDRIZZI (1988) *Combining fuzzy imprecision with probabilistic uncertainty in decision making,* Springer Verlag.

[10] I.B. MACNEILL, G.J. UMPHREY (eds.) (1987) *Actuarial Science,* D. Reidel Publ.

[11] P. MAZZOLENI (1981) "Il ruolo dello Scudo come stabilizzatore della politica monetaria europea" Proceed. IV A.M.A.S.E.S. Meeting Roma, February 13-15, pp. 183-195.

[12] E. PITACCO (1988) "Assicurazioni vita e fondi d'investimento: analisi del rischio finanziario" Proceed. A.I.R.O. Meeting, Pisa, October 5-6, pp. 573-584.

[13] A.P. SAGE, C.C. WHITE (1977) *Optimum Systems Control* Prentice Hall.

[14] C.S. TAPIERO (1987) "A system approach to insurance company management" in [4].

[15] H.J. ZIMMERMANN (1984) *Fuzzy set theory and its applications,* Kluwer Nijhoff Publ.

APPENDIX

EXCHANGE RATE LIRA/ECU

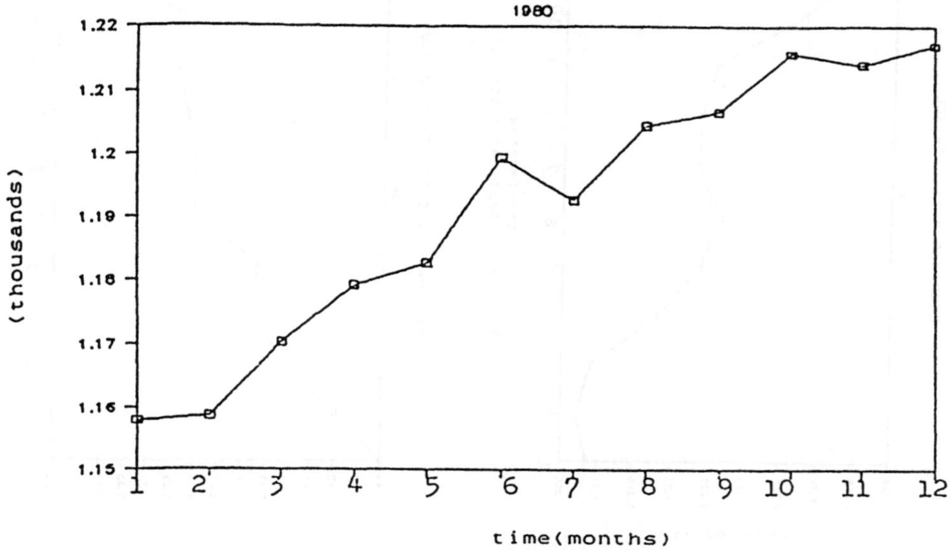

year percentage variation 5

EXCHANGE RATE DEUTCH MARK/ECU

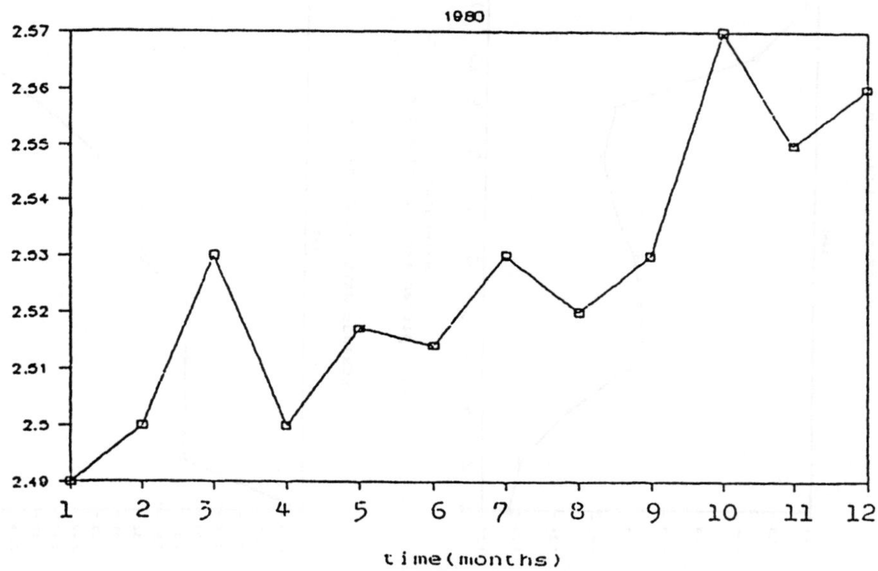

year percentage variation 2.8

EXCHANGE RATE LIRA/ECU

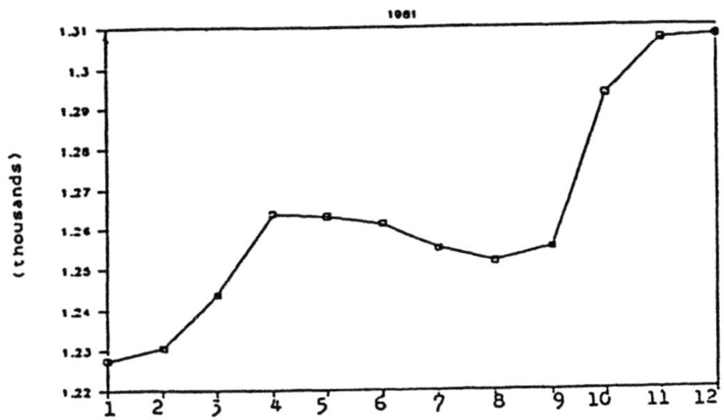

time(months)
year percentage variation 5.6

EXCHANGE RATE LIRA/ECU

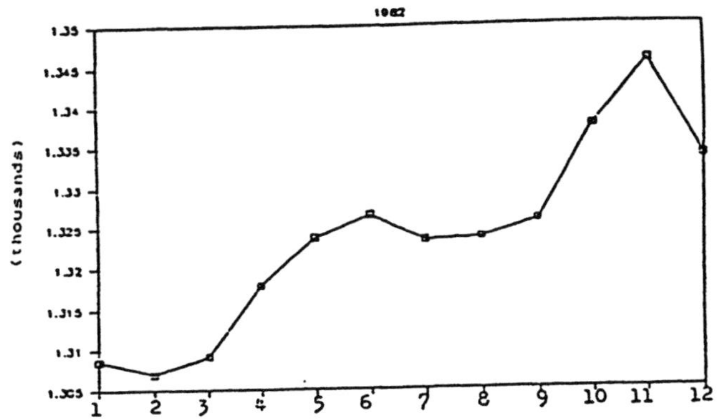

time(months)
year percentage variation 1.1

EXCHANGE RATE DEUTCH MARK/ECU

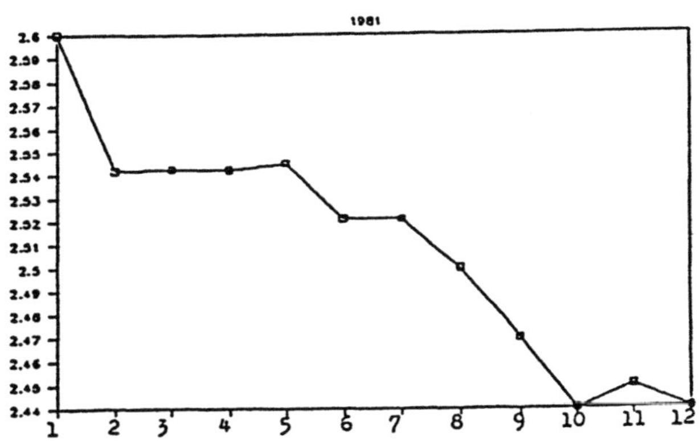

time(months)
year percentage variation -0.3

EXCHANGE RATE DEUTCH MARK/ECU

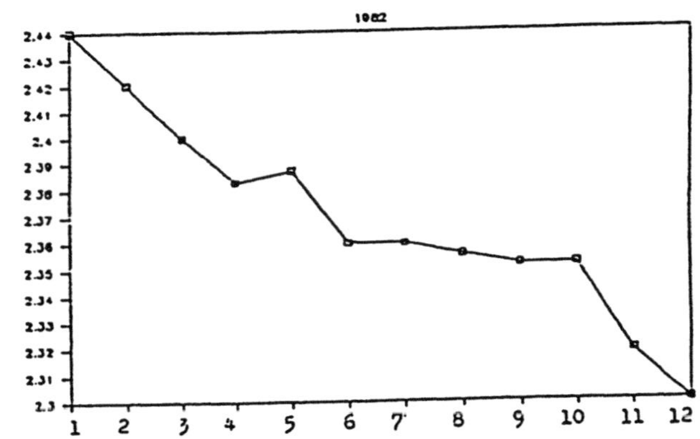

time(months)
year percentage variation -0.5

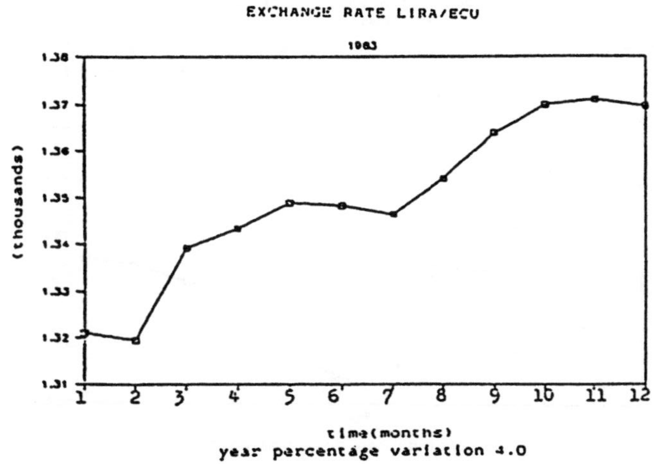
EXCHANGE RATE LIRA/ECU
1983
(thousands)
1.38
1.37
1.36
1.35
1.34
1.33
1.32
1.31
1 2 3 4 5 6 7 8 9 10 11 12
time(months)
year percentage variation 4.0

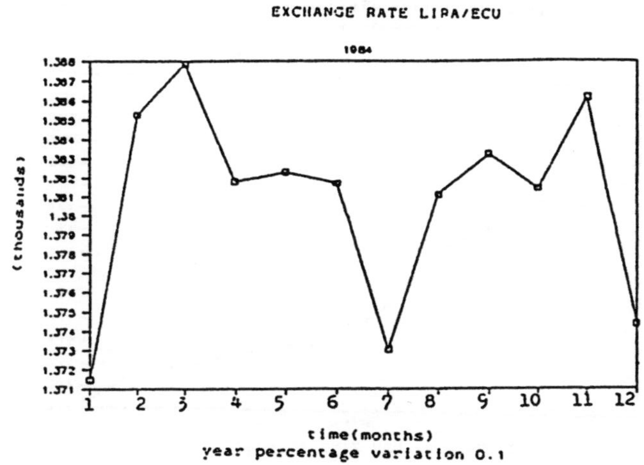
EXCHANGE RATE LIRA/ECU
1984
(thousands)
1.388
1.387
1.386
1.385
1.384
1.383
1.382
1.381
1.38
1.379
1.378
1.377
1.376
1.375
1.374
1.373
1.372
1.371
1 2 3 4 5 6 7 8 9 10 11 12
time(months)
year percentage variation 0.1

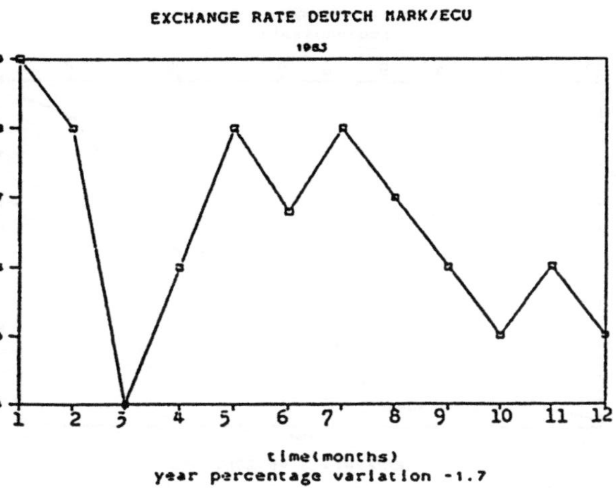
EXCHANGE RATE DEUTCH MARK/ECU
1983
2.29
2.28
2.27
2.26
2.25
2.24
1 2 3 4 5 6 7 8 9 10 11 12
time(months)
year percentage variation -1.7

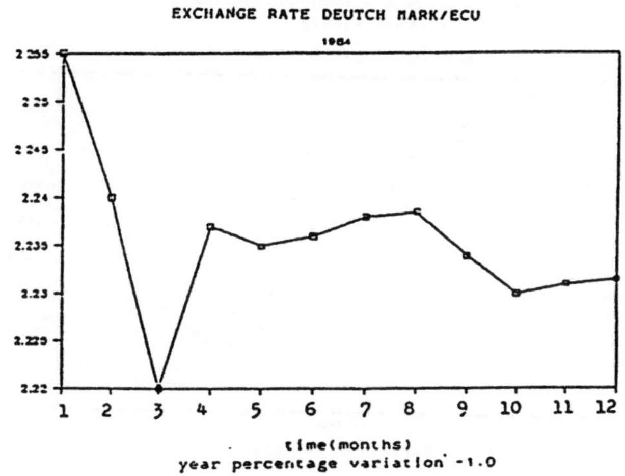
EXCHANGE RATE DEUTCH MARK/ECU
1984
2.255
2.25
2.245
2.24
2.235
2.23
2.225
2.22
1 2 3 4 5 6 7 8 9 10 11 12
time(months)
year percentage variation -1.0

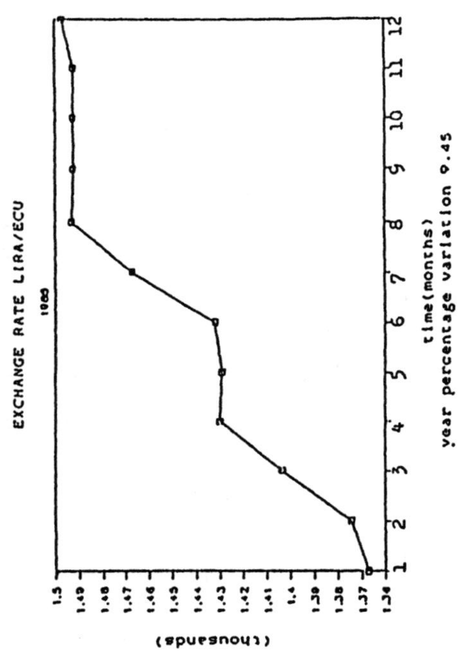
EXCHANGE RATE LIRA/ECU
1985
(thousands)
time(months)
year percentage variation 9.45

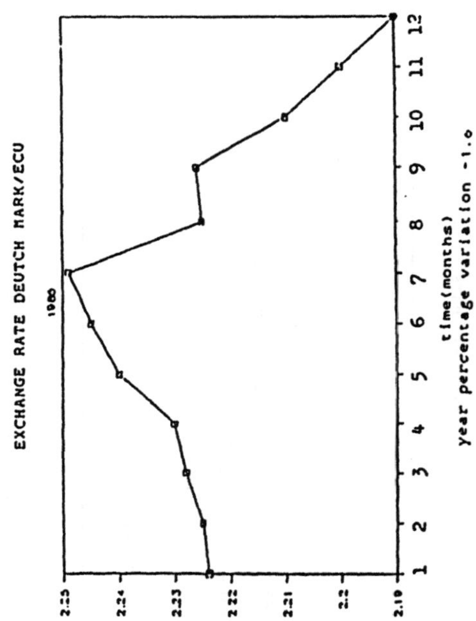
EXCHANGE RATE DEUTCH MARK/ECU
1985
time(months)
year percentage variation -1.6

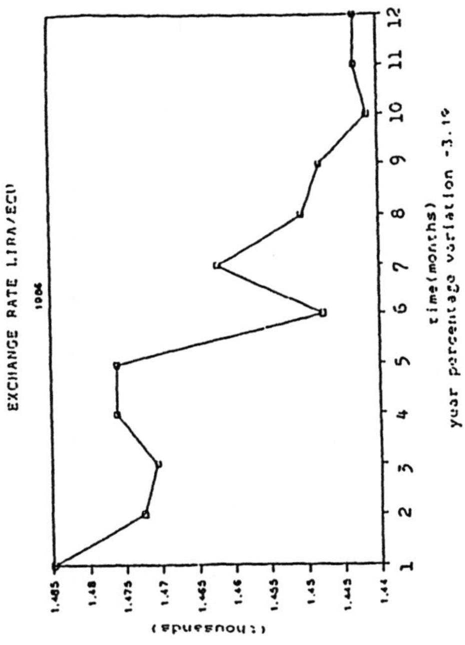
EXCHANGE RATE LIRA/ECU
1986
(thousands)
time(months)
year percentage variation -3.19

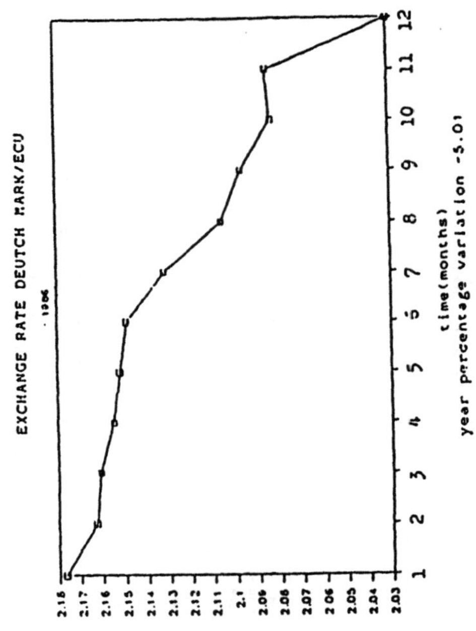
EXCHANGE RATE DEUTCH MARK/ECU
1986
time(months)
year percentage variation -5.01

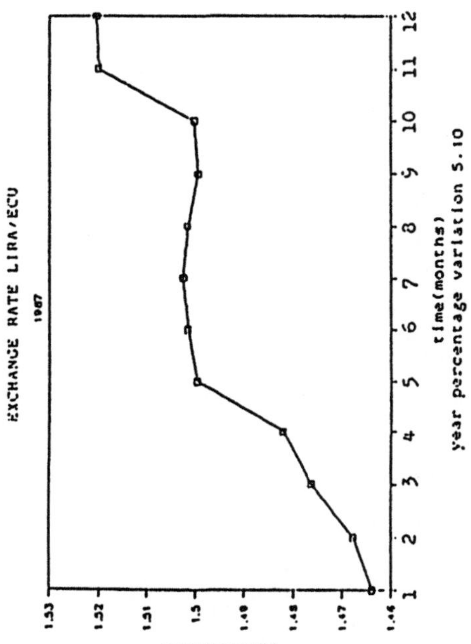
EXCHANGE RATE LIRA/ECU
1987
(thousands)
time(months)
year percentage variation 5.10

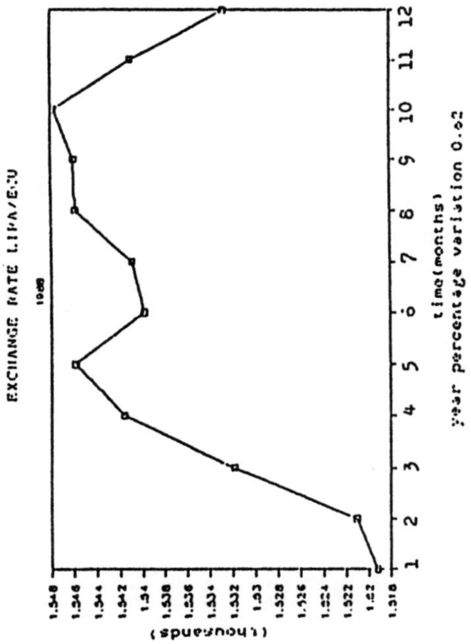
EXCHANGE RATE LIRA/ECU
1988
(thousands)
time(months)

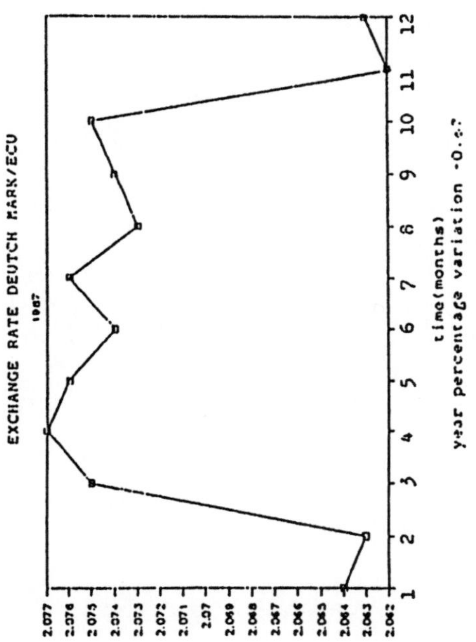
EXCHANGE RATE DEUTCH MARK/ECU
1987
time(months)

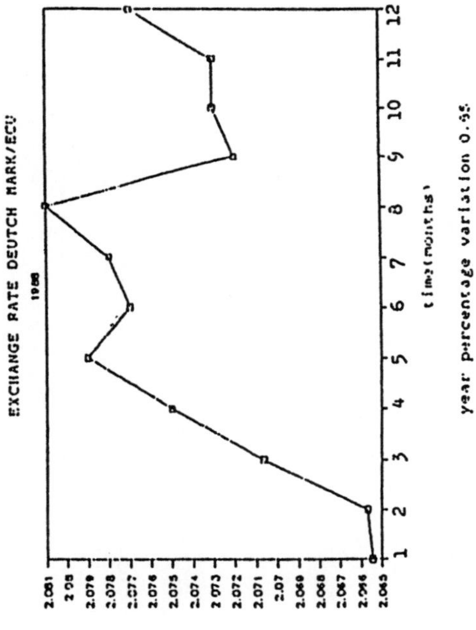
EXCHANGE RATE DEUTCH MARK/ECU
1988
time(months)

MULTIPERIOD ANALYSIS OF A LEVERED PORTFOLIO

LORENZO PECCATI
Turin and "Bocconi" Universities

The notion of Internal Financial Law for an investment is introduced. Through this generalization of the IRR a general notion of outstanding capital is obtained. After the introduction of a generalized version of NPV a decomposition of this parameter is offered which is strictly connected to the notion of ROE.

Some applications to yield averaging for portfolios is provided.

0. Introduction

In project evaluation a particular role is played by the *discounted cash-flow* (*DCF*). Under quite reasonable hypothesis which are often met in practice, *DCF* is substantially the only correct financial indicator to be used (see, for instance, M. BROMWICH (1970), H. LEVY - M. SARNAT (1978), J.C.T. MAO (1970), F.M. WILKES (1983)). This necessity appears to be mainly logical. Sometimes managers do prefer to use single year parameters of accountancy flavour or pseudo-objective indices like the well known *internal rate of return (IRR)*. In practice there are further problems arising from the fact that often one has to evaluate many investments made at different times and with different characteristics. Other troubles come both from the fact that the investment activity may be partially levered through a mix of financial instruments and from the usual delay between income formation and tax payment epochs.

This paper offers a possible solution to all of these problems, where the various aforementioned aspects appear to be harmonically combined. This is possible through a convenient generalization of previous results by the Author (L. PECCATI (1987)). The basic model is described in Section 1. The main results are proved in Section 2, while in Section 3 some applications of practical importance are indicated mainly with reference to average portfolio yield evaluation. The last Section contains a brief description of possible further research.

1. The model

Consider a sequence of equispaced epochs $s = 0, 1, 2, \dots, N$ and denote by f_s the cash-flow of investment I at epoch s, with the usual convention that $f_s < 0$ means that at epoch s there is a money outflow, while $f_s > 0$ has the opposite meaning. By allowing the possibility of zero cash-flows at some epochs, we can suppose that the epochs $0, 1, 2, \ldots, N$ are the same for every investment of a portfolio. We shall suppose that $f_0 < 0$. We can consider, for simplicity's sake, a single investment. In Section 3 a portfolio of many investments will be studied. Suppose that in the period from s to $s+1$ interest rate R_s (in some sense) prevails and define the discount coefficient:

$$\Phi(s, t) = \prod_{u=t}^{s-1} 1/(1 + R_u) \quad (s \geqq t)$$

The *DCF* of I computed through Φ is:

$$G[\Phi] = \sum_{s=0}^{N} f_s \, \Phi(s, 0)$$

We shall speak of *internal financial low (IFL)* for the investment I with reference to any function Φ^* such that $G[\Phi^*] = 0$. Let $\rho_0, \rho_1, \ldots, \rho_{N-1}$ be the interest rates characterizing Φ^*, i.e.;

$$\Phi^*(s, t) = \prod_{u=t}^{s-1} 1/(1 + \rho_u) \ (s \geqq t)$$

Particular attention deserves the case of constant interest rates: $\rho_s = \rho \ \forall s = 0, 1, \ldots, N-1$. In this case, one may write $G(\rho)$ instead of $G[\Phi^*]$ and ρ is said *internal rate of return (IRR)* for the investment I. To develop our approach it is not necessary that an *IRR* exists. It suffices that an *IFL* exists. This fact circumvents some difficulties connected with the possible non existence of an *IRR*. If there is some problem it is of opposite type, because for a given investment I there is an infinity of *IFL* $\Phi^* : G[\Phi^*] = 0$. There are many possibilities to pick up one of them to be used in the analysis (see, for instance DIALE (1989)) and this point deserves some attention. The choice of an *IFL* is simply the attribution to the single periods of the rentability of an investment. The usual choice to assign to each period the same degree of rentability corresponds to the choice of equal interest rates $\rho_s = \rho \ \forall s$. When there is no reason to make differences among the different years it may be the best choice, although it is quite not compulsory. When we study, for instance, the value of a pension fund and we observe empirically different yields in different years, the most natural description of this investment process is not the constant interest rate one. The classical troublesome problem of non existence or of multiplicity of *IRR* arises from the basic and historical error consisting in the aim to describe through a *unique* parameter what happens in *quite different* time periods. The well known oil-pump problem depictes very well the situation. After a positive year comes a disastrous one. It is hard to think of a unique interest rate which describes both. A more reasonable criterion should rely on two interest rates: one positive for the first year and one negative for the second. The fact that there is an infinity of possible interest rates couples bringing to a zero *DCF* is not a deficiency of this approach. It simply gives some degrees of freedom in the choice of parameters. This choice must be made by the person making investment appraisal on the basis of criteria he/she thinks are correct case by case. The problem of existence of an *IFL* is investigated in P. MANCA (1990).

Suppose to have chosen an *IFL* Φ^*. Then it is possible to compute $\forall s = 0, 1, \ldots, N$ the *outstanding capital* (o.c.) w_s at time s for I through the difference equation:

$$w_s = w_{s-1}(1 + \rho_{s-1}) - f_s$$

The initial condition is $w_0 = -f_0$. A bit of algebra allows to prove that $w_N = 0$.

One easily obtains for w_s the "forward" representation:

$$w_s = \sum_{t=s+1}^{N} f_t \, \Phi^*(t, s)$$

Now we pass to the liability side of the problem by considering debt and equity. For the moment we allow only one type of debt, but in n. 3 we shall remove this assumption.

We admit the possibility of leverage of the investment and we suppose that during the life of investment the debt fraction may vary. This, of course, depends on the possibly different evolutions in time of the o.c. of the investment and of the sinking fund of the debt.

Let δ_s be the cost of debt capital between s and $s + 1$. If we denote by D_s the sinking fund at s (precisely, at s^+), the sequence of sinking funds obeys the difference equation:

$$D_s = D_{s-1}(1 + \delta_{s-1}) - \alpha_s \quad (s = 1, 2, \ldots, N)$$

The initial condition for the difference equation is determined by the initial amount of debt. The amounts α_s are the total payments (capital + interest). It is easy to prove that for D_s too a "forward" representation holds:

$$D_s = \sum_{t=s+1}^{N} \alpha_t \, H(t, s)$$

where:

$$H(t, s) = \prod_{u=s}^{t-1} 1/(1 + \delta_u)$$

one gets also easily that $D_N = 0$. It will be necessary to define also α_0. A natural definition is $\alpha_0 = -D_0$.

For any epoch $s = 0, 1, \ldots, N-1$ the leveraged share of the o.c. is given simply by $\theta_s = D_s/w_s$. Although it is common to define as leverage the ratio $\theta_s/(1-\theta_s)$, we shall call leverage the ratio θ_s.

In practice, very often, while carrying on a financial activity one has to pay or to receive money for reasons not strictly dependent on investment and debt. We shall denote by Ω_s the net nonfinancial cash-flow at s ($s = 0, 1, 2, \ldots N$). Concrete cash-flows of this kind are determined, for instance, by salaries, taxes, etc. They may also include collateral returns, so that they may be positive as well as negative. Otherwise, these cash-flows may be thought of as a correction of f_s and/or α_s, and in this case $\Omega_s = 0 \ \forall s$. However it is not restrictive to allow the possibility to consider them separately. It is convenient to assume that $\Omega_0 = 0$.

We are now ready to determine cash-flows on determined by the shareholders through a simple balance equation.

Let e_s denote the equity cash-flow at s. We have necessarily:

$$e_s = f_s - \alpha_s + \Omega_s$$

2. Some results

Let us examine the investment from the viewpoint of the shareholders. Through the interest rates R_s ($s = 0, 1, \ldots, N-1$), which determine the discount factors $\Phi(s, 0)$, the owner computes the net *DCF* sometimes known as Adjusted Present Value:

$$\Gamma[\Phi] = \sum_{s=1}^{N} e_s \Phi(s, 0)$$

A deeper insight into the financial meaning of $\Gamma[\Phi]$ may be obtained following PECCATI (1987) It is possible in fact to break up $\Gamma[\Phi]$ into N addenda, corresponding to the N periods we are considering.

We derive simply the decomposition of $\Gamma[\Phi]$. First consider the investment side. The corresponding *DCF* is given by:

$$G[\Phi] = f_0 + \sum_{s=1}^{N} f_s \Phi(s, 0)$$

From the difference equation for w_s one gets:

$$f_s = w_{s-1}(1 + \rho_{s-1}) - w_s$$

By substituting this expression for f_s in $G[\Phi]$, after some obvious manipulations, one gets:

$$G[\Phi] = \sum_{s=1}^{N} w_{s-1} (\rho_{s-1} - R_{s-1}) \Phi(s, 0)$$

Let $\Delta[\Phi]$ be the analogous *DCF* for the debt (where payments are positive and the initial collection negative). One gets analogously:

$$\Delta[\Phi] = \sum_{s=1}^{N} (\delta_{s-1} - R_{s-1}) \Phi(s, 0) =$$

$$= \sum_{s=1}^{N} \theta_{s-1} w_{s-1} (\delta_{s-1} - R_{s-1}) \Phi(s, 0)$$

If we let $\Omega_s / w_{s-1} = \omega_s$, and:

$$\Psi(\Phi) = \sum_{s=1}^{N} \omega_s \Phi(s, 0)$$

we are able to express the net *DCF* for the shareholders:

$$\Gamma[\Phi] = G[\Phi] - \Delta[\Phi] + \Psi[\Phi]$$

as follows:

$$\Gamma[\Phi] = G[\Phi] + \Psi[\Phi] + \sum_{s=1}^{N} \theta_{s-1} w_{s-1} (R_{s-1} - \delta_{s-1}) \Phi(s,0)$$

This formula gives us a *DCF*- and multiperiod version of the most elementary leverage effect proposition (see, for instance: WESTON-BRIGHAM (1978)). Suppose $\Omega_s = 0 \ \forall s$. $\Gamma[\Phi]$ reduces to:

$$\Gamma[\Phi] = G[\Phi] + \sum_{s=1}^{N} \theta_{s-1} w_{s-1} (R_{s-1} - \delta_{s-1}) \Phi(s, 0)$$

If not levered investment I gives $G[\Phi]$, so that the second addendum appears to be the leverage contribution. If the debt cost is lower than the opportunity cost, and if leverage and outstanding are positive then $\Gamma[\Phi] > G[\Phi]$ and the *DCF*-leverage effect gives $\Gamma[\Phi] - G[\Phi]$.

To get an *IRR*- and multiperiod version of this result we must first assume that the *IFL* Φ^* of I is an exponential one and let ρ^* be the *IRR*. It is easy to prove that under the same hypothesis of the *DCF* case the equation $\Gamma(\rho) = 0$ has at least one root $\rho^{**} > \rho^*$. This follows the fact that $\Gamma(\rho^*) > 0$ and that $\Gamma(+\infty) < < 0$ and that Γ is continuous.

Other interesting consequences of the decomposition can be easily obtained as follows.

If we call $\gamma_s[\Phi]$, the contribution to $\Gamma[\Phi]$ of the period from s to $s + 1$, and we observe that both $G[\Phi]$ and $\Delta[\Phi]$ and $\Psi[\Phi]$ are sum of period contributions, we get:

$$\gamma_s[\Phi] = w_s[(1 - \theta_s)(\rho_s - R_s) + \theta_s(\rho_s - \delta_s) + \omega_{s+1}]\, \Phi(s + 1, 0)$$
$$s = 0\ 1\ \ldots, N - 1$$

The contribution to $\Gamma[\Phi]$ of period from s to $s + 1$ is shown to be proportional to the o.c. in s and to consist of three parts. The first is determined by the equity part of the operation and stems from the spread between the yield of the *IFL* of the investment ρ_s and the opportunity cost R_s. The second is due to the "intermediation" dimension of the activity implied by the leverage and is analogously proportional to the spread between ρ_s and the cost of debt. The two weights θ_s and $(1 - \theta_s)$ split w_s in correct shares. The third addendum concerns the nonfinancial part of the business. The factor $\Phi(s + 1, 0)$ simply brings the financial margins of the various periods to epoch zero.

It is remarkable that the expression of $\gamma[\Phi]$ brings to our attention full and new connections among financial indicators:

* multiperiod financial results;
* single period financial results;
* *IFL* or, in particular, *IRR*;
* *DCF*;
* opportunity cost of equity;
* cost of debt.

Precisely we have that global financial results (gross *DCF*, without taking account of $\Psi[\Phi]$) may be thought of as sum of present values of period results. These period components are determined by the amount of the o.c. at the beginning of the period and by the capital structure. To each part of the o.c. a spread between interest rates has to be applied. The spread is simply the difference between period yield of the *IFL* and the cost of capital of each type of source. The simple consideration of *IRR* or of the mentioned spreads, a practice which is common in finance, is insufficient because it frequently ignores the effect of the o.c. level and of the leverage ratio.

Note that *DCF* and *IRR*, which are usually thought of as in alternative are clearly strictly connected: a period contribution to *DCF* can be defined only through an *IFL* and the *IRR* gives us the most natural way to choosen an *IFL*.

Remark another useful aspect of the representation formula for $\gamma_s[\Phi]$ we have found: for given interest rates the $\gamma_s[\Phi]$'s are linear in the outstandings while for given outstandings they are linear in the interest rates ρ_s and δ_s. In the next paragraph we shall make large use of these facts.

3. Some applications

A simple application of this approach may be made to solve a general problem in finance. Consider a portfolio made up of A assets, numbered with $a = 1, 2, \ldots A$ and financed through a combination of equity and debt. Let J be the number of indebtment sources, numbered with $j = 1, 2, \ldots, J$.

For simplicity's sake, in this section, we work, for the investments, with *IRR*'s instead of using *IFL*'s. The less generality is repaid by grater proximity to the practice. However it is not difficult to rewrite all of this section through *IFL*'s. ,

For each asset a and for each period from s to $s + 1$ one has to consider the outstanding at the beginning of the period w_{sa}, the *IRR* of the asset ρ^*_a, the quota of the o.c. being financed through the debt of type j, denoted by θ_{saj} and the corresponding period cost of capital δ_{sj}. Of course the quota financed by equity is obtained as the complement to unity of the sum of θ_{saj} over index j and results:

$$(1 - \theta_{sa}) = 1 - \sum_{j=1}^{j} \theta_{saj}$$

The possibility that the o.c.'s and/or the leverages are zero for some values of their indices allows from assets and liabilities starting and/or ending at different epochs.

Usual problems concerning such general setting are the evaluation of the average rate of return on a portfolio and/or the average cost of capital.

Following our approach it is possible to find satisfactory answers to these questions. Some of these answers do not coincide with the standard ones. The logic of our approach explains all of these discrepancies.

On the basis of L. PECCATI (1987) in a recent paper (A. CERQUETTI (1988)) some steps in this direction have already been made. What we present here may be seen as their refinement.

The key-formula is a generalization of the expression we gave for the period contributions to the case we are considering. Let $\gamma_{sa}[\Phi]$ denote the contribution to the global *DCF* of the portfolio coming from asset a in the period from s to $s + 1$, given the capital structure. We have:

$$\gamma_{sa}[\Phi] = w_{sa}\left[(1-\theta_{sa})(\rho_a{}^* - R_s) + \sum_{j=1}^{J} \theta_{saj}(\rho_a{}^* - \delta_{sj})\right]\Phi(s+1, 0)$$

First assume we are interested in evaluating the average yield of the various assets constituting the portfolio (or a sub-portfolio) in the period $(s, s+1)$ and/or the average cost of capital in that period.

The average yield ρ^*_s is naturally defined as that interest rate which could be substituted to the $\rho_{sq}{}^*$'s without altering $\gamma_s[\Phi] = \Sigma_a\ \gamma_{sa}[\Phi]$. From simple computations we get:

$$\rho_s{}^* = \frac{\sum_a \rho_{sa}\, w_{sa}\, \theta_{sa}}{\sum_a w_{sa}\, \theta_{sa}}$$

The problems of the average cost of capital is treated analogously, both with reference to a single asset and with reference to the whole portfolio or to sub-portfolios with intuitive and standard results.

It is worthwile to stress that the average yield of a portfolio may vary over time. This is quite natural and is due to the changes in the portfolio composition.

Suppose now that we are interested in the evaluation of the average yield of the portfolio over more than one period $(s, s+1)$. Let $\mathcal{S}$ be the set of indices s characterizing the relevant time set. Generally S will be a sequence of consecutive integers $\mathcal{S} = \{s', s'+1, \ldots, s''\}$ (for instance when s counts the months and one is interested to a yearly portfolio performance), but this is not strictly necessary.

From the same viewpoint as before, we can get the following expression for the average rate of return $r_{\mathcal{S}}{}^*$:

$$\rho_{\mathcal{S}}{}^* = \frac{\sum_s \sum_a \rho_{sa}\, w_{sa}\, \theta_{sa}\, \Phi(s, 0)}{\sum_s \sum_a w_{sa}\, \theta_{sa}\, \Phi(s, 0)} \quad \ldots$$

where in the double summation $s \in \mathcal{S}$ and to $a = 1, \ldots, A$.

Note that the average yield rate is not independent of Φ. This fact may appear quite strange, but one has to accept it owing to the fact that aggregation over time implicitly requires time-transfer prices. Often the *IRR* themselves, or a null interest rate ($\Phi(s, 0) = 1\ \forall s$) are used, but these choices have no serious basis.

Furthermore, note also that *even if* $\rho_{\mathcal{S}}{}^*$ *concerns more than one period, its meaning is that of interest rate for a unitary period* (e.g. averages of monthly yields are monthly yields). It may seem natural to refer interest rates to other time measures units with standard methods. For instance, if $(s, s+1)$ has lenght $1/m$ years, one could obtain a yearly rate ρ through:

$$\rho = (1+ \rho^*)^m - 1$$

The use of such a formula however assumes that reinvestments from period to period are made precisely at interest rate r^*. This is, in general, contrary to our hypothesis.

The case of the average cost of capital again can be faced in an analogous way.

4. Directions of future research

At present some interesting research directions may be suggested.

The first direction concerns the solution of some problems concerning the existence of *IRR*, when one wishes not to work with a general *IFL*. With many well known results on this topic (SOPER (1959), LEVI (1964) and NORSTROM (1970), for good surveys see LONZI (1986) and LONZI (1988)) one can mention some theorems (PECCATI (1989a)) concerning this specific problem. General conditions are derived which guarantee the uniqueness of a useful *IRR*. In specific relevant cases more particular conditions should hold.

Other research directions concern the application of the method to particular types of financial to better understand, evaluate and control their profitability. Some initial results concerning the life insufance activity are explored in L. PECCATI (1989b).

Further theoretical research may be made in a dynamic optimization context, for instance to choose optimally the leverage, and hence the α_s's, given the f_s's, or the f_s's, given the α_s's. The expression of $\gamma_s(\Phi)$ should help in treating the corresponding hamiltonian. See, for instance, E. LUCIANO (1989).

In forthcoming papers (E. LUCIANO - L. PECCATI (1990)) the case of random cash-flows will be analyzed and the method will be applied to the analysis of investments in foreign currencies (M. UBERTI (1990)).

References

M. BROMWICH (1970), *Capital budgeting - a survey*, Journal of Business Finance, 2, n. 3, pp. 3-26.

A. CFRQUETTI (1988), *Tassi medi di rendimento di obbligazioni singole e in portafoglio*, Pubblicazioni dell'Istituto di Matematica, Un. "G. D'Annunziò", Pescara.

G. DIALE (1989), *On multiple IFL*, to appear.

E. LEVI (1964), *Corso di Matematica Finanziaria e Attuariale*, Giuffrè, Milano.

H. LEVY - M. SARNAT (1978), *Capital Investment and Financial Decisions*, Prentice Hall International, Englewood Cliffs.

M. LONZI (1986), *Aspetti Matematici nella Ricerca di Condizioni di Unicità per il Tasso interno di Rendimento*, Rivista di Matematica per le Scienze Economiche e Sociali.

M. LONZI (1988), *Valore Attuale e Montante nei progetti puri,* Presented to Rivista di Matematica per le Scienze Economiche e Sociali.

E. LUCIANO (1989), *A new Perspective on Dynamic Portfolio Policies* in this issue.

E. LUCIANO, L. PECCATI (1990), *The decomposition of random discounted cash-flows,* to be presented at the Fifth International Conference on the Foundations of Utility, Risk and Decision Theory (FUR V), Duke University, Durham, USA.

P. MANCA (1990), *The splitting up of a Financial Project into uniperiodic Consecutive projects,* in this issue.

J.C.T. MAO (1970) *Survey of Capital Budgeting: Theory and Practice,* Journal of Finance, May, pp. 349-360.

C.J. NORSTROM (1972) *A Sufficient Condition for a Unique Nonnegative Internal Rate of Return,* Journal of Financial and Quantitative Analysis, vol. 7, June, pp. 1835-1838.

L. PECCATI (1987), *DCF e risultati di periodo,* Atti dell'XI Convegno AMASES, Torino-Aosta (to appear).

L. PECCATI (1989a), *Di tassi e di tasse,* presented at the "Convegno sulla Matematica Applicata all'Economia e all'Ingegneria", Un. "G. D'Annunzio", Pescara, 26-28 Jan.

L. PECCATI (1989b), *Un metodo di valutazione di un investimento in un portafoglio assicurativo,* presented at the "Giornata di Studio sul tema: Analisi e Gestione del Rischio Finanziario", Istituto Italiano degli Attuari, Roma.

C.S. SOPER (1959), *The Marginal Efficiency of Capital:* A Further Note. In The Economic Journal, vol. 69, March, pp. 174-177.

F. WESTON, E. BRIGHAM (1978), *Managerial Finance,* 6^ ed., Hinsdale, Holt-Saunders International Editions, Dryden Press.

F.M. WILKES (1983), *Capital Budgeting Techniques,* 2nd ed., New York, J. Wiley & Sons.

M. UBERTI (1990), *The decomposition of the present value of foreign currency bonds,* to appear.

THE TIME SERIES CHARACTERISTICS OF QUARTERLY NOMINAL AND REAL LIRA/POUND-STERLING EXCHANGE RATE MOVEMENTS, 1973-1988

ANDREW C. POLLOCK

Glasgow College
Department of Mathematics
Cowcaddens Road
Glasgow
G4 0BA

Time series analysis is applied to quarterly data on nominal and real, lira/pound-sterling exchange rates for the period 1973 Q1 to 1988 Q2. The paper uses logarithmic values which are examined using both time and frequency domain techniques. Trends and cyclical characteristics are examined and related to the concept of purchasing power parity. Furthermore, the validity of the random walk model is considered, as well as the distribution of exchange rate movements. The results suggest that the nominal exchange rate follows a quasi-random walk with drift, whereas real exchange rates show a quasi-random walk without drift. There exists, however, evidence of a non-stationary mean. The frequency domain techniques do not clearly show that cyclical characteristics are a feature of exchange rate movements. The distribution of these movements shows approximate normality.

1. Introduction

Quarterly movements of the lira/pound-sterling exchange rate are of considerable importance to the business community undertaking trade in goods and services between Italy and the UK. An investigation into the time series characteristics of these movements can throw considerable light on the underlying mechanism that influence exchange rate behaviour and provide a starting point for exchange rate modelling and forecasting. The analysis of trends in real and nominal exchange rates can be used to examine the validity of purchasing power parity (PPP) in both the medium- and the long-term. The analysis of low frequency cycles allows investigation into whether business cycle fluctuations exist in exchange rate series and whether or not they are related to similar cycles in relative price series. Examination of randomness can be used to determine whether or not the foreign exchange market is efficient. In addition, the study of exchange rate behaviour requires an understanding of the probability distribution of exchange rate changes and, in particular, the validity of the assumption of normality.

A basic starting point to exchange rate modelling is the concept of PPP. The analysis of the simple relative PPP approach, under a regime of generalised floating, has yielded mixed results. A number of studies, using bilateral exchange rate series, such as Frenkel (1981), Crumby and Obstfeld (1984), Miller (1984) and Daniel (1986), obtained results that suggest PPP broke down during this period. However, studies by Rush and Husted (1985) and Edison (1987) using bilateral rates over a much longer period, obtained results which give more support to PPP. Officer (1982), using effective exchange rate data, obtains results which support the long run validity of PPP. The results obtained by Pollock (1988, 1989) for the UK effective exchange rate also support PPP in the long run. Furthermore, authors such as Davutyan and Pippenger (1985) attributed the results that claim PPP broke down, to a reduction in the importance of monetary shocks in the 1970s compared with other periods, such as the 1920s, rather than a collapse of PPP.

The random walk view is a simple approach to modelling exchange rate behaviour. The basis of this view is that the foreign exchange market exhibits the characteristics of the weak form of the efficient markets hypothesis. This implies that historical exchange rates contain no information that can be used to forecast future exchange rates. The idea that changes in exchange rates follow a random pattern is supported in a number of studies, including Giddy and Dufey (1975), Logue and Sweeney (1977), Crumby and Obstfeld (1984), Junge (1985) and Boothe and Glassman (1987a).

There exists evidence that the distribution of changes in nominal bilateral rates shows evidence of non-normality and non-stationarity, especially when daily or weekly data are used. These problems of stationarity and non-normality of bilateral rate changes are examined in Burt, Kaen and Booth (1977), Hakkio (1981) and Boothe and Glassman (1987b). They found evidence of non-normality in the distribution of exchange rate changes and have noted changes in the variance over time. Westerfield (1977), Calderon-Rossel and Ben-Horrim (1982) and Pozo (1984) found that the variability of exchange rate behaviour is best described by the Paretian distribution. This distribution tends to have longer tails than those of the normal and has some degree of leptokurtosis. The non-normality in exchange rate movements has been attributed to non-constant variance. This is because exchange rate series are often characterised by a mixture of stable and unstable periods. In stable periods, only small deviation occur whilst, large deviations occur in unstable periods. A number of studies have used the Autoregressive Conditional Heteroscedastic (ARCH) model of Engle (1982) to explain exchange rate movements. These studies include Bollerslev (1987) and Milhoj (1987). It is argued that the ARCH model gives a better fit to daily bilateral exchange rate data and can be used to explain the apparent non-normality in the distribution of exchange rate movements. There exists, however, evidence that exchange rate changes, using quarterly data, follow approximately a normal distribution. Officer (1982) and Pollock (1988, 1989) obtained results that support the hypothesis that real exchange rate movements and deviations from purchasing power parity approximately follow normal distributions.

There has been relatively less literature on the presence of cyclical behaviour in exchange rate movements, especially involving the use of spectral techniques. Logue and Sweeney (1977) used spectral analysis in their examination of foreign exchange market efficiency and more recently Metghelchi and Im (1986) and Pollock (1988) used spectral techniques to examine PPP. However, there are a number of studies that have examined stock market movements using spectral techniques, such as Praetz (1979), who set out a procedure to test for randomness in the frequency domain.

This paper undertakes time series analysis on lira/pound, nominal and real exchange rates. Trends and cyclical characteristics are considered and related to the concept of PPP. The cyclical characteristics in real and nominal lira/pound exchange rates are examined using spectral techniques. The study also examines whether or not exchange rates follow a random walk or martingale process. Finally, as analysis of the distribution of changes in nominal and real exchange rates is undertaken.

The empirical analysis involves the lira/pound real and nominal exchange rate, using quarterly data, for the period 1973 Q1 to 1988 Q2. Two measures of relative prices are used, one based on the consumer price index and the other based on the wholesale price index.

2. Time Series Approaches to Examining Real and Nominal Lira/Pound Exchange Rate Movements

The aim of this section is to examine procedures that can be used to identify the time series properties of quarterly lira/pound exchange rate movements. The quarterly data horizon is choosen because it is generally of more interest to the business community involved in the trade of goods and services than more frequent sampling periods. The day-to-day or week-to-week horizons are of more interest to groups such as currency traders or financial institutions operating in the foreign exchange market. The data for the nominal lira/pound exchange rate consists of quarterly series for the end-of-period middle closing rate in London. The period extends from 1973 Q1 to 1988 Q2. To obtain the real lira/pound exchange rate the nominal exchange rate series is multiplied by the ratio of Italy Consumer Prices Index (Wholesale Prices Index) to UK Consumer Prices Index (Wholesale Prices Index). The wholesale prices index relates to the prices of a range of goods, some of which are not directly traded between countries. It includes potential tradable goods and non-traded goods, but excludes services. The broader based consumer price index incorporates a greater proportion of non-tradables, but often excludes services provided by the state. The price indices are based at 1980 = 100, therefore the real rate is at 1980 relative prices [(1)]. Diagram 1 shows the path of the lira/pound exchange rates over the period.

Some discussion is perhaps required as to the nature of the consumer and wholesale prices indices used in this study. A problem arises in using these price indices for two countries when obtaining relative price indices. If both countries have the same weighting pattern, there is no problem. In practice, this is extremely unlikely due to variations in tastes, economic structure and data construction between countries, hence bias can result when calculating the purchasing power parity. If the expenditure patterns of one country are used, then the weights may not be suitable to represent the expenditure patterns of the other country.

In practice, the calculation of weights in price indices is a very lengthy procedure, requiring a large scale sample. In empirical analysis, using the available consumer and wholesale price indices implies that the weights relate to each country's expenditure patterns. Consequently, if countries with similar expenditure patterns are considered, as in the case of industrialised western nations, the bias is not great. However, if the countries considered are at different stages of development, these biases can be substantial. As this study involves Italy and the UK, which are both developed industrialised nations, it is reasonable to use the available data on the consumer and wholesale price indices for each country, as variations between the weighting patterns are not substantial.

In the analysis of exchange rate behaviour many of the economic and statistical problems can be overcome by using first differences compared with non-differenced values. On economic grounds, it can be argued, that differencing is an appropriate procedure as the exchange rate series is influenced strongly by expectations in a foreign exchange market, that is, it is at least quasi-efficient. First differencing is further supported on statistical grounds as exchange

(1) A problem arises, due to data construction, in using price indices with the lira/pound exchange rate, due to non-compatibility. The end-of-period exchange rate series is obtained from the middle closing rates at the last day of trading of the month or quarter. However, the price series are indices obtained from samples taken in the middle of the month or quarter. Therefore, in the construction of the real monthly end-of-period exchange rates approximately a two week lag exists with respect to the price series. In the case of quarterly data used in this study, the value of the price series in the last month of the quarter are used, instead of the period-averaged price series, to obtain series that are more consistent with the exchange rate series.

Diagram 1. Lira/Pound-Sterling Exchange Rates

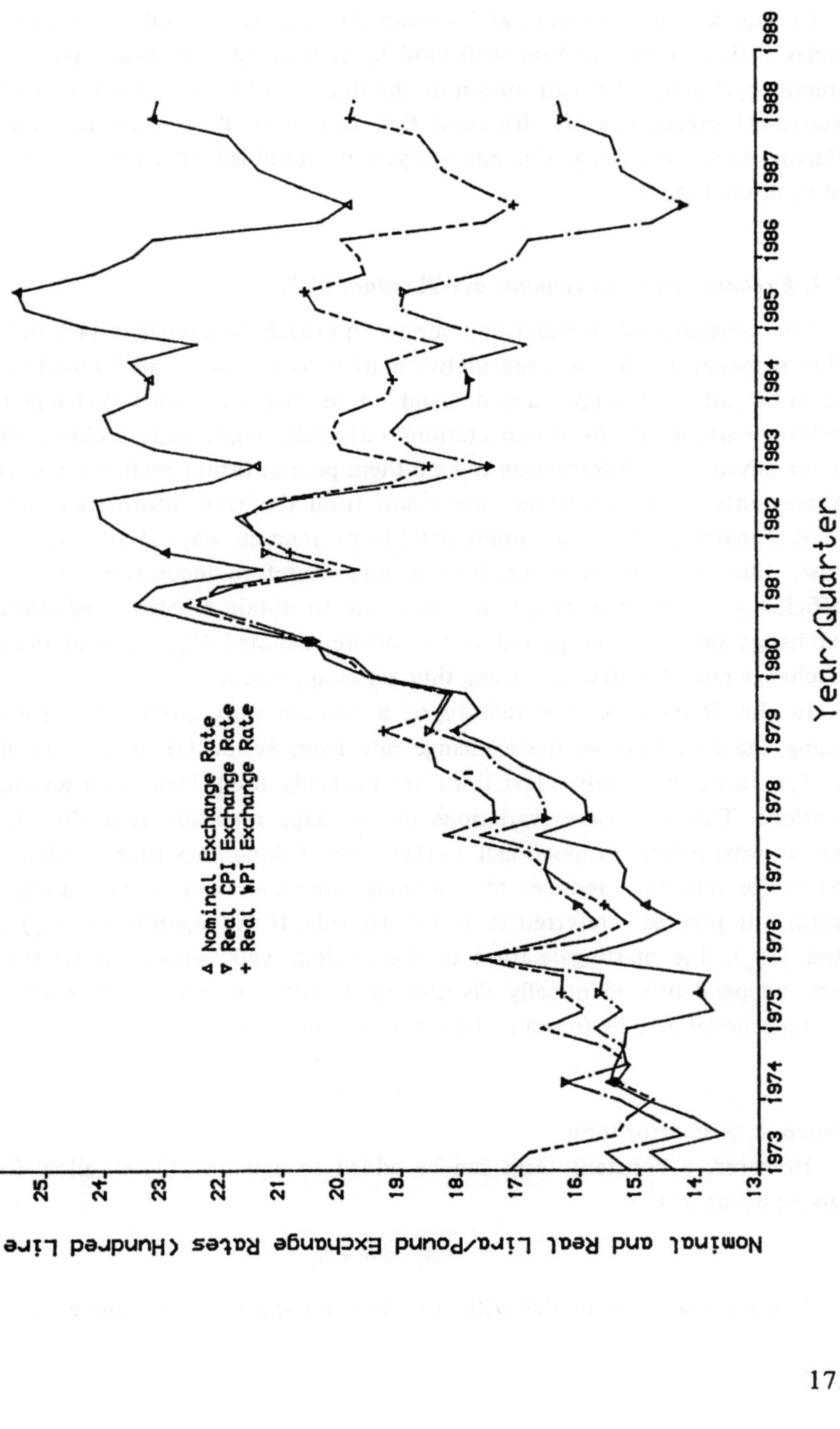

rate series show the characteristics of a random walk. First differencing, as well as removing a linear trend in the undifferenced series, substantially reduces autocorrelation problems that arise when actual values are used.

In this section, the time series characteristics attributable to exchange rate series including the random walk model, stationarity, purchasing power parity, trends, cycles and the distribution of the lira/pound exchange rate are examined. Statistical procedures are discussed that can be used to examine these issues. Furthermore, frequency domain analysis is examined to detect the existence of cycles in the series.

2.1. Exchange Rate Movements as a Random Walk

The conventional demand and supply approach to exchange rate determination is inappropriate for a speculative market, where prices are formed according to anticipation of supply and demand. In an efficient foreign exchange market, market participants form expectations rationally, continually seeking, obtaining and analysing new information to help them predict future exchange rate changes. Movements of the exchange rate result from this new information coming to market participants in an unpredictable or random way. If this were not the case, this information is predictable and therefore inconsistent with market efficiency. In other words, it is impossible to obtain a better prediction of the exchange rate for one period in the future, denoted (S_{t+1}), than the current exchange rate, denoted (S_t), using time series approaches.

In this framework, the validity of a random walk model can be examined using the deviations in the exchange rate from period (t) to ($t-1$), denoted (ΔS_t). However, relative deviations are normally used, instead of absolute deviations. This is because variations in exchange rates are generally viewed to be approximately proportional to their level. Taking logarithmic values of the exchange rate thus reduces the variance compared with actual values. In this form, the process is referred to as a martingale. If the logarithm of (S_t) is denoted (Δs_t), the martingale form of the random walk model implies that (Δs_t) are independently identically distributed. In other words, (Δs_t) is white noise.

This model may be formally described as equation (1).

$$\Delta s_t = v_t \tag{1}$$

where v_t is an error term.

However, a constant term can be added to equation (1) to allow for drift, giving equation (2).

$$\Delta s_t = b + v_t \tag{2}$$

The random walk model with drift is more appropriately applied to nominal exchange rate movements. A negative constant or drift term reflects a fall in the nominal exchange rate over the period, a positive term reflects a rise.

The random walk hypothesis can be tested by measuring statistical dependence of successive changes in exchange rates. That is, testing whether past rates contain useful information for the prediction of future rates, implying that a general pattern repeats itself at regular intervals.

In this study, a number of tests of randomness are applied to the first differenced natural logarithmic values of the nominal lira/pound exchange rate, in end-of-period form. Furthermore, the tests are applied to logarithmic first differences of the real lira/pound exchange rate obtained using consumer and wholesale price indices.

The first test applied is the runs test. This is a simple non-parametric test for randomness on the median, giving a statistic that can be considered to be normally distributed in large samples, if the null hypothesis of randomness applies. This test requires no assumptions about the distribution and provides a simple approach to measuring any departures from the random walk model.

The second test applied to the data is the Ljung-Box test. This is a test based on the first set of serial correlations up to a given lag. If the serial correlations are independently distributed in large samples, the Ljung-Box statistic follows a Chi-squared distribution, with degrees of freedom equal to the length of the lag period. The test is used to examine both high and low order serial correlations and therefore provides an indication of nature of any departures from the random walk model. This test is discussed in Harvey (1981a).

The third test used, the cumulative periodogram, which examines non-randomness in the frequency domain, such as seasonal variation, is discussed in Section 2.4.

2.2. Stationarity and Structural Change

Stationarity is a weaker characteristic of a time series process than randomness. When a series of observations is generated by a stationary process, it fluctuates around a constant level and there is no tendency for the spread to increase or decrease over time. Weak stationarity is a condition where the mean, variance and autocovariance are constant over time. Strict stationarity is a stronger property which implies that the joint probability of a set of observations at one period in time is the same as the joint probability of the observations at another period in time. If a series shows weak stationarity and is distributed normally, then the series is also strictly stationary.

In this analysis, the data is divided into three sub-periods based on the trend patterns of the nominal lira/pound exchange rate. Sub-period 1, which shows no clear trend in the undifferenced values of the nominal exchange rate, extends from 1973 Q1 to 1976 Q3. Sub-period 2, which shows a clear upward trend, extends from 1976 Q4 to 1981 Q2. Sub-period 3, which shows no clear trend, extends from 1981 Q3 to 1988 Q4.

There are a number of factors that could be argued to cause a structural change in the lira/pound exchange rate. For example, it could be argued that Italy joining the EMS not only reduces exchange rate variation between Italy and other member countries, but also has an influence on exchange rates outside the EMS. That is, in such a managed system, a general weakness in the lira, may result in less variation of the lira/pound exchange rate than may otherwise have been the case. On the other hand, the positive impact of North Sea Oil and oil prices on pound-sterling exchange rates, since the end of the 1970's, could be argued to be a factor that caused a structural change in the lira/pound exchange rate, tending to increase the variation in the series.

To consider if the nominal and real exchange rates show stationarity the Mann-Whitney test is applied using the three sub-periods defined above. The Mann-Whitney test is a test of strong stationarity. It is used to test whether the underlying populations from which the two samples are drawn, are distributed differently. The test is applied to three pairs of data sub-periods. A statistic can be obtained that is approximately standard normally distributed for large samples.

However, non-stationarity may result from changes in one of the parameters in the distribution, such as the variance, rather than all the parameters. The Mann-Whitney test can be modified to take into account both changes in the mean by subtracting the sub-period mean from the original values and changes in the standard deviation by dividing the original values by the sub-period standard deviation. The Mann-Whitney test can then be applied to the transformed series.

2.3. *Purchasing Power Parity*

Purchasing Power Parity is founded on the idea that the value of a currency is determined by the amount of goods, services or other assets that a unit of currency can buy in the country of issue. The foreign currency has a value, relative to domestic currency, because the foreign currency reflects a purchasing power, which may be used to acquire these goods, services or assets in the foreign country. The relative PPP theory implies that changes in the purchasing power of one country's currency will be the same as that of another country, in terms of the numeraire currency.

More formally, relative PPP may be defined as expression (3).

$$s^r = s + p - p' = k \tag{3}$$

where

s^r is the logarithm of the real exchange rate at constant prices,
s is the logarithm of the nominal exchange rate,
p is the logarithm of the domestic price index,
p' is the logarithm of the foreign price index and
k is a constant.

In the case where relative PPP holds, the nominal exchange rate will be dependent on relative prices and the real exchange rate will be constant. Movements of the logarithms of real exchange rates, in the absence of non-PPP factors are effectively random. This is set out in expression (4).

$$s^r_t = k + w_t \tag{4}$$

where k is a constant and w_t is an error term.

However, relative PPP is only useful as a description of the long run equilibrium exchange rate, either when short – and medium– term relative price effects have diminished, or when inflationary forces dominate real effects, such as in the case of hyperinflations.

The view that the real exchange rate follows a random walk is compatible with relative PPP. However, the presence of drift in the real exchange rate implies that a long-term trend occurs which invalidates the hypothesis, under PPP, that the real exchange rate returns to its equilibrium level in the long run.

To examine relative PPP and the random walk hypothesis it is necessary to consider whether or not a trend exists in the non-differenced exchange rate series. The process or differencing effectively removes a linear trend from a non-differenced series. A linear trend in the non-differenced series will be reflected by a non-zero measure of location in the first difference values.

In this study two tests for trend are applied, the sign test and the Student t test.

The sign test is a simple non-parametric test that can be used to test the hypothesis that the median is zero against the alternative that it is non-zero. It requires no assumptions about the distribution of exchange rate changes. If a trend exists in the non-differenced series, the first differenced series will give a median significantly different from zero. A statistic can be obtained that can be considered to be approximately standard normally distributed under the null hypothesis of zero median.

The simple Student t test is the parametric equivalent of the sign test and can be used to test the hypothesis that the mean is zero against the alternative that it is not. The resulting statistic can be tested using the Student t tables with degrees of freedom equal to the total number of observations less one.

2.4. Cyclical Characteristics Cumulative Periodogram and Spectral Analysis

The trend is not the only regular time series characteristic of data. Economic data often show evidence of seasonal and business cycle activity, as well as other cycles.

One such characteristic, that can cause short term movements in the nominal and real exchange rate, is seasonal variation. For example, seasonal variation in relative price indices, may cause seasonal patterns to be present in real exchange rates.

Another characteristic that can cause longer term movements in the nominal and real exchange rate is business cycle activity. This type of cycle is commonly found in aggregate economic series. For example, the presence of a business cycle in the nominal exchange rate index, with the absence of a cycle in relative prices, may cause medium-term movements in real exchange rates.

The analysis of cyclical activity is undertaken in the present study by the use of periodogram and spectral analyses. Periodogram and spectral analyses are processes by which the time series profile of a variable can be represented by pure sine waves summed over different frequencies, with different amplitudes and phases at each frequency. The technique involves Fourier transforms of the time series data to coefficients of the sinusoids at discrete frequencies.

The cumulative periodogram is a frequency domain alternative to the Ljung-Box test that detects whether cyclical non-randomness exists in the data. The cumulative periodogram, when plotted against frequency, lies close to the 45 degree line for a white noise process. For a process with an excess of low frequency cyclical behaviour, it will tend to lie above the 45 degree line and with an excess high frequency cyclical behaviour, it will tend to lie below the line. A two sided test can be carried out by rejecting the null hypothesis of randomness in the frequency domain if the maximum absolute value of the difference between the cumulative periodogram and the respective value from the 45 degree line is greater than the critical value. This test is discussed in Harvey (1981a) and critical values for this test are contained in Harvey (1981b).

The sample periodogram is closely related to the sample spectrum. The spectrum is essentially the periodogram divided by 4π. However, to apply spectral analysis, it is usually desirable to preadjust the data to give a zero mean, which is undertaken in the study. Another desirable refinement is the grouping of frequencies. Neighbouring frequencies can be grouped into frequency bands and the quantities from the Fourier transformed data can be estimated in one frequency band. This grouping of frequencies is undertaken to improve the statistical stability of the estimates. The weighting procedure used in this study is set out in Henstridge (1982) and discussed more fully in Koopmans (1974).

In the application of frequency domain techniques, the effect of first differencing of the data needs to be discussed. First differencing, as well as removing a linear trend in a series, causes amplitude reductions for low frequencies and amplitude increases for high frequencies. This reduces the spectral estimates in the low frequency range and increases the spectral estimates in the high frequency range.

In this study, the smoothed spectral estimates are obtained for the first differenced natural logarithmic series to examine cyclical variation. This smoothing process involves the averaging of the periodogram over a range of adjacent frequencies. An equal weighted average is used. Smoothing the spectrum estimates gives more stable estimates with lower variance, but the resolution is lowered as wider frequency bands are used in the averaging process. Smoothing is appropriate for the examination of non-discrete cycles, such as the business cycles. Comparison is made with the theoretical spectrum of a white noise process to examine departures from randomness in the frequency domain. This procedure is discussed in Koopmans (1974) and Harvey (1981a).

2.5. Exchange Rate Movements and Their Distribution

An assumption frequently made about a distribution is that of normality, which forms the basis for parametric tests. There exists strong evidence that the distribution of bilateral exchange rate changes in logarithms, show evidence of non-normality. Tests that make the normality assumption in considering the weak form of market efficiency may not be appropriate. Accordingly, skewness and normality tests are applied to examine whether differences in the lira/pound exchange rate exhibit asymmetry and non-normality.

The skewness test is a test of symmetry of the data. Movements of the exchange rate can show non-symmetry due, for example, to the presence of a strong trend. The skewness statistic used in this study follows approximately a standard normal distribution in large samples when the null hypothesis of symmetry applies [2].

However, symmetry in the data need not imply normality. The Stable Paretian and Student t distribution will also show symmetry. Normality is a stronger assumption about a distribution than symmetry. In this study, the test suggested by Lilliefors (1967) is applied to examine whether the distribution of changes in exchange rate variables is normally distributed. This test is a modification of the Kolmorgov goodness of fit test which can be applied when the population mean and variance are unknown. This test involves comparing the norma-

(2) The skewness statistic (ZSK) is defined as

$$ZSK = [c/n - 1/2]\,[2\sqrt{(n)}]$$

Where c denotes the number of observations below the mean.

lised relative cumulative frequency distribution of the data with the cumulative frequency distribution of the standard normal. The hypothesis of normality is rejected if a Lilliefors test statistic value, in absolute terms, is critical. Critical values for this test are given in Lilliefors (1967).

3. Results

The statistical analyses discussed in the previous section are applied to quarterly movements of the nominal and real lira/pound exchange rates, in natural logarithmic form, using end-of-period data. The results are presented for the whole period and the three sub-periods defined in the previous section.

3.1. Basic Summary Statistics and Stationarity

To undertake a preliminary examination of exchange rate movements, the means and standard deviations of first differences of the logarithms of the series are presented (in Tables 1 and 2 respectively) for the real and nominal exchange rates series. In addition, the Mann-Whitney test is applied to the three combinations possible for the sub-periods. These tests are applied with the data, (i) unadjusted, (ii) adjusted by the mean and (iii) adjusted by the standard deviation. The results are presented in Table 3.

The mean values show substantial variations between the three sub-periods. Sub-periods 1 and 3 give mean values close to zero, while sub-period 2 shows

Table 1. Mean Values

	Whole period $n = 62$	*Sub-period 1* $n_1 = 15$	*Sub-period 2* $n_2 = 19$	*Sub-period 3* $n_3 = 28$
Nominal	0.00366	0.00137	0.01089	0.00003
Real (CPI)	0.00078	0.00214	0.00777	– 0.00468
Real (WPI)	0.00110	– 0.00302	0.00819	– 0.00151

Table 2. Standard Deviations

	Whole period $n = 62$	*Sub-period 1* $n_1 = 15$	*Sub-period 2* $n_2 = 19$	*Sub-period 3* $n_3 = 28$
Nominal	0.02192	0.02784	0.01547	0.02169
Real (CPI)	0.02172	0.02493	0.01432	0.02325
Real (WPI)	0.02091	0.02398	0.01564	0.02179

Table 3. Mann-Whitney Test Results

$n_1 = 15, n_2 = 19$ and $n_3 = 28$

		Sub-periods 1/2	*Sub-periods 1/3*	*Sub-periods 2/3*
Nominal	– unadjust.	1.21	0.01	1.80
	– mean adj.	0.14	0.09	0.16
	– s.d. adj.	1.98	0.06	2.16
Real (CPI)	– unadjust.	0.62	0.73	1.81
	– mean adj.	0.24	0.01	0.34
	– s.d. adj.	1.18	0.73	2.33
Real (WPI)	– unadjust.	1.46	0.27	1.57
	– mean adj.	0.03	0.16	0.27
	– s.d. adj.	1.91	0.32	1.88

Critical Values, two tailed test at 5% = 1.96, at 1% = 2.58.

relatively high positive value reflecting the clear trend in the undifferenced values in this sub-period. The real exchange rate shows a similar pattern in terms of the mean values, although for the period as a whole the mean values are fairly small. These results are roughly consistent with relative PPP in the long run but the high mean values for the first differences in the real exchange rate, for both consumer and wholesale price measures, in sub-period 2 do not support relative PPP in the medium term.

The standard deviations have roughly similar values for real and nominal exchange rate movements for all three sub-periods. However, there appears to be slightly lower variation in sub-period 2. These results do not imply that the variance of the lira/pound exchange rate showed any marked change over the period.

This is reinforced by the Mann-Whitney test results. The data adjusted by the standard deviation show significance for the nominal exchange rate for the sub-period combinations 1/2 and 2/3. The results, however, are insignificant for the sub-period combination 1/3 and for all combinations of the sub-periods with respect to the mean adjusted data. The data also gives significant results for the sub-periods combination 2/3 for the real (CPI) exchange rate. In addition, the unadjusted data gives values relatively close to significance over the sub-periods 1/2 and 2/3, but low values for sub-periods 1/3. The mean adjusted values are clearly insignificant.

The above results imply that any non-stationarity over the whole period is largely caused by a non-stationary mean, rather than a non-stationary variance.

This non-stationarity in the mean appears to be attributed to sub-period 2 when the pound-sterling supported by large balance of payments benefits from North Sea Oil revenues showed considerable strength against most major currencies. However, it is interesting to note that stationarity between sub-periods 1 and 3 is supported by the results. This implies that sub-period 2 may only represent the circumstances arising from North Sea Oil revenues to the UK economy (3). In sub-period 3, this NSO effect is lower, owing partly to lower world oil prices and partly to the increased demand for imports and the decreased demand for exports caused by the high exchange rate itself. The results suggest that the distribution in sub-period 3 is similar to that prior to the structural change caused by North Sea Oil (4).

3.2. Randomness, Time Domain Tests

The results for the two time domain statistical tests for randomness, the runs and Ljung-Box tests, are presented in Tables 4 and 5 respectively. In the case of the Ljung-Box test, owing to space limitations, Table 5 gives only a summary of the results.

Table 4. Runs Test Results

	Whole period $n = 62$	*Sub-period 1* $n_1 = 15$	*Sub-period 2* $n_2 = 19$	*Sub-period 3* $n_3 = 28$
Nominal	– 1.02	0.56	0.00	– 1.54
Real (CPI)	0.00	0.56	1.46	– 1.54
Real (CPI)	– 0.51	0.56	0.97	– 1.54

Critical Values, two tailed test at 5% = ± 1.96, at 1% = ± 2.58.

(3) A number of empirical studies have examined the impact of North Sea Oil on the UK effective exchange rate. The results imply that North Sea Oil increased the real effective exchange rate by 10% or more in the late 1970s and early 1980s. A review of these studies and the impact of oil on the UK economy and the exchange is contained in Atkinson and Hall (1983).

(4) Oil prices will influence both the exchange rate and relative prices. High (low) oil prices will tend to increase (decrease) the lira/pound exchange rate as the actual and expected income from UK oil revenues increase (decrease). On the other hand, high (low) oil prices also cause increases (decreases) in domestic prices in both Italy and the UK. However, as both countries have similar standards of living and development, the effect on relative prices can be assumed to be small.

Table 5. Ljung-Box Test Results

Lag	*Nominal*	*Real (CPI)*	*Real (WPI)*
Whole Period ($n = 62$)			
1	0.01	0.00	0.00
2	2.43	2.88	3.23
4	3.33	5.14	4.19
12	14.48	17.61	14.22
20	16.92	21.60	21.02
Sub-Period 1, ($n_1 = 15$)			
4	2.88	4.36	1.68
Sub-Period 2, ($n_2 = 19$)			
4	3.17	2.86	2.09
Sub-Period 3, ($n_3 = 28$)			
4	4.07	3.73	3.85

Critical Values, Chi-squared

lag	5%	1%	lag	5%	1%	lag	5%	1%
1	3.84	6.64	4	9.49	13.28	20	31.41	37.57
2	5.99	9.21	12	21.03	26.22			

Table 6. Sign Test Results

	Whole period $n = 62$	*Sub-period 1* $n_1 = 15$	*Sub-period 2* $n_2 = 19$	*Sub-period 3* $n_3 = 28$
Nominal	1.65	0.00	2.29	0.57
Real (CPI)	1.40	0.52	1.84	0.00
Real (CPI)	1.40	− 0.52	2.29	0.57

Critical Values, two tailed test at 5% = ± 1.96, at 1% = ± 2.58.

The results for the runs test indicate insignificance in all cases and the Ljung-Box results show insignificance for all lags and for all cases. These results support the view that exchange rate movements are random.

These results are consistent with the hypothesis that the exchange rate follows a random walk or martingale process.

3.3. Trends

The results for the two statistical test for trend; the sign test and Student t

Table 7. Student t Test Results

	Whole period $n = 62$	*Sub-period 1* $n_1 = 15$	*Sub-period 2* $n_2 = 19$	*Sub-period 3* $n_3 = 28$
Nominal	1.65	0.19	3.07	– 0.01
Real (CPI)	0.28	0.33	2.36	– 1.07
Real (CPI)	0.41	– 0.49	2.28	– 0.37
Critical Values				
5%	± 2.00	± 2.15	± 2.10	± 2.05
1%	± 2.66	± 2.98	± 2.88	± 2.77

Table 8. Cumulative Periodogram Test Results

$n = 62$	*Maximum Positive Diff.*	*Maximum Negative Diff.*
Nominal	0.241	– 0.194
Real (CPI)	0.257	– 0.203
Real (WPI)	0.273	– 0.145

Critical Values, at 5% = ± 0.221, at 1% = ± 0.268 .

test, are presented in Tables 6 and 7 respectively.

The results for the sign test show significance for the nominal exchange rate for sub-period 2, but insignificance in all other cases, although the results for the period as a whole are almost significant. The results for the real exchange rates show less significance although, for both consumer and wholesale price measures, significance is indicated for sub-period 2 and for the case of the wholesale price measure.

The Student t test gives similar results although, it must be pointed out that, the validity of this test depends on the assumption that exchange rate movements are approximately normally distributed. The results set out in Sub-section 3.5 show that this assumption is approximately satisfied for the whole period and the sub-periods.

The higher values for the sign and t test for the nominal exchange rates, compared with the real exchange rates, tend to support the view that the trend in the nominal exchange rate partly reflects the trend in relative prices, which is consistent with relative PPP. The upward trend in the nominal exchange rate tends to be concentrated in sub-period 2. In this sub-period the rise in the nominal exchange rate also coincides with a rise in relative prices, both in terms of consumer and wholesale price measures. However, although the nominal exchange rate shows that no clear trend exists in sub-period 3, relative prices increased with the result that, for the period as a whole, the overall trend in relative prices appears similar to the overall trend in the nominal exchange rate. Therefore, for real exchange rates, sign and t test values are close to zero for the whole period. The results suggest that the pound-sterling was overvalued in terms of the lira at the end of sub-period 2, but this overvaluation gradually diminished in sub-period 3 as both the relative Italy/UK consumer and wholesale prices indices increased.

The results are consistent with a drift in the lira/pound nominal exchange rates over the period, although this drift is not constant but concentrated in sub-period 2. However, the real exchange rates do not show an overall drift over the period, but show a drift in sub-period 2 which is, to some extent, reversed in sub-period 3. The results overall are consistent with relative PPP in the long run but variations between the sub-periods imply that relative PPP did not apply in the medium term to the lira/pound exchange rate.

3.4. Cyclical Activity, the Cumulative Periodogram and Spectral Analysis

The cumulative periodogram is estimated for the whole period data. However, it is not estimated for the sub-periods, due to the limited data length that does not allow clear identification of low frequency cycles. Unlike time domain tests, the cumulative periodogram gives results, presented in Table 8, are significant in all cases, with the highest spectral estimates in the low frequency range. This is illustrated by the significant positive values, with less significant negative values. These results suggest that non-randomness exists in the frequency domain with the implication that low frequency cycles may be more important than high frequecy cycles. Although, first differencing tends to reduce the power of low frequency cycles, the remaining effects from, for example, a business cycle in the undifference series, may still be present in the data.

The presence of cyclical activity of a low or high frequency nature violates the assumption of a random walk. To examine this issue further, it is necessary to apply spectral analysis, as well as the cumulative periodogram, such that the frequencies where violation of the assumption of a white noise process occurs can be examined. Furthermore, it is also necessary to consider the implications of the smoothing process as averaging the spectrum estimates is often a more suitable procedure for non-discrete cycles. That is: does smoothing increase or decrease some of this implied non-randomness? This gives an indication as to whether the apparent cycles are «pure» cycles or whether they only result from the chance timing of peaks and troughs in the lira/pound exchange rate series.

Spectral analysis with and without smoothing is applied to first-differenced mean-adjusted real and nominal lira/pound exchange rate series. The mean-

Diagram 2. Spectral Estimates for the Nominal Lira/Pound-Sterling Exchange Rate

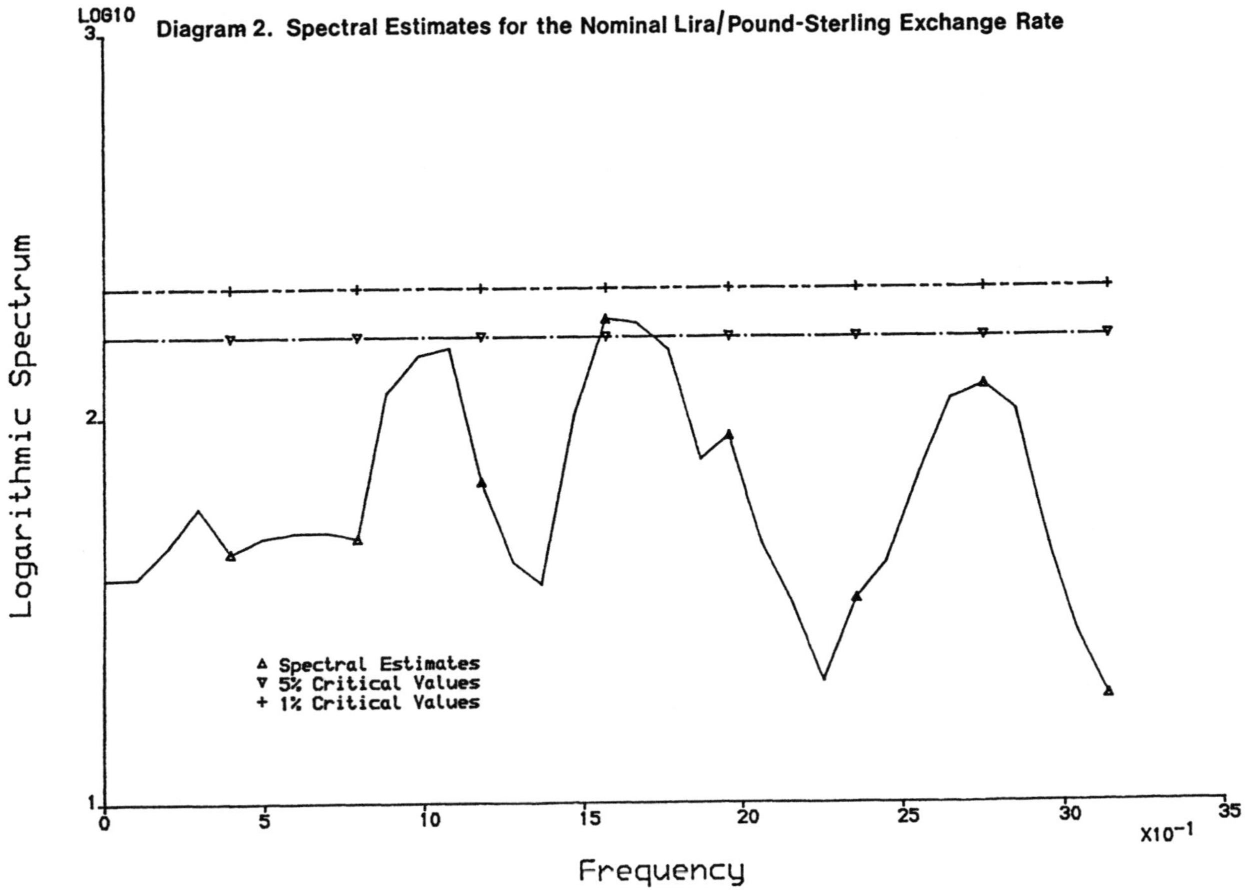

Diagram 3. Spectral Estimates for the Real CPI Lira/Pound-Sterling Exchange Rate

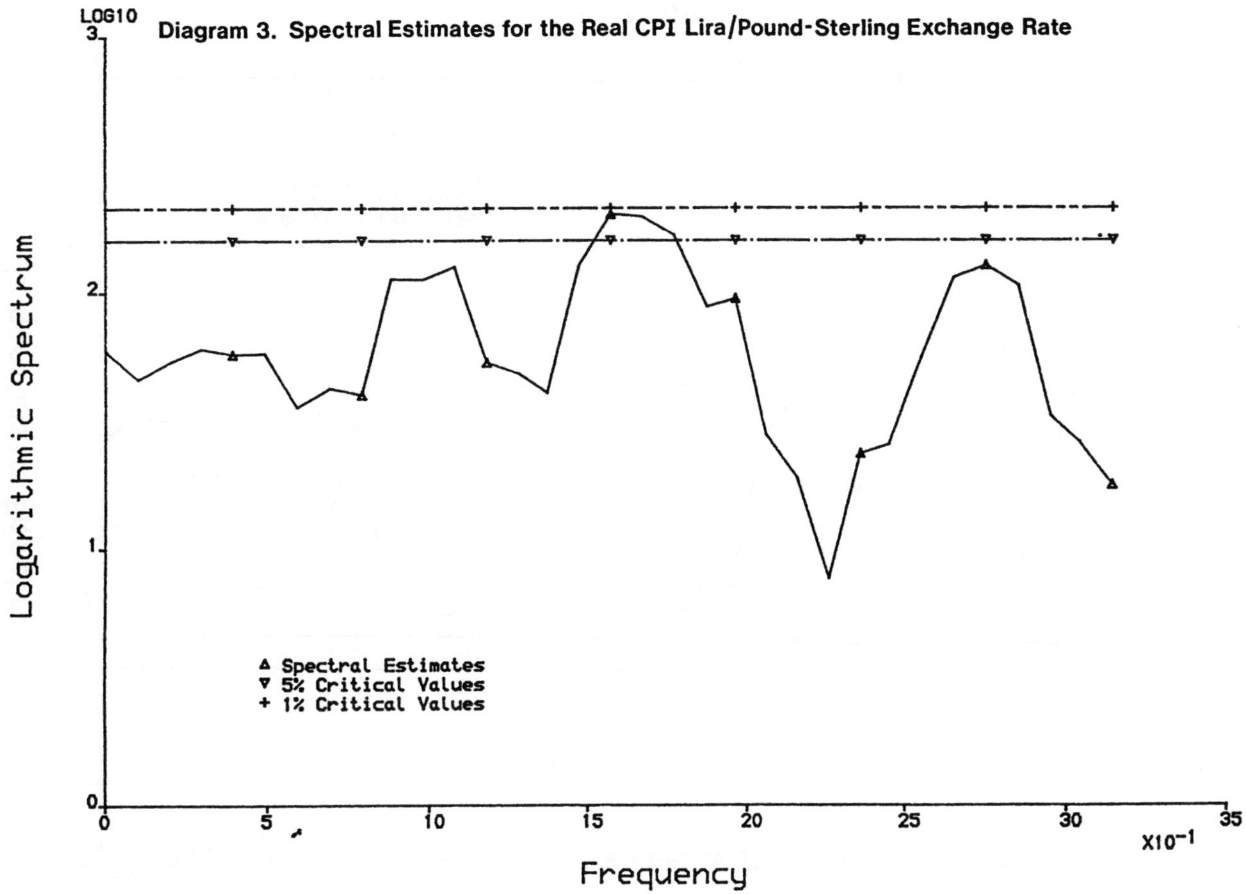

Diagram 4. Spectral Estimates for the Real WPI Lira/Pound-Sterling Exchange Rate

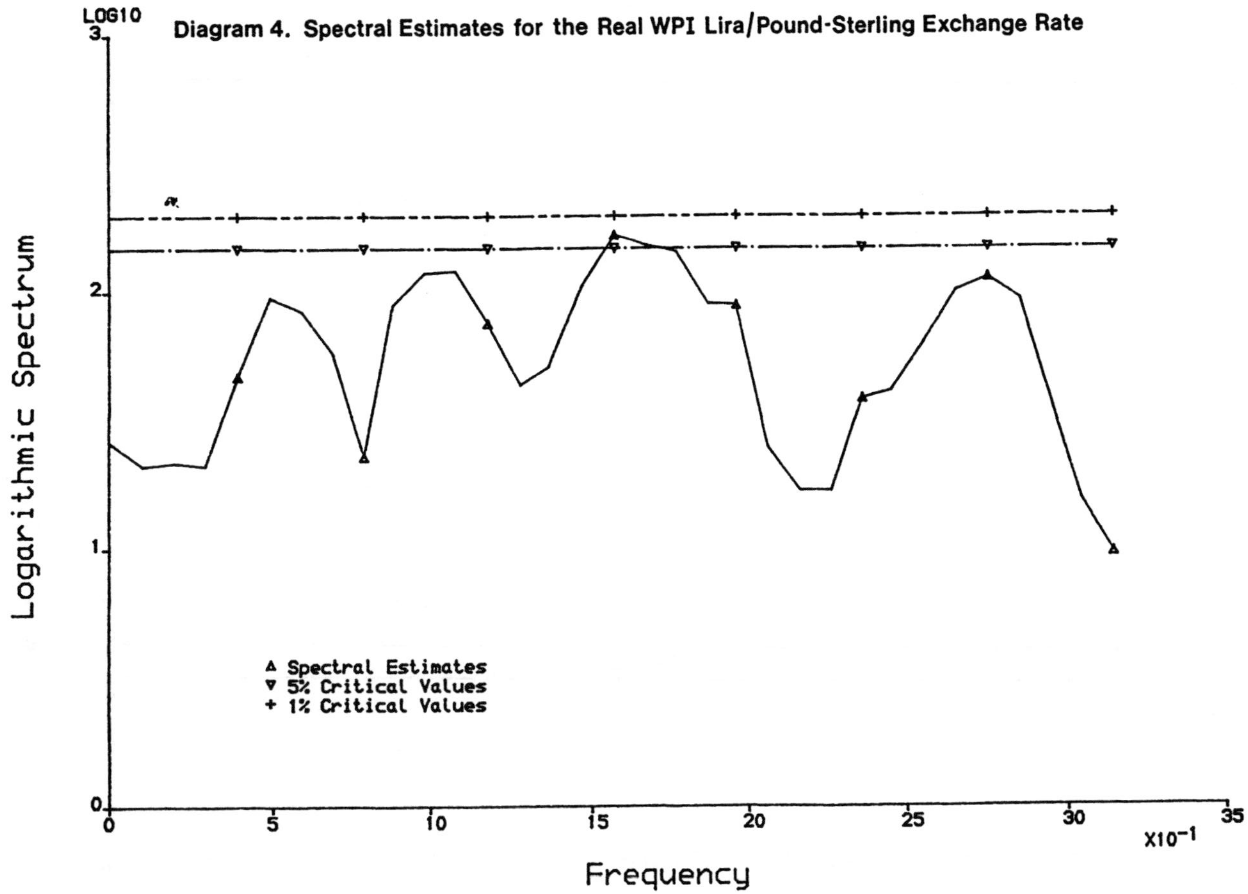

-adjustment takes out the influence of a constant drift. However, the results presented in Diagrams 2, 3 and 4 only relate to the case with smoothing. The unsmoothed spectra are not included partly owing to space limitations and partly because they provide little additional information. Furthermore, to improve the presentation of the graphs, the spectral estimates are presented on a logarithmic scale y-axis.

The spectra show a peak at the seasonal frequency range (1.57 frequency) with the estimated spectra moving outside the 5% white noise bound at the seasonal frequency in all three cases. A smaller peak also occurs at the 1.5 year cycle range (0.98 frequency) but this is insignificant. However, the spectra stays within the 1% bound in all cases and for all frequencies. This could be interpreted as indicating that limited seasonal variation exists in exchange rate series. Seasonal variation in the exchange rate can arise through the influence of balance of payments movements. For example, bilateral trade flows between Italy and the UK show clear seasonal patterns. Seasonal influence may also occur in the flows of invisible items such as travel and tourism. However, the seasonal patterns in exchange rate movements may also reflects the timing of peaks and troughs in the lira/pound exchange rate, rather than true seasonal variation.

Overall, there does not appear to be clear evidence of business cycle activity in the first differenced quarterly data but some seasonal variation may be present. The significant result obtained for the cumulative periodogram tests may partly reflect the timing of peaks and troughs in the lira/pound exchange rate, partly reflect the higher spectral estimates in the low frequency range and partly reflect seasonal patterns. It is reasonable to conclude that the series appears only quasi-random in the frequency domain. The effect of using real exchange rates does not appear to have any clear impact on the spectra compared with nominal exchange rates. This implies that there exists no evidence that cycles in nominal exchange rates are offset by cycles in relative prices when real exchange rates are used.

3.5. Distribution of Exchange Rate Movements

To examine the distribution of logarithmic first differences in the real and nominal exchange rates, the skewness test and the Lilliefors test of normality are applied. The results for these tests are presented in Tables 9 and 10 respectively.

The results for the skewness test suggested that the distribution of real and nominal exchange rate movements were approximately symmetrical both for the whole period and the sub-periods, with insignificant results in all cases. A skewed distribution does not appear to be a feature of lira/pound exchange rate movements.

Table 9. Skew Test Results

	Whole Period $n = 62$	*Sub-period 1* $n_1 = 15$	*Sub-period 2* $n_2 = 19$	*Sub-period 3* $n_3 = 28$
Nominal	− 0.76	0.26	0.23	− 0.76
Real (CPI)	− 1.52	− 0.26	0.23	− 0.76
Real (CPI)	− 1.27	0.26	− 0.69	− 1.13

Critical Values, two tailed test at 5% = ± 1.96, at 1% = ± 2.58.

Table 10. Lilliefors Test Results

	Whole period $n = 62$	*Sub-period 1* $n_1 = 15$	*Sub-period 2* $n_2 = 19$	*Sub-period 3* $n_3 = 28$
Nominal	0.074	0.142	0.116	0.079
Real (CPI)	0.101	0.138	0.082	0.087
Real (CPI)	0.076	0.073	0.108	0.111
Critical Values				
5%	0.113	0.220	0.195	0.167
1%	0.131	0.257	0.235	0.195

A stronger assumption about a distribution than symmetry, is that of normality. The Lilliefors test is used to undertake a formal test of this assumption. The results are insignificant for all periods. The results, therefore, support the view that quarterly movements of the logarithms of nominal and real lira/pound exchange rates are approximately normally distributed. That is, the presence of non-constant variance and ARCH effects do not appear to be a problem when using quarterly data for changes in the lira/pound exchange rate. Nevertheless, this does not imply that this is the case for shorter data sampling periods [5].

(5) The analysis was repeated using monthly data. These results, however, showed that the distribution of monthly exchange rate movements was non-normal, but the non-parametric tests, other than the Lilliefors test lead to conclusions similar to the quarterly data case. This implies that the assumption of normality in case of the lira/pound exchange rate movements is not justified for monthly or more frequent data sampling periods.

4. Conclusions, Interpretations and Implications for Modelling and Forecasting

This paper has applied time series analysis to quarterly movements of real and nominal lira/pound, end-of-period exchange rates, for the period 1973 Q1 to 1988 Q2.

It has been shown that nominal lira/pound exchange rate movements follow what can be regarded as a quasi-random walk with drift over the period as a whole. Furthermore, the real exchange rates, using consumer and wholesale relative prices show a quasi-random walk without drift over the period as a whole. The time domain tests support the assumption of randomness, and the frequency domain results do not clearly show that cyclical behaviour is a feature of exchange rate movements. Nevertheless, there exists some evidence of non-randomness and the existence of seasonal variation which may reflect seasonal patterns on the visible and invisible current accounts of the balance of payments between Italy and the UK. However, the Mann-Whitney test illustrates that there exists evidence of a non-stationary mean, owing to a substantial upward trend in the undifferenced values, which partly reflects the impact of North Sea Oil on the UK economy and the exchange rate. This implies that the lira/pound exchange rate has been subject to medium-term structural change which is inconsistent with a pure random walk process.

The test for trends show evidence of non-zero measures of location in the movement of the nominal lira/pound exchange rates for the whole period. This is attributable to the trend in the undifferenced series. However, the upward movement in the exchange rate is concentrated in the middle of the period, rather than over the whole period. Movements of real exchange rate series do not show a clear non-zero mean over the whole period, but still show a clear positive mean in the middle of the period. These results are consistent with long-term relative PPP, but inconsistent with medium-term PPP.

The distributions of quarterly logarithmic values of the nominal and real exchange rate movements show no evidence of skewness and support the assumption of normality.

These conclusions have considerable implications in the modelling and forecasting of the lira/pound exchange rate in the medium-and long-term.

The first point is that there is no evidence to refute relative PPP in the long-term. It is therefore reasonable, when forecasting exchange rates, to base long term forecasts of the changes in the real lira/pound exchange rate on a zero mean and long-term undifferenced values on the mean over a reasonably long period of time, such as 15 years. It is reasonable to base long-term forecasts of the nominal exchange rate on expected relative price movements.

On the other hand, the results do not support medium-term relative PPP. Structural changes can occur in the medium-term, such that, in modelling and forecasting the exchange rate, these factors need to be taken into account. In the data period under consideration a significant factor is the impact of North Sea Oil on the lira/pound exchange rate. However, mechanisms exists that restore the exchange rate to equilibrium in the long-term. It is shown, in Pollock (1988, 1989) that, if the real exchange rate is influenced by balance of payments flows, and trade flow and asset market mechanisms operate, there will be a movement of the real exchange rate to its equilibrium value in the long-term that restores relative PPP. In modelling and forecasting medium-term lira/pound exchange rate movements it is necessary to take into account balance of payments movements and the factors that affect them in order to detect possible structural shifts in exchange rate movements. In other words, to extend the time series analysis to econometric analysis.

Given the absence of medium-term structural factors and major asymmetries in balance of payments flows, it is reasonable to assume that the real exchange rate will drift towards its long-term mean value and the nominal exchange rate will drift towards its equilibrium value, taking into account relative price movements.

The normality of quarterly logarithmic movements in the lira/pound exchange rate also have implications on modelling and forecasting. The assumption of normality implies that more powerful parametric statistical techniques are justified when using quarterly logarithmic changes in lira/pound exchange rates. This implies that for modelling and forecasting, confidence intervals and statistical tests are reasonably straight forward to apply.

On balance, the results are approximately consistent with the view that end-of-period movements of the lira/pound exchange rate over the period exhibit the characteristics of a quasi-random walk. That is, there is evidence that exchange rate movements follow a pattern that is almost random, although non-stationary drift and seasonal patterns may be present, which are not consistent with the weak form of the efficient market hypothesis. Therefore, there appears scope for modelling and forecasting, especially in the medium- and long-term. A suitable starting point to this is the concept of relative PPP.

APPENDIX

DATA; NOTATION, SOURCES AND DEFINITIONS

The data used in this study essentially comes from two sources. First, the lira/pound exchange rate data comes from the Central Statistical Office (CSO) Macroeconomic Databank. This computer database was made available through th ESRC Data Archive at the University of Essex. Second, the price indicies are obtained from the International Monetary Fund publication «International Financial Statistics».

The notation for the variables is set out in the following sections. Capital letters are used for actual values and small letters are used for logarithms. The source of the data series, either CSO or IFS, is given in brackets.

The data used in the analysis is set out below. For each variable, the notation, data source and definition is given.

Exchange Rate and Price Indices

S or s Lira/Pound Nominal Exchange Rate.
End-of-period monthly, middle closing values, monthly and quarterly, in London. (CSO).

P or p U.K. Price Indices.
Obtained using Consumer and Wholesale Prices Indices, (1980 = 100). (IFS).

P' or p' Italy Price Indices.
Obtained using Consumer and Wholesale Prices Indices, (1980 = 100). (IFS).

S^r or s^r Lira/Pound Real Exchange Rate Index, (1980 = 100).

$$S^r = \frac{SP}{P'} \quad \text{or} \quad s^r = s + p - p'$$

Acknowledgements

I would like to thank Dr. G. Riddington and Mr. M. A. Speller of Glasgow College for their constructive comments.

REFERENCES

F. ATKINSON, S. HALL (1983). *Oil and the British Economy.* Croom-Helm, London.

T. BOLLERSLEV (1987). A Conditional Variance Heteroscedastic Time Series Model for Speculative Prices and Rates of Return. *Review of Economics and Statistics,* 69:542-547.

P. BOOTHE, D. GLASSMAN (1987a). Comparing Exchange Rate Forecasting Models, Accuracy versus Profitability. *International Journal of Forecasting,* 3:65-79.

P. BOOTHE, D. GLASSMAN (1987b). The Statistical Distribution of Exchange Rates. *Journal of International Economics,* 22:297-319.

J. BURT, F.R. KAEN, G.G. BOOTH (1977). Foreign Exchange Market Efficiency Under Flexible Exchange Rates. *Journal of Finance,* 32:1325-1330.

J.R. CALDERON-ROSSEL, M. BEN-HORRIM (1982). The Behaviour of Foreign Exchange Rates. *Journal of International Business Studies,* 99-111, Autumn.

R.E. CRUMBY, M. OBSTFELD (1984). International Interest Rate and Price Level Linkages under Flexible Exchange Rates: A Review of Recent Evidence. In Bilson J.F.O. and Marston R.C., (ed). *Exchange Rate Theory and Practice.* Chicago Press, Chicago.

N. DAVUTYAN, J. PIPPENGER (1985). Purchasing Power Parity Did Not Collapse During the 1970s'. *American Economic Review*, 75:1151-1158.

B.C. DANIEL (1986). Empirical Determinants of Purchasing Power Parity Deviations. *Journal of International Economics*, 21:313-326.

H.J. EDISON (1987). Purchasing Power Parity in the Long Run: A Test of the Dollar/Pound Exchange Rate (1890-1978). *Journal of Money Credit and Banking*, 19:376-387.

R.F. ENGLE (1982). Autoregressive Conditional Heteroscedasticity with Estimates of the Variance of United Kingdom Inflation. *Eonometrica*, 50:987-1007.

J.A. FRENKEL (1981). The Collapse of Purchasing Power Parities in the 1970's. *European Economic Review*, 16:145-165. Also Comments on this article by Vaubel R., and Branson W.H., in this issue.

I.H. GIDDY, G. DUFEY (1975). The Random Behaviour of Flexible Exchange Rates: Implications for Forecasting. *Journal of International Business Studies*, 6:1-32.

C.S. HAKKIO (1981). Expectations and the Forward Exchange Rate. *International Economic Review*, 22:663-678.

A.C. HARVEY (1981a). *Time Series Models*. Philip Allan, Oxford.

A.C. HARVEY (1981b). *The Econometric Analysis of Time Series* Philip Allan, Oxford.

J.D. HENSTRIDGE (1982). *TSA, An Interactive Package for Time Series*. Numerical Algorithms Group, Oxford.

G. JUNGE (1985). Trends and Random Walks of Real Exchange Rates. *Weltwirtschaftliches Archiv*, 121:427-437.

L.H. KOOPMANS (1984). *The Spectral Analysis of Time Series*. Academic Press, New York.

H.W. LILLIEFORS (1967). On the Kolmorgorov-Smirnov Test for Normality with Mean and Variance Unknown. *Journal of the American Statistical Association*, 62:399-402.

D.E. LOGUE, R.J. SWEENEY (1977). White Noise in Imperfect Markets: The Case of the Franc-Dollar Exchange Rate. *Journal of Finance*, 32:761-768.

M. METGHELCHI, E.I. IM (1986). Purchasing Power Parity: A Spectral Analysis. *Revista Internationale di Scienze Economiche e Commerciale*, 33:1041-1047.

A. MILHIJ (1987). A Conditional Variance Model for Daily Deviations of an Exchange Rate. *Journal of Business and Economic Studies*, 5:99-103.

S. MILLER (1984). Purchasing Power Parity and Relative Price Variability, Evidence from the 1970s'. *European Economic Review*, 26:353-367.

L.H. OFFICER (1982). *Purchasing Power Parity and Exchange Rates/ Theory, Evidence and Relevance*. Contemporary Studies in Economic and Financial Analysis, Volume 35. J.A.I., London.

A.C. POLLOCK (1988). Modelling the U.K. Real Effective Exchange Rate Index: A Purchasing Power Parity Framework. Ph. D. Thesis. Paisley College of Technology, Paisley.

A.C. POLLOCK (1989). A Model of UK Real Effective Exchange Rate Behaviour. *Applied Economics*, 21: 1563-1587.

S. POZO (1984). Composition and Variability of the SDR. *Review of Economics and Statistics*, 66: 308-314.

P.D. PRAETZ (1979). Testing for a Flat Spectrum on Efficient Markets Price Data. *Journal of Finance*, 34:645-658.

M. RUSH, S. HUSTED (1985). Purchasing Power Parity in the Long Run. *Canadian Journal of Economics*, 23:137-145.

J.M. WESTERFIELD (1977). An Examination of Foreign Exchange Risk Under Fixed and Flexible Exchange Rate Regimes. *Journal of International Economics*, 7:181-200.

EXPLORING EFFICIENT SETS AND EQUILIBRIA ON RISKY ASSETS WITH ABAPO DSS PROTOTYPE VERSION 2.1. (*)

FRANCESCO A. ROSSI
Istituto di Matematica
Facoltà di Economia e Commercio
Università di Verona
Via dell'Artigliere, 8
37129 Verona - Italy

ABAPO 2.1 (Assets/Business(es) Analyser and Portfolio Optimizer) is a DSS prototype for portfolio managers. It assists the decision maker in two important stages of his task. First, it provides an integrated synthesis of the returns scenario in order to support the decision maker in the selection of the assets to retain, in accordance with his strategy. Second, on the retained assets it computes and shows the E-σ efficient solutions. For each efficient portfolio ABAPO supplies immediately a lot of information that should help the decision maker to single out the portfolio which fits his goals best.

ABAPO works on an integration of elements derived from the Portfolio Selection Theory, the Capital Asset Pricing Model, the Utility Theory. ABAPO uses the principal component, the univariate, the bivariate regression and the correlation analysis, a parametric quadratic programming model and an algorithm based on the critical line method.

ABAPO is implemented in C language under AIX operating system and runs on a IBM RT PC 6150. It is a ductile, interactive procedure that involves graphics in order to increase the efficiency and the effectiveness of the "what if" simulations.

This version 2.1 improves upon the previous one by the evaluation of the Security Market Line, some statistics on the returns of the efficient portfolios, the evaluation of the quadratic indifference curves associated to the efficient portfolios.

(PORTFOLIO SELECTION, CAPITAL ASSET PRICING MODEL, UTILITY THEORY, STRATEGIC PLANNING, DECISION SUPPORT SYSTEMS).

(*) Research supported by the Italian National Research Council (CNR), grant n. 88.03065.10. ABAPO DSS 2.1 prototype has been developed with the support of the CNR (grant n. 87.1210.10), of the Banca Popolare di Verona, of the Cassa di Risparmio di Verona Vicenza e Belluno, of the Società Cattolica di Assicurazione, at the Istituto di Matematica, Università di Verona.

1. Introduction

The strategic portfolio planning problem involves two interdependent decisions [8].

First, the decision maker must decide which assets/business(es) should be retained and which should be removed (divested). In this task, statistics are useful to supply the scenario of the returns.

Second, for those assets/business(es) retained in or added to the portfolio, the management must decide the amount to invest in each alternative, subject to constraints (upper and lower bounds).

As well known, under the E-σ framework the primary strategic objective of management in making these two interdependent decisions in maximizing the expected return, for a given risk (standard deviation), or viceversa [8].

At the moment, there are a lot of statistical softwares (i.g. SPSS [16]) available for the first step, while softwares for the evaluation of the E-σ efficient portfolios are not widespread. Furthermore, those available compute the efficient combinations for a given E (or σ) or for fixed increments of E or for the corner portfolios [4, 7, 9, 10, 18]. Generally speaking, both these types of softwares are batch programs.

An integrated and interactive Decision Support System [11, 12] is improved, based on the Portfolio Selection Theory (PST) [2, 5, 6, 14, 17] and on the Capital Asset Pricing Model (CAPM) [2, 15, 17], with the addition of the following elements: Security Market Line (SML)) [15], linear regressions and correlations between efficient portfolio returns and the underlying factor returns [15] and quadratic indifference curves [13, 15] as well.

For the first stage, ABAPO provides an integrated synthesis of the returns scenario using principal component analysis [3], univariate analysis, bivariate regression and correlation analysis with underlying factors, SML, balance sheet ratios. This information should improve the analysis on the assets and help the manager to select the alternatives to be retained in the portfolio, in accordance with his strategy and constraints.

For the second stage, on the assets/business(es) retained in the portfolio, the manager can change the average (expected) returns, set upper and lower bounds on the amount to be invested in the single alternative in order to respect his preferences and legal, institutional and operational constraints. Afterwards, ABAPO computes, using a parametric quadratic programming model and an algorithm based on the critical line method [6, 7, 11], and shows on the screen the efficient set E-σ. The manager, scanning the efficient frontier with the mouse, can easily and immediately have a lot of useful information for each efficient point (portfolio).

The analysis of these data, particularly the risky efficient portfolio returns with the linear [15] and quadratic [13] associated riskless returns, may help the manager to choose the most suitable to his goals portfolio out of the infinite efficient ones. ABAPO increases the efficiency and the effectiveness of the "what if" simulations in the described stages of the controlling (ex-post) or planning (ex-ante) process.

2. METHODS

2.1. Inputs

ABAPO needs ex-post or ex-ante data provided by the user:

– n rates of return (weekly or monthly or ...) for k alternatives ($k \leqslant 125$);

– n rates of return (weekly or monthly or ...) for h underlying factors (market indexes (Dow Jones, ...) or macroeconomic variables (GNP, inflation, ...)) to which the decision maker refers in his analysis ($h \leqslant 8$);

– up to 13 ratios for each alternative (balance sheet ratios or others indexes traditionally used by the analysts: price/earning, price/book value, yield, ROI, ROE, ROS, acid test, etc.).

2.2. Selection of the alternatives

In order to help the manager to decide which assets/business(es) should be kept in the portfolio, ABAPO works "secretly" and supplies a set of information on the scenario of the returns. In particular it provides:

– the r orthogonal subsets of alternatives, $r \leqslant \min(k, n)$. The subset are the principal components extracted from the returns correlation matrix [3]. In other words, each subset of alternatives with high linear correlation on the returns is collected under the same component:

and for each alternative:

– descriptive analysis (minimum, maximum, average (expected) return, standard deviation, coefficient of variation);
– bivariate linear regression and correlation analysis between the alternative returns and the underlying factors returns according to CAPM [14, 15] (a and b, OLS estimates of alpha and beta-sistematic risk), adjusted R-square and its test of significance, std error of the estimate);

showing them on a partitioned screen. The manager analyses the alternative (rows) in the components (columns) using the cursor, Fig. 2.

Pressing different keys, ABAPO integrates this information with a window on the balance sheet ratios or the plot of the SML (used in order to find out an over (under) – or under (over) – estimation of the market price (beta) of the alternative in relation to each of the underlying factors) [15].

Given his strategy and his constraints, the manager analyses the structured information and selects the alternatives pressing a key.

After that, he has to face the problem of deciding the amount to invest in each alternative.

2.3. Identification of the portfolio which fits best the manager's goals

At this stage the manager can:

– change the expected rates of return, if he thinks to have better estimates of the future performance of the alternatives;

– set upper and lower bounds on the funds to be invested in each alternative (default: 0 and 100% respectively) in order to comply with his legal, operational (internal and/or external) constraints and his preferences.

At this point ABAPO has all the parameters, except l_R the risk propensity of the manager, to inform the model

$$\min z = V_p - l_R R_p$$

$$\begin{aligned} \text{s.t.} \quad & \Sigma_i x_i - 1 = 0 && i = 1, \ldots, n \\ & l_i \leqslant x_i \leqslant u_i && i = 1, \ldots, n \\ & 0 \leqslant l_i, u_i \leqslant 1 && i = 1, \ldots, n \\ & x_i \geqslant 0 && i = 1, \ldots, n \end{aligned}$$

where

$V_p = \Sigma_i \Sigma_j x_i x_j \sigma_{ij}$, variance of the portfolio,
$j = 1, \ldots, n$. σ_p standard deviation of the portfolio
σ_{ij}, covariance between returns of alternative i and j
$R_p = \Sigma_i x_i R_i$ average (expected) return of the portfolio
R_i , average (expected) return of the alternative i
x_i , amount to be invested in asset/business i
l_i , lower bound on x_i
u_i , upper bound on x_i

An automatic procedure for solving this quadratic programming model for all the possible values of $l_R \geqslant 0$ is implemented in ABAPO [11]. The DSS "secretely" works out and records the l_Rs and the parameters of the parabola associated to each of the corner portfolios.

Then, in a window ABAPO plots the efficient set (frontier), with the corner portfolios in evidence, and it is ready for the interactivity with the user [12].

The user can visit an efficient portfolio by:

– scanning with the mouse the whole efficient frontier or only the corner portfolios (PST);

– digiting an average (expected) portfolio return or a standard deviation (PST);

– digiting a risk free rate of return R_f (CAPM).

ABAPO marks the visited portfolio on the graph of the efficient frontier and shows immediately in another window (on the left side of the graph):

– portfolio composition (solution vector);

– average (expected) return;

– standard deviation;

– coefficient of variation;

– derivative $d\sigma/dE$;

– risk premium;

– two risk-free rates of return, associated to the linear (R_f) and the quadratic (R_{fq}) functions tangent at the risky efficient portfolio visited [13];

– linear regression and correlation statistics of the portfolio returns with the underlying factors returns.

The user can build a number of different scenarios (feedbacking to the first stage, point 2.2., or modifying the expected returns and/or the upper and/or lower bounds) and analyse them. He can explore the consequences of alternative sets of assumptions, "what if" simulations, until a satisfactory compromise situation is reached, and he can identificate the one which corresponds most to his goals out of the infinite efficient portfolios.

A flow chart of ABAPO DSS PROTOTYPE 2.1. is shown in Fig. 1.

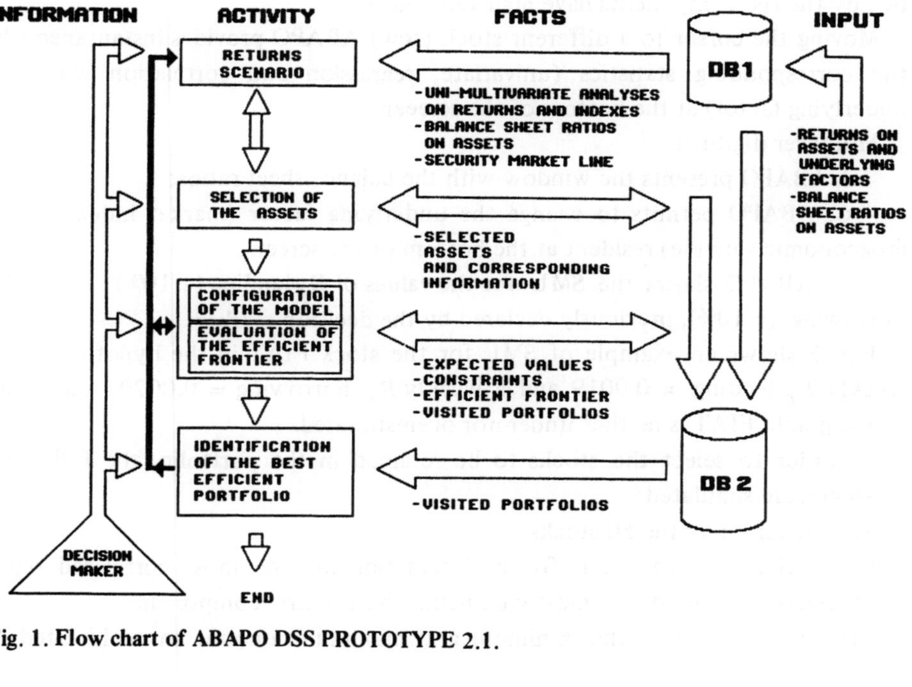

Fig. 1. Flow chart of ABAPO DSS PROTOTYPE 2.1.

3. SIMULATIONS

In this section are presented the results of some simulations obtained using ABAPO DSS 2.1. on Databank SpA data for the period 15/9/1988 - 3/11/1988 [1]:

– 8 weekly rates of return for 50 italian stocks quoted in Milan;

– 8 weekly rates of return for 4 stock/bond market indexes (COMIT, MIB, COFINDI convertible bonds, SFFI);

– 3 balance sheet ratios for each stock (price/earning, price/book value, dividend yield).

The simulations presented have only the aim to show the operativity of the DSS.

3.1. Selection of the alternatives

The synthesis of the returns scenario is graphed in Fig. 2. It can be implemented switching to another stock market index and/or calling the window with the SML in Fig. 3, pressing a key.

Analysing Fig. 2 one can observe that the returns of the 50 stocks are condensed in only 5 orthogonal components extracted in decreasing order of explained variance (total explained 90.76%).

The stocks mostly explained by the first and the second component are typical "market makers" (hight R-square with the market indexes), whereas those described by the last components have high variability.

Moving the cursor to a different stock (row) ABAPO provides instantaneously the corresponding statistics (univariate, regression and correlation with the underlying factor) at the bottom of the screeen.

Moreover digiting:

– *I*, ABAPO presents the window with the balance sheet ratios;

– *C*, ABAPO permits to change the underlying factor (market index or macroeconomic variable) resident at the bottom of the screen;

– *A*, ABAPO shows the SML for the values of R_f lending (± 10%) and R_f borrowing (± 10%), previously declared by the decision marker.

Fig. 3 shows an example of SML for the stock FIAT in the hypothesis of a weekly R_f lending = 0.0019 and a weekly R_f borrowing = 0.0029. According to the graph, FIAT is neither under-nor overestimated.

In order to select the stocks to be retained in the portfolio, the following strategies are simulated:

a) selection of all the 50 stocks;

b) selection of one stock for each component (the most correlated one);

c) selection of the stocks mostly explained by the first component;

d) as in c), but with the minimum and maximum amount to be invested in

BALANCE SHEET RATIOS:
ALTERNATIVE : FIAT
- P/E : 8.6
- P/BOOK VALUE : 1.7
- YIELD : 2.7

Benetton	+0.94				
Latina	+0.89				
Indśfin	+0.86				
Italcable	+0.84				
Cofide	+0.83				
Olivetti	+0.83				
Cir	+0.80				
Eridania	+0.78	-0.53			
Gemina	+0.74				
Marelli	+0.73	-0.62			
Ifil	+0.70	-0.56			
FerruAF	+0.69			+0.48	-0.43
Mondado	+0.69		+0.53		
Monted	+0.69	-0.51		+0.49	
Alitalia	+0.65		+0.48		+0.50
Fiat	+0.62	-0.47			
PirSpA	+0.43	-0.88			
Fidis		-0.87		+0.40	
Italmob		-0.84			
Stet		-0.80			
Alleanza	+0.48	-0.79			
Assital		-0.79		-0.45	
Mediob		-0.78			
Toro		-0.77			
Generali		-0.74		+0.49	
Ras	+0.46	-0.72		-0.41	
Aerital	+0.41	-0.58			-0.56
Fondiar		-0.58			+0.58
Ifilpriv	+0.49	-0.55			
Credit			+0.95		
BLariano			+0.92		
Comit			+0.88		
BcoRoma			+0.88		
BancTosc			+0.87		
Autostr			+0.81		
Burgo			-0.69	+0.47	
PirC	-0.40	-0.43	-0.67		
Rinasc			+0.67	-0.63	
Saipem			+0.67		+0.40
Sme	+0.56		+0.62		
BNA				+0.98	
NBA				-0.95	
FerFin	+0.40			+0.67	-0.46
Italcem	+0.61			+0.64	
SniaBPD		-0.46	+0.52	-0.62	
Espresso				+0.56	-0.40
Sip					+0.88
Sirti					-0.80
Italgas	+0.51				+0.71
Sai		-0.43		+0.47	-0.58

Stock: FIAT
Min:-0.0143 Max:+0.0614 A/E: +0.0158 σ: 0.0223 c.v.: 1.4114

Underlying factor: COMIT A/E: +0.0169 σ: 0.0164 c.v.: 0.9704
FIAT=(a:-0.0071) + (b:+1.0590) * COMIT; R^2: 0.69 std e: 0.0133**

Fig. 2. Example of returns scenario when the user is interested in the stock FIAT (cursor on row FIAT).

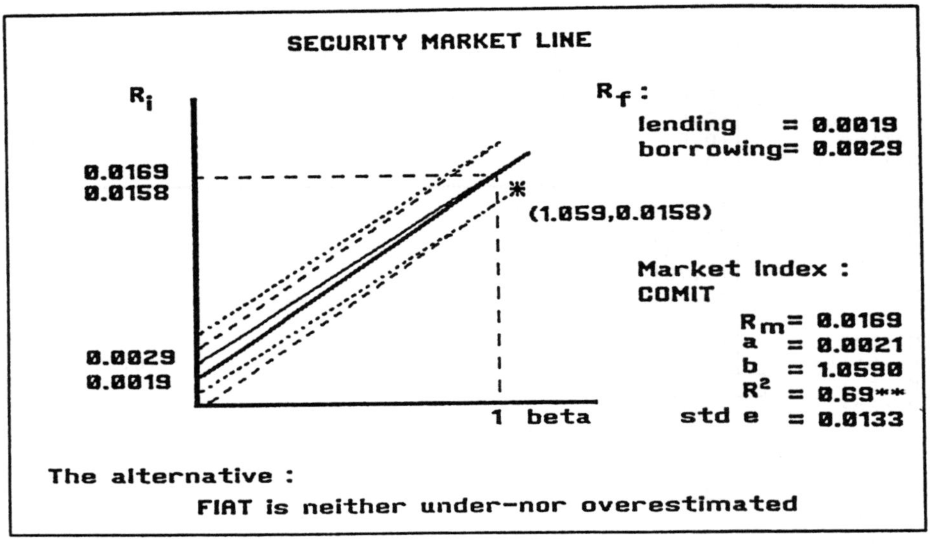

Fig. 3. Example of Security Market Line for FIAT.

the alternatives constrained to 5% and 10% respectively (10% and 20% for the FIAT).

3.2. Identification of the portfolio which fits best the manager's goals

For the four strategies in 3.1 ABAPO has calculated the efficient frontiers and here it is proposed to visit the portfolios corresponding respectively to:

a) a weekly $R_f = 0.0019$ (bounds 0, 100%);

b) a weekly average rate of return of 0.033 (bounds 0, 100%);

c) a weekly standard deviation of 0.0265 (c1) and 0.0252 (c2) (bounds 0, 100%);

d) the corner portfolio (of two) with the lowest standard deviation.

In case a), as shown in Fig. 4, ABAPO:

– presents, on the right of the screen, the graph of the efficient frontier;

– marks the efficient portfolio corresponding to a weekly lending $R_f = 0.0019$ on the market at that time;

– draws the linear and the quadratic indifference functions tangent at this efficient portfolio.

In this case, the efficient frontier contains 14 corner portfolios, points on the dotted frontier, and returns and standard deviations range from 0.0147 to 0.043 and from 0.0014 to 0.0743 respectively.

Then, immediately ABAPO opens a window, on the left of the graph, with

Average return	0.0156
Standard deviation	0.0014
Coefficient of var.	0.0896
Derivative	0.1020
Risk premium	9.8078
R_f	0.0019
R_{fq}	0.0144

Underlying factors	R^2	a	b
COMIT	0.00	0.0100	0.3356
MIB	0.00	0.0104	0.3033
COFINDI	0.00	0.0123	0.4426
IFMI	0.00	0.0102	0.8822

Portfolio composition	%
NBA	34.5828
BNA	21.3649
Burgo	18.3907
BancTosc	9.2408
SIP	8.5308
Sirti	4.8703
Benetton	3.0197

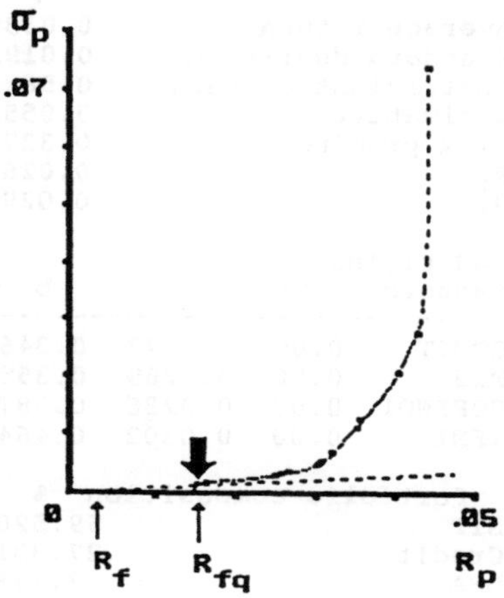

Fig. 4. Strategy a): efficient portfolio corresponding to a weekly R_f = 0.0019.

the information in Fig. 4. Note:

– one hand the high risk premium and on the other the low coefficient of variation;

– the portfolio returns are not linearly correlated with those of the market indexes (underlying factors);

– the quadratic indifference function tangent at this efficient risky-portfolio has R_{fq} = 0.0144;

– the stocks contained in this portfolio represent 4 of the 5 components (columns in Fig. 2).

The comments on the results of the other cases are let to the reader (Fig. 5 to Fig. 8 in Appendix).

4. FINAL CONSIDERATIONS

ABAPO is very ductile and effective in the interactivity with the user. On the 50 alternatives and with default lower and upper bounds, it takes about 35 seconds to prepare the returns scenario and about 20 seconds to compute the efficient frontier on a IBM RT PC 6150/125 computer.

The DSS is certainly a useful simulation instrument and it could also be used to increase the efficiency and the effectiveness of the decision process of portfolio managers.

Average return	0.0330
Standard deviation	0.0192
Coefficient of var.	0.5828
Derivative	3.0556
Risk premium	0.3273
R_f	0.0267
R_{fq}	0.0299

Underlying factors	R^2	a	b
COMIT	0.00	0.0272	0.3463
MIB	0.00	0.0269	0.3557
COFINDI	0.00	0.0286	0.5872
IFMI	0.00	0.0302	0.4648

Portfolio composition	%
SIP	69.5204
Credit	27.3311
BNA	3.1485

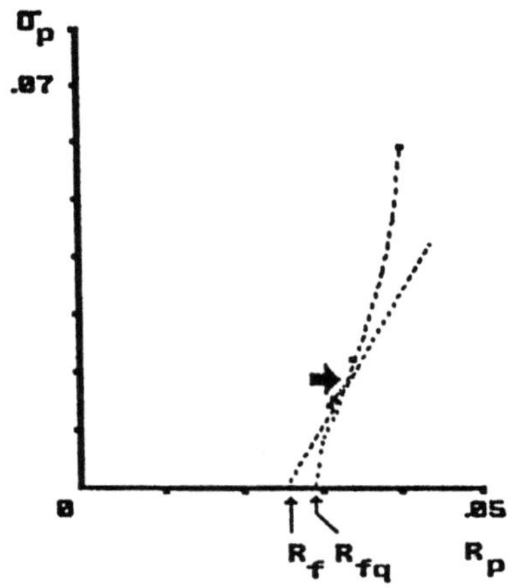

Fig. 5. Strategy b): efficient portfolio corresponding to a weekly average rate of return of 0.033.

Average return	0.0335
Standard deviation	0.0265
Coefficient of var.	0.7904
Derivative	5.5622
Risk premium	0.1798
R_f	0.0288
R_{fq}	0.0312

Underlying factors	R^2	a	b
COMIT	0.46	0.0169	0.9841
MIB	0.48	0.0170	0.9567
COFINDI	0.62	0.0178	2.0911
IFMI	0.37	0.0197	2.2346

Portfolio composition	%
Gemina	88.8937
FerruAF	6.0441
Italcabl	5.0622

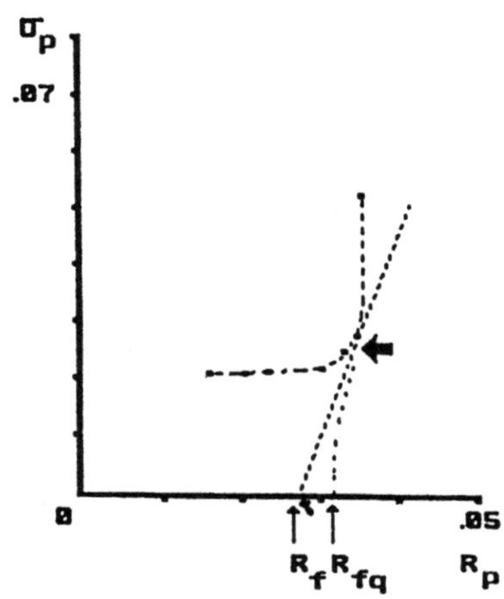

Fig. 6. Strategy c1): efficient portfolio corresponding to a weekly standard deviation of 0.0265.

Average return	0.0328
Standard deviation	0.0252
Coefficient of var.	0.7674
Derivative	0.7252
Risk premium	1.3790
R_f	-0.0019
R_{fq}	0.0200

Underlying factors	R²	a	b
COMIT	0.43	0.0171	0.9324
MIB	0.45	0.0172	0.9055
COFINDI	0.60	0.0179	1.9837
IFMI	0.35	0.0195	2.1569

Portfolio composition	%
Gemina	85.5360
FerruAF	11.5683
Italcabl	2.8957

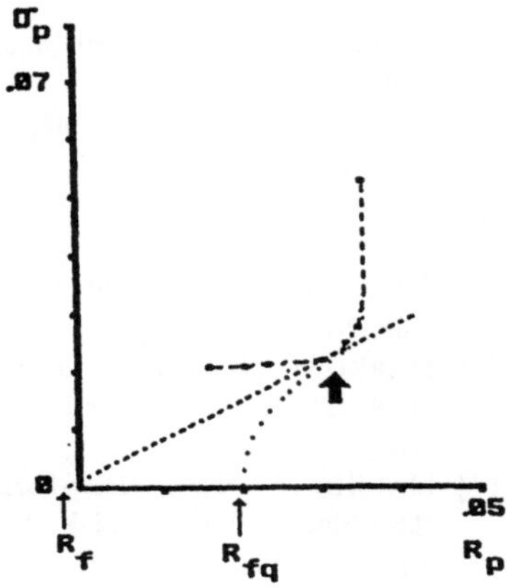

Fig. 7. Strategy c2): efficient portfolio corresponding to a weekly standard deviation of 0.0252.

Average return	0.0188
Standard deviation	0.0292
Coefficient of var.	1.5521
Derivative	1.4523
Risk premium	0.6886
R_f	-0.0013
R_{fq}	0.0097

Underlying factors	R²	a	b
COMIT	0.96	-0.0056	1.4478
MIB	0.96	-0.0050	1.3786
COFINDI	0.97	-0.0020	2.7652
IFMI	0.95	-0.0021	3.3986

Portfolio composition	%
Fiat	20.0000
Gemina	10.0000
Benetton	5.0000
Olivetti	5.0000
Marelli	5.0000
Cir	5.0000
Mondado	5.0000
Cofide	5.0000
Eridania	5.0000
FerruAF	5.0000
Ifil	5.0000
Italcabl	5.0000
Monted	5.0000
Indsfin	5.0000
Alitalia	5.0000
Latina	5.0000

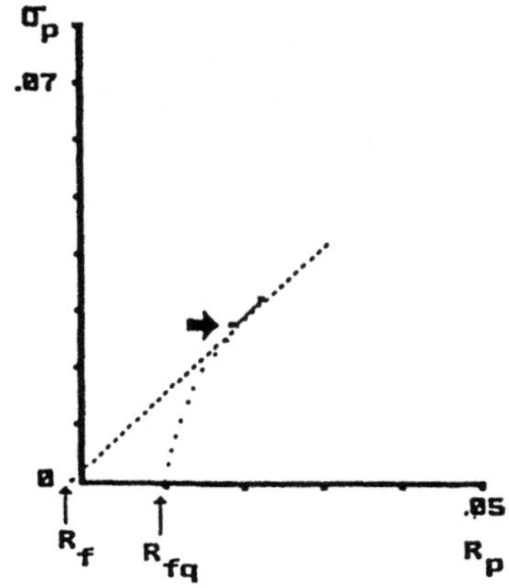

Fig. 8. Strategy d): information available on the corner portfolio with the lowest standard deviation.

REFERENCES

[1] CANDIA B., *Risk-Return Analysis* 15/9/1988 - 3/11/1988, Databank SpA, Milano, 1988.

[2] ELTON E., GRUBER M., *Modern Portfolio Theory and Investment Analysis*, J. Wiley, N.Y., 1984.

[3] HARMAN H.H., *Modern Factor Analysis*, The University of Chicago Press, Chicago, 1968.

[4] IBM, *1401 Portfolio Selection Program* 1401-F1-04X, Program Reference Manual, IBM, New York, 1965.

[5] MARKOWITZ H.W., *Portfolio Selection*, J. of Finance, 1952.

[6] MARKOWITZ H.W., *Portfolio Selection: Efficient Diversification of Investments*, J. Wiley & Sons, 1959.

[7] MARKOWITZ H.W., *Mean-Variance Analysis in Portfolio Choice and Capital Markets*, Basil Blackwell, Oxford UK, 1987.

[8] NAYLOR T.H., TAPON F., *The Capital Asset Pricing Model: an Evaluation of its Potential as a Strategic Planning Tool*, Management Science, Vol. 28, n. 10, Oct. 1982.

[9] PANG J.S., *A New and Efficient Algorithm for a Class of Portfolio Selection Problems*, Operational Research, 28, 1980.

[10] PEROLD A.F., *Large-Scale Portfolio Optimization*, Management Science, October 1984.

[11] ROSSI F.A., CHAVAN A.M., *Una procedura per la valutazione della frontiera efficiente in problemi di selezione del portafoglio*, in AIRO, Annual Meeting, Pisa 1988.

[12] ROSSI F.A., *Un prototipo di DSS per l'analisi e l'ottima composizione di un portafoglio di attività rischiose: ABAPO*, in AIRO, Annual Meeting, Pisa 1988.

[13] ROSSI F.A., *Valutazione della avversione al rischio del decisore dell'analisi dell'insieme delle alternative non dominate*. in AMASES, Annual Meeting, Palermo 1988.

[14] SHARPE W.F., *A Simplified Model for Portfolio Analysis*, Management Science, 1963.

[15] SHARPE W.F., *Portfolio Theory and Capital Markets*, Mc Graw-Hill, New York, 1970.

[16] SPSS SPSS/PC+, SPSS Inc., Chicago, Illinois, 1987.

[17] SZEGO G.P., *Portfolio Theory with Application to Bank Asset Management*, Academic Press, N.Y., 1980.

[18] WILLIAMSON J.P , DOWNS D H., *Manuals for Computer Programs in Finance and Investments*, Dartmounth College Hannover, New Hampshire, 1970.

A STOCHASTIC CASH MODEL WITH DETERMINISTIC ELEMENTS (*)

WILLEM-MAX VAN DEN BERGH and WINFRIED HALLERBACH
Erasmus University Rotterdam

In this paper we present a simple model which gives a solution to a (one period) stochastic cash problem with a fixed cash outlay at the end of the period. We focus on the role of options as insurance contracts, as to value a constraint on the minimum cash level. It is argued that a cash level adjustment is optimal where the sum of the marginal cost of liquidity and the marginal insurance premium (options value) is zero.

I. Introduction

The basic objective in cash management is to keep the investment in cash as low as possible while still operating the firm's activities efficiently and effectively. Numerous models have been developed to operationalize this objective. The most widely known approach (Miller and Orr [1966]) tries to minimize the cost of liquidity by determining the amount by which the available cash has to be reduced (by depositing) or extended (by loaning) at the appropriate moments. Constantinides [1976] has formulated a continuous time model of cash management with stochastic elements and allowing for positive and negative cash balances. However, these models' practical usefulness is limited because it rests on the assumption that cash inflows and outflows are entirely unpredictable. This may be well the case for day-to-day and relatively modest fluctuations but not for some distinct and important cash receipts or outlays. Another group of models departs from a deterministic cash flow pattern and seeks to identify an optimal strategy with respect to the amounts and time moments that deposits or loans have to be made. (cf. Chand and Morton [1982]). Again the assumed (un) predictability of (parts of) the cash flow may

(*) We like to thank Edwin O. Fischer, Jaap Spronk and three anonymous referees for helpfull comments. Excellent computational assistance by Henk Hofmans is hereby acknowledged. Of course, the usual disclaimers apply.

be unrealistic. Obviously a more practical approach to the cash management problem has to incorporate both stochastic and deterministic elements.

In this paper, we present a simple model which gives a solution to a (one period) stochastic cash problem with a fixed cash outlay at the end of the period. Suppose a treasurer of a firm faces a future liability, for instance the repayment of a loan, to be met at time T. His problem is to adjust the initial level of cash under the restriction that this liability can be met, considering existing overdraft facilities. Apart from the fixed outflow at T, the level of the cash balance is supposed to be a stochastic variable: the variability of the cash inflows and outflows induce the variability of the total cash level over time.

The risk this treasurer faces is that the variability of the cash evolves in such a way that at time T the level of the cash, including the existing overdraft facility, is lower than the liability. To eliminate this risk, the treasurer could make an additional risk free investment by the amount of the present value of the liability. This solution to the cash problem, however, will be costly since the firm's cost of capital will in general be higher than the risk free interest rate and since transaction costs will be involved.

In a more global way, the treasurer could strive to limit the risk (probability) of unfunded liabilities at a specified horizon date T. The treasurer then could adjust the initial cash balance under the restriction that this probability is smaller than or equal to, say, 5% given the estimated parameters of the stochastic cash development. Unfortunately, the probability of an unfunded liability is not very informative. Surely a relatively high probability of underfunding at T by \$ 1. – will *ceteris paribus* be preferred to a rather small probability of not being alble to meet the liability by \$ 10,000. –! To count for this missing dimension of the problem, the additional assumption of a type of loss function could be made. However, the question then arises what kind of loss function would be appropriate. Typically some objective valuation measurement should be available, taking into account all possible cash levels beyond the funding restriction. An elegant solution to this valuation problem would be the availability of a fairly priced insurance contract that secures funding at each state of nature on the horizon date.

In this paper, we propose a way to incorporate both the risk dimension and the value dimension of an unfunded liability at a specified horizon date based on the ideas mentioned above. In particular, we focus on the role of options as insurance contracts, as to value a constraint in the sense of evaluating the (financial) consequences of not meeting this constraint. The basic proposal is that the smaller the value of the «fair» [1] insurance premium to meet the liability by the adjusted cash at time T, the less evidence

---

[1] «Fair» in the sense of a fair gamble in a risk neutral world: the expected loss from the underlying risk against which insurance is effected equals the insurance premium.

exists for an extension of the current cash balance. If the cash balance is large enough, the premium will ultimately reach to zero. On the other hand, holding too much funds in a more or less liquid form involves an oppurtinity cost since the interest proceeds (if any) generally will be lower than the firm's cost of capital. It can be argued that the cash level adjustment is optimal where the sum of the marginal opportunity cost of liquidity and the marginal insurance premium against the funding risk equals zero.

II. The model

We start from the following

Assumptions:

(i) The decision maker (treasurer) faces a single deterministic liability, L_T, due at $t = T$ (in terms of years).

(ii) There exists a constant overdraft facility. We define the *funding potential*, C_t, as the level of the cash balance at t plus the constant overdraft facility.

(iii) The current ($t = 0$) funding potential is C_0. The variability of both cash inflows and outflows, CF_t, induce the variability of the total funding potential over time. Thus the level of the total funding potential is a stochastic variable. More in particular, we assume that the instantaneous percentual rate of change of the cash, c, follows a Wiener process with drift μ_c and variance σ_c^2, which are constant over $t \in [0,T]$:

$$c = dC/C_t = \mu dt + \sigma_c dz, \tag{1}$$

where z is a standard Gauss-Wiener process. So, the cash balance (the funding potential) is a random variable in continuous time and follows an Itô process. The resulting distribution of the funding potential is log-normal. A property of this distribution is that always $C_t > 0$.

(iv) The goal of the decision maker is to adjust the initial level (i.e. at $t = 0$) of the cash balance by selecting a level of the cash, such that the present value of the expected cost of not being able to meet L_T at time T and the opportunity cost of holding cash is minimized.

This total cost can be split into two components:

(v) The *insurance premium*; The fair price of an insurance contract that guarantees that the liability L_T can be met from the funding potential.

(vi) the *opportunity cost* of increasing the current level of the cash balance by a specific amount. The opportunity cost per dollar cash is the difference between the (continuosly compounded) cost of capital of the firm, r_i, and the (continuously compounded) leding rate (or return on safe investments), r_f.

Clearly, in funding the liability L_T, the treasurer faces a *downside risk*: the probability of underfunding, $Pr\{C_T < L_T\}$, is relevant. This expected present value of the loss on the liability incorporates both the risk/probability dimension and the value dimension of the unfunded liability. Basically, the expected present value of the loss, $E\{PV(\max[0, L_T - C_T])\}$, is the value of a put option. We can elucidate this in a more heuristic way.

As an insurance against interest rate risk, the treasurer could buy a put option on the funding potential C_t (assuming for a moment that these options are available in the market). To insure against defaulting on the liability , it would have to be a European put option with underlying asset C_t (where C_0 equals the initial funding potential), exercise price L_T, volatility σ_c and maturity T : $P(C_t, L_T, \sigma_c, T)$. If $C_T < L_T$, this option would enable the treasurer to exchange C_T for an aumont of L_T, which suffices exactly to meet the liability when due. If $C_T \geq L_T$ the option expires worthless.

If the (European) put option is «fairly» priced, its value P reflects the *market value* of the risk that $C_T < L_T$, i.e. the value of the put is the present value of the expected payoffs on the exercise date (see for example Jarrow & Rudd [1983, section 7.6]):

$$\begin{aligned} P(C_t, L_T, \sigma_c, T) &= PV(E\{\max[L_T - C_T, 0]\}) \\ &= PV(L_T) * Pr(C_T < L_T) - PV(E\{C_T | C_T < L_T\}) \qquad (2) \\ &\quad * Pr\{C_T < L_T\} \end{aligned}$$

In words: if $C_T < L_T$, you exchange the funding potential for the liability, so you give up C_T and you receive L_T. The value of the put thus reflects the expected present (market) value of the loss that can arise from the difference between the values of L_T and C_T at the liability date. Note that the interpretation of the «fair» put value in eq. (2) is only valid in a *risk neutral* world; in this situation the return on a fully hedged portfolio should be the riskless rate while each deviation will be eliminated by profitable arbitrage opportunities. The value of a (put)-option, however, will be the same in a risk neutral as in a risk averse world.

From this point of view, the probability of defaulting on L_T equals the probability of exercise of the put. As C_T is a log-normal variable and L_T is a constant, we can evaluate the probability as:

$$Pr\{C_t < L_T\} = N\{[\ln(L_T) - \ln(C_T)]/\sigma_c\sqrt{T}\} = 1 - N\{\ln(C_T/L_T)/\sigma\sqrt{T}\} \quad (3)$$

where: $N\{y\}$ = the (cumulative) standard normal distribution function:

$$N\{y\} = \int_{-\infty}^{y} \frac{1}{\sqrt{2\pi}} \exp\left(-\frac{1}{2}x^2\right) \mathrm{d}x$$

Given the stochastic process for the funding potential as specified in eq. (1), we known that $C_T = C_0 \exp(\mu T + \sigma\sqrt{T} \cdot z)$, so

$$Pr\{C_T < L_T\} = 1 - N\{[\ln(C_0/L_T) + \mu T]/\sigma\sqrt{T}\} \tag{4}$$

For our purpose, the value of the put option is more informative than this probability of exercise because it combines the probabilities and the possible losses in one number: as a probability weighted average of the losses, it is a ready to interpretate amount of current dollars.

It is very likely, however, that this kind of put option is not available in the market. This means that we cannot observe the real market values of the options, so that we cannot deduct the *market* value of the insurance contract. Given the stocastich process for the funding potential, however, we can compute the *theoretical* value of the contract with the Black & Scholes [1973] - formula. Note, however, that the cash balance is not a traded asset. As McDonald & Siegel [1984] have argued, the μ_c in eq. (1) is not equal to the expected return μ_c^* of a *traded* asset with risk σ_c. The rate of return short fall equals $\delta = \mu_c^* - \mu_c$, assumed to be constant. δ can be seen as a dividend: a portion of the total required rate of return that does not accrue to the option holder and thus affects the option prices.

Combining Put Call Parity and the Black & Scholes formula yields:

$$P(C_t, L_T, \sigma_c, T) = C_0[N\{h\} - 1] - L_T \exp(-r_f T)[N\{h - \sigma_c\sqrt{T}\} - 1] \tag{5}$$

where: $h = \{\ln(C_0/L_T) + (r_f - \delta)T\}/\sigma_c\sqrt{T} + \frac{1}{2}\sigma_c\sqrt{T}$.

Crucial in the derivation of eq. (5) is the absence of riskless arbitrage opportunities and the ability to construct a perfect risk free hedge or arbitrage portfolio with the funding potential and an insurance contract to switch the future funding potential against a specific amount of money that is necessary to meet liability L_T (2).

Recall that we have assumed that the variability of the total funding potential over time, C_t, is induced only by the variability of the cash inflows and outflows, CF_t (cf. eq. 1). Because CF_t is a stochastic variable, the funding potential C_t is also stochastic. We assume that the instantaneous percentual rate of change of the cash inflows and outflows, *cf*, follows a Wiener process with mean μ_{cf} and variance σ_{cf}^2, which are constant over $t \in [0,T]$ (cf. eq. 1).

$$cf = dCF/CF_t = \mu_{cf}dt + \sigma_{cf}dz \tag{6}$$

(2) For that reason, eq. (2) is evaluated in a risk neutral world, i.e. the geometric mean of the relative change in the cash level, (cf. eq. 1) equals the risk free rate corrected for the return short fall δ.

Care must be taken in transferring this cash flow generating process to the funding potential generating process: when the level of the current funding potential C_0 is adjusted to a higher (lower) level, the variance of the instantaneous percentual rate of change of the funding potential, dc, decreases (increases). This is true because the percentual rate of change of the funding potential over a very small time interval ΔT can be written as:

$$c = \frac{\Delta C}{C} = \frac{CF}{C} \tag{7}$$

It can be shown (cf. Mood, Boes & Graybill [1974, p. 181]) that, given eq. (7), the variance of the instantaneous percentual rate of change of the funding potential can be approximated as:

$$\mathrm{Var}(CF/C) \approx \left\{\frac{E(CF)}{E(C)}\right\}^2 \cdot \left\{\frac{\mathrm{Var}(CF)}{E(CF)^2} + \frac{\mathrm{Var}(C)}{E(C)^2} - \frac{2\,\mathrm{Cov}(CF,C)}{E(CF)\cdot E(C)}\right\} \tag{8}$$

As the variability of the cash inflows and cash outflows in the only source of uncertainty with respect to the total funding potential, it follows that the correlation between the cash flows and the funding potential is perfectly positive. Hence,

$$\mathrm{Cov}(CF,C) = [\,\mathrm{Var}(CF)\cdot \mathrm{Var}(C)]^{\frac{1}{2}} \tag{9}$$

Substituting eq. (9) in (8) and recognizing the factored squares, we get:

$$\begin{aligned} \mathrm{Var}(CF/C)^{\frac{1}{2}} &\approx \frac{E(CF)}{E(C)} \cdot \left\{\frac{\mathrm{Var}(CF)^{\frac{1}{2}}}{E(CF)} - \frac{\mathrm{Var}(C)^{\frac{1}{2}}}{E(C)}\right\} \\ &= \frac{\mathrm{Var}(CF)^{\frac{1}{2}}}{E(C)} - \frac{\mathrm{Var}(C)^{\frac{1}{2}}\cdot E(CF)}{E(C)^2} \end{aligned} \tag{10}$$

Under the assumption that the expected value of the cash flow (i.e., the expected change of the cash balance) equals zero, eq. (10) reduces to:

$$\mathrm{Var}(CF/C)^{\frac{1}{2}} \equiv \sigma_c \approx \frac{\mathrm{Var}(CF)^{\frac{1}{2}}}{E(C)} = \frac{\mathrm{Var}(CF)^{\frac{1}{2}}}{C_0} \tag{11}$$

where the latter equality follows from the fact that $E(C_t + CF_t) = E(C_0) = C_0$.

The implication of eq. (11) is that the volatility of the underlying value of the put option changes as the initial (and thus the expected) level of the cash balance is adjusted.

The assumptions (v) and (vi) imply a trade-off between the value of the insurance premium and the opportunity cost of cash as the curent level of the cash balance is adjusted. Increasing the level of the cash balance increases the opportunity cost but lowers the value of the insurance premium. This decrease in the value of the put option has two sources: first, increasing the cash level potential means increasing the exercise price of the option; second, increasing the cash level means decreasing the volatility (the standard deviation of the instantaneous percentual rate of change of the funding potential) according to eq. (11).

The current cash balance will be adjusted until the sum of the marginal opportunity costs and the marginal change in the value of the put option equals zero. As the opportunity costs for a cash level C equal $C \cdot [\exp(r_i T) - \exp(r_f T)]$, the marginal costs equal

$$d\{C_0[\exp(r_i T) - \exp(r_f T)]\}/dC_0 = \exp(r_i T) - \exp(r_f T) \qquad (12)$$

The marginal change of the value of the put option resulting from a change in the current cash level equals

$$dP/dC_0 = \frac{\partial P(C_0)}{\partial C_0} + \frac{\partial P(\sigma_c)}{\partial \sigma_c} \cdot \frac{\partial \sigma_c}{\sigma C_0} \qquad (13)$$

Using eq. (11) and the (standard) derivatives of a put with respect to the underlying value and the volatility (cf. Jarrow & Rudd [1983, p. 209]), we evaluate eq. (13) as

$$\begin{aligned} dP/dC_0 &= \{N(h) - 1\} + \{C_0\sqrt{T}N'(h)\} \cdot \{-\operatorname{Var}(CF)^{\frac{1}{2}}/C_0^2\} \\ &= N(h) - N'(h) \cdot \operatorname{Var}(CF)^{\frac{1}{2}} \cdot \sqrt{T}/C_0 - 1 \end{aligned} \qquad (14)$$

with

$$N'\{y\} = \frac{1}{\sqrt{2\pi}} \exp\left(-\frac{1}{2}y^2\right)$$

Given the necessary inputs, the goal is now to select a level C_0 such that the value of the sum of (12) and (14) is zero.

III. Behaviour of the Model and Conclusions

The simple cash model set out in the previous sections should be extended to make it more realistic. A first extension might be the incorporation of transaction costs. In that case, adaptions of the cash level will not occur continuosly but only when the decrease in cost of holding cash (opportunity cost plus insurance premium) will be higher than the transaction costs. Another possible extension is the incorporation of more than one deterministic cash flow, i.e. a whole scenario of relatively important projected cash receipts and outlays. We will not elaborate these extensions here since they do not seem to affect the basic concepts. To get more insight in the behaviour of the simple model under various parameter settings we will present some simulation results. In figure 1, we have plotted the combinations of initial cash levels and total costs involved for various levels of cash flow variance with $r_f = 8\%$ and $\delta = 1\%$. Note that at low levels of the funding potential the cost of the insurance contract clearly dominates; at high levels of the initial cash, the effect of the opportunity cost of holding cash is more important. The optimal initial cash level (at the minimum value of the function) moves to the right when the cash flow variance increases, cet. par. In figure 2, the cash flow variance level is held constant at a level of 30 while the opportunity cost varies. It can be observed that the minimum of the total cost function is less pronounced for low opportunity costs: the penalty for holding too large amounts of cash is low.

In figure 3 and figure 4, we have plotted the evolution of the actual funding potential following a simulated Wiener precess (using the same seed for the random generator). In both plots we have also depicted the development of the ex-ante optimal cash level based on the simple model set out above. In figure 3, the variability of the cash flow simulation is relatively low and in figure 4 relatively high.

To get a more realistic impression of the behaviour of the model, we have assumed that the exact variability parameter of the simulation is not known to the decision making part of the model. Based on the actual outcome of the simulation, the standard deviation, σ_t, of the funding potential has been re-estimated each t, with the following weighted average approach:

$$\mu_n = C_n + \frac{(n-1)}{n}(\mu_{n-1} - C_n), \qquad n = 1, 2, \ldots N \tag{15}$$

$$\sigma_n = (n-1)\left[\frac{1}{n}\sigma_{n-1} + \frac{1}{n^2}(\mu_{n-1} - C_n)^2\right] \tag{16}$$

where n refers to the period simulated thus far (we start the simulations with a history of 30 days). In both simulations the liability L_T, the risk free rate r_f and the firm's lending rate have been set equal to each other. It is interesting to learn from these plots an interesting feature of the model, namely that the optimal ex-ante cash level is strongly influenced by the magnitude of the estimated variability in the cash flow pattern. The reason for this is of course that the first derivative of the option price (insurance premium) with respect to the variance of the underlying value is positive, while the opportunity cost of liquidity is not affected.

A final remark concerns the absolute nature of the constraint on the overdraft facility. In reality there will often be no limits but extra funding can only be obtained at a significantly higher interest rate. This implies that the insurance contract does not need to hedge the total amount of the liability, but only the higher interest cost that must be paid over the difference between the liability and the funding potential at maturity. In this case only the extra interest over the premium of the original insurance contract has to be considered.

REFERENCES

F. BLACK and M. SCHOLES, 1973: *The Pricing of Options and Corporate Liabilities*, Journal of Political Economy Vol. 81, pp. 637-654.

S. CHAND and T.E. MORTON, 1982: *A Perfect Planning Horizon Procedure for a Deterministic Cash Balance Problem*, Management Science Vol. 28/6, pp. 652 ff.

G.M. CONSTANTINIDES, 1976: *Stochastic Cash Management With Fixed and Proportional Transaction Costs*, Management Science Vol. 22/12, pp. 1320-1331.

R.A. JARROW and A. RUDD, 1983: *Option Pricing*, Dow Jones-Irwin, Homewood Illinois.

R. McDONALD and D. SIEGEL, 1984: *Option Pricing When the Underlying Asset Earns a Below-Equilibrium Rate of Return:* A note, The Journal of Finance, Vol. 39/1, pp. 261-265.

M.H. MILLER and D. ORR, 1966: *A model of the Demand for Money by Firms*, Quartely Journal of Economics, Vol. 80, pp. 413ff.

A.M. MOOD, D.C. BOES and F.A. GRAYBILL, 1974: *Introduction to the Theory of Statistics*, McGraw-Hill, Auckland.

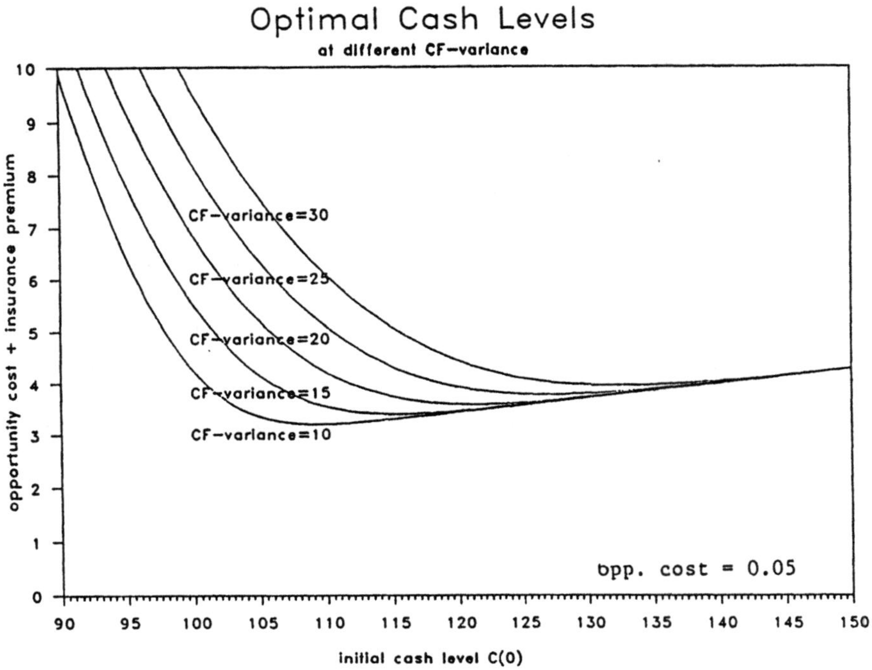

Figure 1.

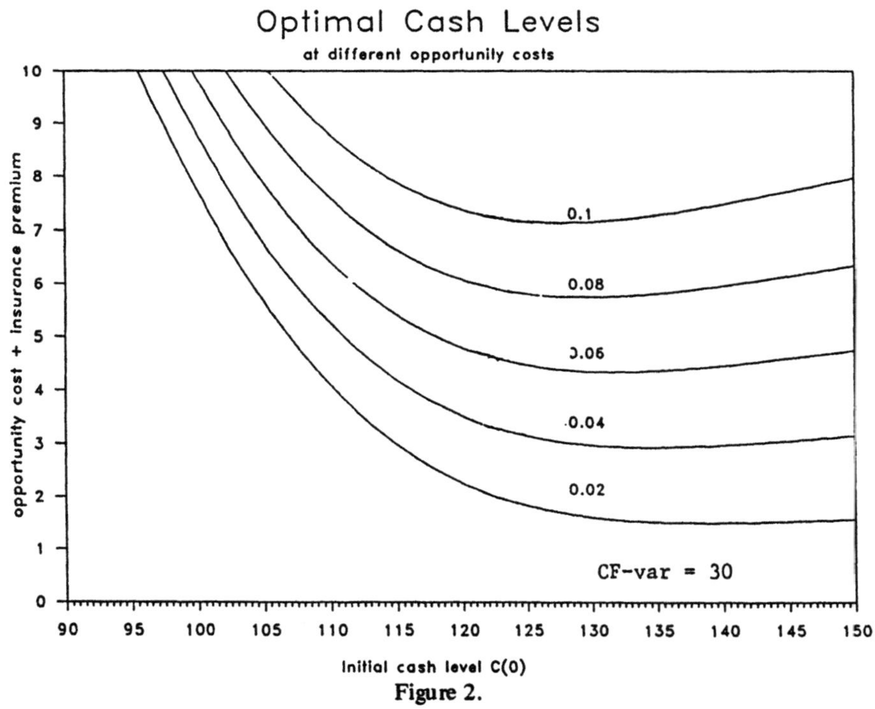

Figure 2.

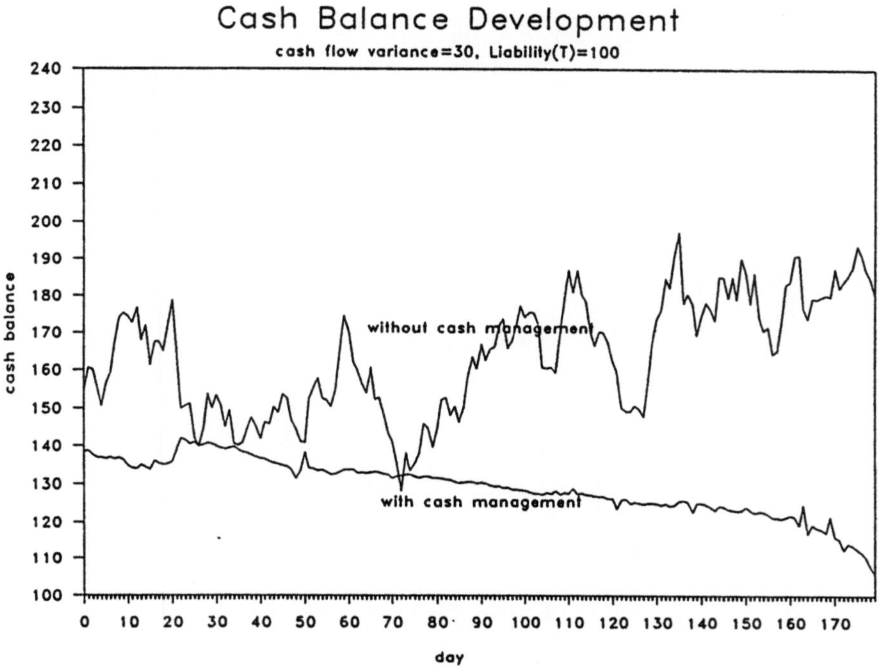

Figure 3.

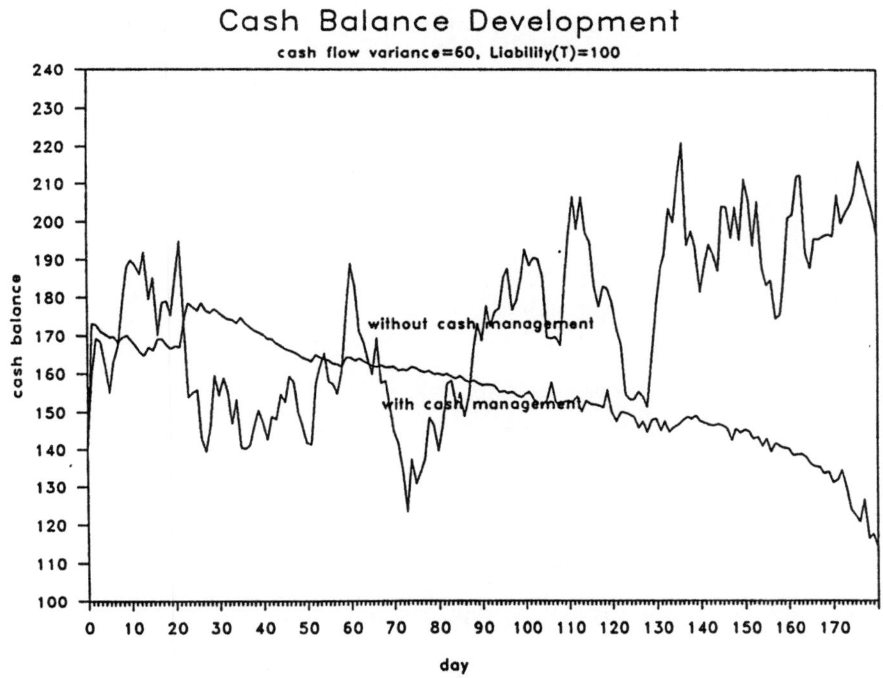

Figure 4.

UTILITY OF WEALTH AND RELATIVE RISK AVERSION: OPERATIONALIZATION AND ESTIMATION (*)

NICO L. VAN DER SAR

Department of Business Finance,
Erasmus University Rotterdam

Next to expectations, preferences play an important part in explaining individual investment decision making. In contrast with the case of expectations, most financial models do not presuppose homogeneity with respect to preferences, but leave room for variation between individuals. In this article we employ the social filter theory to model the concept of utility. The investor group on which we focus consists of a sample drawn from the members of the Dutch Central Union of Investment Study Clubs. By means of verbal choice behavior we operationalize and determine empirically the utility function of wealth as a function of club-specific characteristics, and we analyze the implications for the corresponding relative risk aversion.

1. Introduction

The theory of rational decision behavior assumes that decision makers choose their best collection of investment projects consistent with the limited resources available to them. To determine which collection is «best» a preference or utility function is introduced. When making an investment decision the various alternatives are ranked by the decision makers and the one with the highest utility is the preferred choice.

In this paper we will focus on the utility that is derived from different amounts of wealth. It is assumed that every individual n evaluates amounts of wealth according to a cardinal wealth utility function $U_n(.)$. Then, the investor's optimal financial position is represented by the alternative that generates the highest utility. In the case of a choice between *risky* alternatives characterized by various possible outcomes with associated probabilities, next to preferences, also (sub-

(*) We express our gratitude to Jelle Koolstra, who created the dataset with the help of the Dutch Central Union of Investment Study Clubs (NCVB). Programming support by Rob Flik is gratefully acknowledged. We like to thank Gerrit Antonides and Winfried Hallerbach for stimulating discussions on the subject. Responsability for remaining errors is that of the author.

jective) expectations play an important part. Then, choice behavior may be rationalized by (subjective) expected utility analysis (for an overview see e.g. Schoemaker [1982]).

In recent years, various theories of choice behavior have been developed wherein the requirement of the properties of mathematical probability is relaxed. Although some of them attracted a great deal of attention and provided explanations for until then unexplained phenomena (e.g., the prospect theory as proposed by Kahneman and Tversky [1979] offers a useful framework for the analysis of explaining investor preference for cash dividends (see Shefrin and Statman [1984]), utility theory still is the dominant paradigm for decision making under risk. In most applications the individual utility function over wealth, which captures his attitude toward risk, is assumed to be strictly concave with the degree of curvature being indicative of the individual degree of risk aversion. Pratt [1964] and Arrow [1970] introduced the so-called relative risk aversion (rra). This specific risk aversion measure is useful because it provides some insight into people's behavior in the face of risk. In Van der Sar and Antonides [1989] it is shown that in a world where decision making is based on only the first two statistical moments of the probability distribution of return, an individual's rra almost completely pins down his (return, risk)-attitude and therewith his optimal portfolio on the Capital Marked Line.

The purpose of this article is, first, to determine empirically if and how the utility function of wealth varies among investors, and, second to analyze the implications for the corresponding rra. The investor group on which we shall focus consists of a sample drawn from the members of the Dutch Central Union of Investment Study Clubs (NCVB).

Section 2 provides a description of the data. In section 3 we present the social filter theory. This theoretical approach which is used to model the investor's utility of wealth differs from the one applied by Van der Sar and Antonides [1989]. Section 4 presents the empirical results. In section 5 consequences for the rra are discussed, while section 6 ends with some concluding remarks.

2. The data

The investor group at issue is a subset of the Dutch Central Union of Investment Study Clubs (NCVB). It comprises the members of the NCVB in the western part of the Netherlands, viz. the provinces of North Holland, South Holland, North Brabant and Utrecht. While the sample is not representative of the Dutch investors as a whole, it represents an investor-category that is of great interest, among others, in studying the influence of groupthink on investment decision making. The data used in our study were collected via a mail questionnaire created by Koolstra in April 1987. A total of 63 responses appeared to be amenable to analysis for a response rate of 23%. For each club information was obtained on its expectations with respect to the future value of financial assets, and with respect to various financial and macro-economic factors. However, our specific interest lies in the questions concerning the club's profile of both its attributes and its attitudes on amounts of invested wealth. The data contain a record of the club's current circumstances like, e.g., the amount of invested wealth (on average about 15,400 Dfl.), the mean age (approximately 39 years), the size of the club (ca. 12 members per club), and the percentage of men being club member (about 74%). To reveal the club preferences, viz. their evaluation of different amounts of invested wealth, the so-called Wealth Evaluation Question (WEQ) has been supplied. It will be used as an instrument for the measurement of the respondent's utility function of wealth. Responding to the WEQ falls under verbal choice behavior. Usually, research on the investor's preferences is based on trading statistics (cf. among others Lewellen, Lease and Schlarbaum [1979].

However, in this paper we shall not use *revealed* preferences which go together with the investor's actions. Instead we shall study *stated* preferences, which have to do with the investor's belief. The WEQ is a set of attitude questions which is offered to the respondent who is asked to associate an amount of wealth, which according to him fits in best with each qualification. This particular question module falls under the Evaluation Question Approach (see Van der Sar and Van Praag [1987]), which is a more general questioning device for measuring people's attitudes toward social, psychologic and economic issues. The WEQ that has been supplied by Koolstra in 1987 to Dutch investment study clubs runs as follows.

«For a club like ours, in our circumstances, we consider an amount of wealth to be

VERY SMALL	if it is about	. . . Dfl.
SMALL	if it is about	. . . Dfl.
NEITHER BIG, NOR SMALL	if it is about	. . . Dfl.
BIG	if it is about	. . . Dfl.
VERY BIG	if it is about	. . . Dfl.»

The response vector being composed of five amounts of wealth, to be denoted by $(w_{1n}, \ldots, w_{5n})$, expresses the wealth judgments of study club n, and will be used to estimate the wealth utility function $U_n(.)$.

3. The social filter process

Often, a distinction is made between the objective reality which concerns the way things truly are and the subjective perception which has to do with the way people believe things are. The investor's subjective wealth distribution applies to the way he perceives the objective wealth distribution. The evaluation of amounts of wealth may be seen as a fairly relative affair. An amount of wealth is evaluated as VERY BIG if it is perceived to be in the upper tail of the wealth distribution, and as VERY SMALL if it is believed that only a few have invested less, or to put it more accurately, if according to our perceived distribution 70% of the wealth levels is below 40,000 Dfl., then we evaluate the amount of wealth 40,000 Dfl. with 0.70 on a zero-one scale.

The wealth utility function $U_n(.)$ shows how an investor perceives and evaluates amounts or wealth, and reflects as such the subjective wealth distribution. The subjective wealth distribution function $U_n(.)$ may be regarded as the outcome of an individually determined process which transforms the objective wealth distribution $U(.)$. The way an investor filters reality and derives his own perception and evaluation of it may be explained by the social filter model. We shall briefly present the social filter process and the theory underlying it. In Van Praag [1981] and Van der Sar, Van Praag and Dubnoff [1988] a more detailed description is given. Let $u(.)$ and $u_n(.)$ respectively denote the objective and subjective wealth density function. Then, the social filter function $\xi_n(.)$ is implicitly defined by

$$u_n(w) = \xi_n(w)\, u(w), \tag{1}$$

where w stands for wealth.

Actually $\xi_n(.)$ describes the varying importance weights that are assigned by the respondent to all members of society in conformity with his view of th wealth distribution function. In order to develop a model that can be estimated we shall make a few assumptions.

First, we assume that $U_n(.)$ is a lognormal distribution function with parameters τ_n, ϕ_n^2, viz.

$$U_n(w) = N\,(ln\ w;\ \tau_n, \phi_n). \tag{2}$$

Second, we adopt the equal interval hypothesis, meaning that the verbal qualifications of the WEQ are equally spaced in the [0, 1]-interval. This yields

$$\frac{ln\ w_{in} - \tau_n}{\phi_n} = u_i \qquad (i = 1, \ldots, 5), \tag{3}$$

where $u_1, \ldots, u_5$ equal the quantiles 1/10, 3/10, 5/10, 7/10 and 9/10 of the standard normal distribution, viz.

$$N(u_i; 0, 1) = \frac{i - 1/2}{5} \qquad (i = 1, \ldots, 5). \tag{4}$$

The plausibility of specifying the utility function of wealth $U(.)$ by a lognormal distribution function and the adoption of the equal interval hypothesis rests on arguments similar to the ones used in research on utility of income (cf., among others, Van Praag [1968], and Kapteyn and Wansbeek [1985] for a review of research on the so-called individual welfare function of income). In view of the foregoing we obtain

$$ln\, w_{in} = \tau_n + \phi_n\, u_i \qquad (i = 1, \ldots, 5). \tag{5}$$

It is to be expected that the study club's answers will not satisfy this equation exactly.

Third, we also assume that the objective wealth distribution $U(.)$ is lognormal with parameters τ_0, ϕ_0^2 as is approximately true. Then, in view of (1) and (2) we may write

$$ln\, \xi_n(w) = -\, 1/2\, ln\, q_n^2 + \frac{1/q_n^2 - 1}{2\phi_0^2}\, (ln\, w - \tau_n^*)^2, \tag{6}$$

where $q_n^2 = \phi_n^2 \,/\, \phi_0^2$, and τ_n^* is implicitly defined. It can easily be shown that

$$\tau_n = (1 - q_n^2).\tau_n^* + q_n^2 \tau_0. \tag{7}$$

The so-called presbyopia factor q_n^2 is linked up with the subjective wealth horizon. In case $q_n^2 > 1$, we have that the larger q_n^2 is, the broader the range of wealth levels that are weighted substantially different from zero. At the so-called social dispersion point τ_n^* the social filter function has a minimum, which corresponds with the wealth level whereto a minimum weigth is given. The investor's situation displays far-sightedness: actually, only (high) wealth classes far away from his own are considered to be of importance.

4. Empirical results

If we put (5) and (7) together, we can write

$$ln\, w_{in} = (1 - q_n^2)\, \tau_n^* + q_n^2\, \tau_0 + u_i\, q_n\, \phi_0 + \epsilon_{in} \quad i = 1, \ldots, 5;\; n = 1, \ldots, N, \tag{8}$$

where ϵ_{in} is the error term, which is assumed to be independent identically distributed having a normal distribution with mean 0 and variance ϕ_ϵ^2. We hypothesize the following equations

$$\tau_n^* = \beta_0 + \beta_1\, ln\, w_n + \beta_2\, ln\, age_n + \beta_3\, ln\, men_n + \beta_4\, ln\, cs_n \tag{9}$$

and

$$q_n^2 = exp\, (\gamma_0)\, cs_n^{\gamma 1}\, age_n^{\gamma 2}\, men_n^{\gamma 3} \tag{10}$$

where w_n is the investment study club's own amount of invested wealth, cs_n the club size, age_n the mean age, and men_n the percentage of men being club member. Minimizing $\Sigma_{i.n}\ \epsilon^2_{in}$ with respect to β_0, β_1, β_2, β_3, β_4, γ_0, γ_1, γ_2 and γ_3 yields the maximum likelihood estimates and corresponding standard deviations that are given in Table 1.

Table 1. Estimation results for $N = 40$ investment study clubs, with standard deviations between brackets.

β_0	= 24.412 (0.079)	γ_0	= 1.647 (0.016)
β_1	= -0.661 (0.094)	γ_1	= -0.258 (0.046)
β_2	= -2.882 (0.640)	γ_2	= -0.133 (0.060)
β_3	= -1.127 (0.429)	γ_3	= 0.045 (0.008)
β_4	= 0.357 (0.146)		

$\bar{R}^2 = 0.469$

With respect to the estimation results the following observations can be made:

1. the presbyopia factor $q_n^{\ 2}$

– in general $q_n^{\ 2} > 1$, implying that the investment study club's attention is mainly focused on far away (high) wealth levels; this differs from earlier results on utility of income, where in general $q_n^{\ 2} < 1$ being characteristic for short-sightedness appears to hold (cf., e.g., Van der Sar, Van Praag and Dubnoff [1988]); it may be explained by the fact that investment study clubs are aware of the fact that they fall into a very specific investor-category with, on average, a relatively low amount of invested wealth;

– $q_n^{\ 2}$ is negatively correlated with the size of the study club reflecting a smaller subjective wealth horizon in larger clubs;

– $q_n^{\ 2}$ varies negatively with the mean age of the club members and positively with the percentage of men being club member;

2. the social dispersion point τ_n^*

– since on average $q_n^{\ 2} > 1$, the social filter function generally has a minimum at τ_n^*, which shows the investment study club's tendency to put its mind especially on far away wealth classes;

– generally $\tau_n^* < ln\ w_n$ which reflects the fact that the investment study club's attention is mainly concentrated on the wealthy ones;

– τ_n^* is negatively affected by own wealth level w_n, the mean age and the percentage of men, and positively by the club size cs_n;

reflecting that relatively less weight is given to the investment study club's own wealth class in the case of a decrease of w_n, age_n and/or men_n, and in the case of an increase of cs_n;

3. the parameter τ_n

it may be interpreted as a want/need parameter, i.e. a higher value of τ_n shows that more wealth is needed in order to reach a specific utility level; by combining (7) with (9) and (10), it is possible to obtain τ_n in terms of club-specific characteristics;

– the coefficient $(1 - q_n^2)\ \beta_1$, on average being 0.441, is indicative of the degree whereto investment study clubs adapt their wealth judgments to their own wealth circumstances; this so-called preference drift phenomenon has been operationalized earlier with respect to income judgments by Van Praag [1971];

– τ_n varies positively with mean age and percentage of men, and negatively with club size cs_n, the size of the effects not being constant but depending on q_n^2.

5. Relative risk aversion

The relative risk aversion which has been introduced by Pratt in 1964 is defined by

$$rra(w) = -\frac{U''(w)}{U'(w)}\, w. \tag{11}$$

It directly measures the insistence of an individual for more-than-fair odds, at least when the bets, being measured not in absolute terms but in proportion to w, are small (see Arrow [1970]). Substituting the first and second derivative of the lognormal utility function of wealth we obtain *rra* in terms of club-specific characteristics, viz.

$$rra_n(w) = \frac{ln\, w - (1 - q_n^2)\, \tau_n{}^* - q_n^2\, \tau_0}{q_n^2\, \phi_0^2} \tag{12}$$

In view of the estimation results of Table 1, the following observations seem pertinent:

– the investment study club's rra_n generally has a position value, meaning that in general the club's position on the *S*-shaped utility curve falls within the terminal concave segment; on average it approximately equals 0.76;

– since economists generally agree on only some of the reasonable important intuitively plausible properties utility functions of wealth should exhibit, different types of utility functions have been used, and as a consequences there is no consensus about rra_n, i.e. whether it should increase, remain constant, or decrease; e.g. Friend and Blume [1975] estimated rra_n to be 2 and roughly constant across different levels of wealth, while our findings show that rra_n is positively affected by the club's own level of invested wealth w_n which is in conformity with Arrow's [1970] hypothesis of an increasing relative risk aversion;

– the size of the investment study club cs_n has a positive effect on rra_n, indicating that group decision making leads to a shift toward greater caution, which can be rationalized by the fact that caution is a socially approved value; Vinokur [1971] suggested that group discussion strengthens an already existing tendency which may explain the existence of both the phenomena of a cautious and a risky shift (see also Steiner [1982]);

– rra_n is negatively correlated with the investment study club's mean age, which reflects the fact that the older clubs are less risk averse than the younger ones;

– rra_n varies negatively with the percentage of men, which suggests that men are more inclined to take risks than women.

6. Summary and discussion

With respect to individual investment decision making financial theoretical analysis, modelling and empirical application has focused mainly on information, beliefs and objective probabilities of possible outcomes which determine the investor's expectations. However, there is another side to the matter, namely that of the values or utilities of the possible outcomes which for the greater part has been ignored.

The preceding sections have been devoted .to a study of a theoretical model of investors' preferences with respect to invested wealth, and an analysis of the empirical results for members of the Dutch Central Union of Investment Study Clubs (NCVB). Verbal choice behavior is employed to estimate the club's cardinal utility function of wealth, which appears to vary among the investment study clubs, depending on club-specific characteristics. The relative risk aversion (*rra*) which may be used to capture the investor's risk attitude generally has a positive value, indicating that the club's own financial position falls within the concave segment of the S-shaped wealth utility function. Our results empirically support Arrow's hypothesis of an increasing *rra* (as a function of wealth). *Rra* appears to vary negatively with the mean age of the club and the percentage of men being a club member. The size of the club affects rra positively, indicating a cautious shift, i.e. group decision making leads to a shift toward greater caution. Our results are more or less consistent with the empirical findings of Van der Sar and Antonides (1989), who used a different less complex model.

Van der Sar and Antonides [1989] found that in the mean-variance world the *rra* almost completely pins down the indifference curves and therewith the (return, risk)-attitude of an investor, and used this result to derive the subjective price of risk by empirically determining the «subjective Capital Market Line». In view of Loistl [1976] who showed that the Taylor series approximation is not necessarily accurate or might even be erroneous, it is of importance that in this study we did not make any presuppositions on the distribution of returns. The implication which arises is that, though we didn't put it into effect in this article, it is possible to employ our model to derive the subjective price of risk in the way Van der Sar and Antonides did.

The foregoing suggests that the use of verbal choice behavior, including the application of attitude questions, may contribute to the understanding of the concepts of utility and risk aversion which are basic to investment decision making.

REFERENCES

K.J. ARROW, 1970, *Essays in the Theory of Risk-Bearing,* North-Holland Publishing Company, Amsterdam.

I. FRIEND, M. BLUME, 1975, The Demand for Risky Assets, *American Economic Review,* Vol. 65, pp. 900-922.

D. KAHNEMAN, A. TVERSKY, 1979, Prospect Theory: an Analysis of Decision under Risk, *Econometrica,* Vol. 47, pp. 263-291.

A. KAPTEYN. T.J. WANSBEEK, 1985, The Individual Welfare Function: A Review, *Journal of Economic Psychology,* Vol. 6, pp. 333-363.

W.G. LEWELLEN, R.C. LEASE, G.G. SCHLARBAUM, 1979, Investment Performance and Investor Behavior, *Journal of Financial and Quantitative Analysis,* Vol. 14, pp. 29-57.

O. LOISTL, 1976, The Erroneous Approximation of Expected Utility by Means of a Taylor's Series Expansion: Analytic and Computational Results, *Americal Economic Review,* Vol. 66, pp. 904-910.

J.W. PRATT, 1964, Risk Aversion in the Small and in the Large, *Econometrica,* Vol. 32, pp. 122-126.

P.J.H., SCHOEMAKER , 1982, The Expected Utility Model: Its Variants, Purposes, Evidence and Limitations, *Journal of Economic Literature,* Vol. 20, pp. 529-563.

H.M. SHEFRIN, M. STATMAN, 1984, Explaining Investor Preference for Cash Dividends, *Journal of Financial Economics,* Vol. 13, pp. 253-282.

I.D. STEINER, 1982, Heuristic Models of Groupthink, in: H. Brandstätter, J.H. Davis and G. Stocker-Kreichgauer, *Group Decision Making,* Academic Press, London, pp. 503-524.

N.L. VAN DER SAR, B.M.S. VAN PRAAG, S. DUBNOFF, 1988, Evaluation Questions and Income Utility, in: B. Munier (ed.), *Risk, Decision and Rationality,* D. Reidel Pub. Cy., Dordrecht, pp. 77-96.

N.L. VAN DER SAR, B.M.S. VAN PRAAG, 1987, The Evaluation Question Approach, report

8753/A, Econometric Institute, Erasmus University Rotterdam.

N.L. VAN DER SAR, G. ANTONIDES, 1989, The Price of Risk Empirically Determined by the Capital Market Line, report 8915/F, Centre for Research in Business Economics, Erasmus University Rotterdam.

B.M.S. VAN PRAAG, 1968, *Individual Welfare Functions and Consumer Behavior,* North-Holland Publishing Company, Amsterdam.

B.M.S. VAN PRAAG, 1981, Reflections on the Theory of Individual Welfare Functions, report 81.14, Center for Research in Public Economics, Leyden University, proceedings of the *American Statistical Association*

B.M.S. VAN PRAAG, 1971, The Welfare Function of Income in Belgium: An Empirical Investigation, *European Economic Review,* Vol. 2, pp. 337-369.

A. VINOKUR, 1971, Review and Theoretical Analysis of the Effects of Group Processes upon Individual and Group Decisions Involving Risk, *Psychological Bulletin,* Vol. 76, pp. 231-250.

ON THE ROBUSTNESS OF MODELS OF OPTIMAL CAPITAL STRUCTURE

D. VAN DER WIJST
Research Institute for Small Business
Department of Fundamental Research
P.O. Box 7001
2701 AA Zoetermeer The Netherlands

This paper investigates the robustness of models of optimal capital structure i.e. their sensitivity for small changes in their specification. This question is addressed by incorporating well known models of optimal capital structure within a uniform framework of assumptions and definitions. Using both a single and a multi-period setting, the effects of limited liability, risk of default, bankruptcy costs and agency costs are investigated. In contrast with published models, virtually all of which are well behaved, many models in this study appear to produce inderminate results. It is concluded that the robustness of models of optimal capital structure leaves much to be desired, so that the prospects of extending the models with more realistic assumptions than the ones used here are rather questionable.

1. Introduction

Since the 1958 publication of the famous Modigliani-Miller irrelevance theorem, many models of optimal capital structure have been published. The general result of these studies, which is now widely accepted in the profession, is that the combination of leverage related costs and a tax advantage of debt produces an optimal capital structure at less than a 100 % debt financing, as the tax advantage is traded off against the likelihood of incurring the costs. This theoretical result is hardly contentious, although the question arose whether or not the various leverage related costs and benefits are economically significant enough to have an appreciable effect on optimal leverage. The question that is generally ignored in the literature on optimal capital structure is now robust the various theoretical contributions are, i.e. how sensitive the published models are for small changes in their specification. This paper addresses that question by incorporating well known models of optimal capital structure within a uniform framework of assumptions and definitions. This procedure should produce a tree-structured family of interrelated models, but in view of the general tendency to publish only well-behaved models, this may not be the case.

The framework adopted in this paper is the extended Modigliani-Miller theory, modelled within the so-called mean-variance approach under a set of fairly restrictive assumptions. This particular framework is chosen because it is comparatively simple and because, over the years, it has been used to model a considerable part of the contributions to the theory. Of course, the analyses have to be limited in several respects in order to keep the paper within limits. The question of corporate debt capacity is not addressed here: it is assumed that the lenders do not chicken out before the shareholders. No comparative statics analyses are performed for the «well behaved» models, the effects of information asymmetries are not modelled and the discussion of the models is restricted to their qualitative results (i.e. the existence of optimal capital structure and not the locus of the optimum). Derivations and proofs and the elaboration of some models with indeterminate results are not included. Extensive discussions and mathematical treatments of all models presented here can be found in Van der Wijst (1986 and 1989).

2. Assumptions and definitions

The assumptions made to facilitate the construction of the models attempt to capture, as simply as possible, the essence of the economic phenomena they seek to describe. Hence, no detailed technical realism is aimed at. It should be noted, however, that the assumptions are not as restrictive as they may seem at first glance, because the results of the analyses can be interpreted in broader terms. For instance, a very simple tax structure can be thought of as the net taxes that, over a certain range, result from a more complex tax system, involving both corporate and personal taxes.

Capital markets are assumed to be costless and competitive. In costless capital markets there are no transaction costs and financial assets are costlessly and infinitely divisible. In competitive markets, no buyer or seller is large enough to individually influence prices. Corporate profits are taxed at a fixed rate and personal taxes are neutral, i.e. there are no personal taxes or the effective tax rates on interest, dividends and capital gains (realized or unrealized) are equal. The tax system used is a wealth tax system which allows the deduction of all payments to the debholders, including principal repayments, from the firm's taxable income, but depreciation charges and other non-debt tax shields are not deductible.

The firm is considered at a point in time at which the investment decisions have already been made, whereas the financing decision has not yet been made. Hence, the firm's set of income generating assets (comprising both the physical assets in place and the future investment opportunities, if any) is assumed to be fixed. Firms only issue debt and equity; debtholders are protected against unanticipated transfers of their wealth to stockholders by protective convenants in the bond indenture. Debt claims are only subject to the risk of default; other risks, e.g. price level risk, are not explicitly dealt with in this study. The firm's optimal capital structure is defined as the degree of leverage that maximizes the wealth of the (existing) shareholders, which is, in most instances, equivalent to maximizing the value of the firm [1]. The firm's management is assumed to act in the best interest of the existing shareholders.

Investors are assumed to share the same subjective expectations regarding future events (i.e. they have homogeneous expectations) and to be indifferent to risk. Further, all market participants are assumed to be insatiable and to act rationally. The effect of the combined assumptions is a very simple financial world. Modelling the leverage decision under this set of restrictive assumptions provides an insight into the robustness of the various models which, in turn, may throw some light on the prospects of extending the models with more realistic assumptions.

3. Single period models

3.1. Introduction: the MM-position

In this section, the financing decision is analysed in a one period-two moment context. Because there is only one period, payments to debtholders comprise both interest and redemption of the principal sum. Under the tax system introduced in the previous section both are tax deductible. In addition to the permanent assumptions discussed in the previous section, the following temporary assumptions are made. All market participants are assumed to have equal and costless access to all relevant information. Bankruptcy is assumed to be costless. Further, it is assumed that the firm's owners have unlimited liability and that their personal wealth is sufficient to meet the contractual obligations to the debtholders if these cannot be met out of the cash flow. The result of the latter assumption is that debt is riskless and that the stockholders always receive the, positive or negative, cash flow after interest and taxes. In combination, these assumptions are equivalent to the MM tax case. The valuation formulae for this case can be derived as follows. If we assume that the fiscal authorities pay a tax rebate if the firm suffers a loss, the after tax end of period value of equity, Y_e, is equal to:

$$Y_e = (1 - \tau)(\tilde{x} - R),$$

in which τ is the corporate tax rate, $\tilde{x}$ is the random variable representing the firm's cash flow before interest and taxes and R represents the contractual payments to the debtholders. For risk neutral investors, the equilibrium value of equity, V_e, is the present value, discounted at the risk free interest rate, of the expectation of Y_e :

$$V_e = \frac{E(Y_e)}{(1+r)} = \frac{(1-\tau)\int_{-\infty}^{\infty}(\tilde{x} - R)f(\tilde{x})\mathrm{d}\,\tilde{x}}{(1+r)}$$

---

[1] In some instances, maximizing firm value is not equivalent to maximizing the existing owner's wealth (see e.g. Haley and Schall, 1979, p. 477-82). These instances are discussed later on.

in which $f(\tilde{x})$ is the probability density function (continuous and twice differentiable) of $\tilde{x}$. This expression can be written as:

$$V_e = \frac{(1-\tau)(\bar{x}-R)}{(1+r)}. \tag{3.1}$$

The end of period value of debt, Y_d, can be derived in a similar way and equals the payments to the debtholders:

$$Y_d = R.$$

For risk neutral investors, the equilibrium value of debt, V_d, is the present value of the expectation of Y_d :

$$V_d = \frac{R}{(1+r)}. \tag{3.2}$$

The value of the firm is the sum of the values of equity and debt ($V = V_e + V_d$) :

$$V = \frac{(1+\tau)\bar{x} + \tau R}{(1+r)}. \tag{3.3}$$

The first term in the numerator of (3.3) represents the value of the unlevered firm (V_u), while the second term represents the tax advantage of debt, i.e. the well known MM result $V = V_u + \tau V_d$. Differentiating (3.3) with respect to R produces the well known MM result:

$$\frac{\partial V}{\partial R} = \frac{\tau}{(1+r)} > 0, \tag{3.4}$$

which implies that the level of payments to debtholders that maximizes the value of the firm (optimal capital structure) is reached at a 100% debt.

3.2. The effect of risk of default and limited liability

The influence of the risk of default on the valuation of corporate claims is closely connected with the influence of limited liability; they are, so to speak, opposite sides of the same coin. In the previous subsection, debt was not subject to the risk of default because stockholders were assumed to have unlimited liability and sufficient personal wealth to meet the contractual obligations to the debholders. If either of these assumptions is relaxed, debt automatically becomes subject to the risk of default (2). In the sequel, stockholders are assumed to have limited liability. This means that the firm's cash flow is the only source out of which the obligations to the debtholders can be met. Consequently, if the obligations to the debtholders exceed the firm's cash flow, the firm

(2) In the literature, the assumption of unlimited liability for stockholders is sometimes combined with risky debt (e.g. Castanias, 1983).

defaults and is declared bankrupt. This makes the bankruptcy condition, b, in single-period models:

$$b = R > \tilde{x} \tag{3.5}$$

If b obtains, stockholders are protected by limited liability and receive nothing. So, the end of period value of equity, Y_e, is

$$\begin{aligned} Y_e &= 0 && \text{if} \quad \tilde{x} < b \\ &= (1-\tau)(\tilde{x} - R) && \text{if} \quad \tilde{x} \geq b(b = R). \end{aligned}$$

The equilibrium value of equity, V_e, is the present value of the expectation of Y_e, which equals:

$$V_e = \frac{(1-\tau)\int_b^{\infty}(\tilde{x} - R)f(\tilde{x})\mathrm{d}\tilde{x}}{(1+r)} \tag{3.6}$$

If stockholders are protected by limited liability, it is reasonable that debtholders are granted the same protection. Limited liability for debtholders means that, if the bankruptcy condition obtains, they only receive a positive cash flow; they are not required to accept a negative one. In the literature, frequently no distinction is made between a positive and a negative cash flow [(3)]. This means that in those cases it is implicitly assumed either that the debtholders bear the loss in case of a negative cash flow or that the cash flow is always positive [(4)]. On the other hand, the assumption of limited liability for all security holders means that a negative cash flow is included in neither the value of equity nor the value of debt and, hence, constitutes a leak in the model [(5)]. Under the assumption of limited liability for all security holders the end of period value of debt is:

$$\begin{aligned} Y_d &= 0 && \text{if} \quad 0 \geq \tilde{x}, \\ &= \tilde{x} && \text{if} \quad 0 < \tilde{x} < b, \\ &= R && \text{if} \quad b \leq \tilde{x}(b = R). \end{aligned}$$

The equilibrium value of debt is the present value of the expectation of Y_d:

$$V_d = \frac{\int_0^b \tilde{x}f(\tilde{x})\mathrm{d}\tilde{x} + \int_b^{\infty} Rf(\tilde{x})\mathrm{d}\tilde{x}}{(1+r)}$$

Using the following definition of the probability of bankruptcy F:

---

(3) For example by Kim (1978), Jonkhart (1980) and Chen and Kim (1979).

(4) A strictly positive cash flow is, of course, incompatible with the use of an open ended distribution for $\tilde{x}$, such as the normal distribution. Kim (1978) for instance, uses such a set of inconsistent assumptions.

(5) One may think of this leak as the losses borne by e.g. employees, government and social security institutions.

$F = \int_{-\infty}^{b} f(\tilde{x})\,\mathrm{d}\,\tilde{x}$, this can be written as:

$$V_d = \frac{\int_0^b \tilde{x} f(\tilde{x})\,\mathrm{d}\,\tilde{x} + R(1 - F)}{(1 + r)}. \tag{3.7}$$

Adding up (3.6) and (3.7) and rearranging terms produces the following expression for the value of the firm:

$$V = \frac{\int_0^\infty \tilde{x} f(\tilde{x})\,\mathrm{d}\,\tilde{x} - \tau \int_b^\infty \tilde{x} f(\tilde{x})\,\mathrm{d}\,\tilde{x} + \tau R(1 - F)}{(1 + r)}. \tag{3.8}$$

Optimal capital structure is found by differentiating (3.8) with respect to R

$$\frac{\partial V}{\partial R} = \frac{\tau(1 - F)}{(1 + r)} > 0; \tag{3.9}$$

Since (3.9) only contains benefits (tax savings), the conclusion of optimal capital structure at a 100% debt financing remains unchanged. This repeats the well known conclusion that the introduction of risky debt alone does not cause an optimal capital structure at below a 100% debt financing (6). To ensure an «internal» optimal capital structure a cost of debt financing is needed.

3.3. The effect of bankruptcy and agency costs

The specification of bankruptcy and agency costs

In models of optimal capital structure, bankruptcy costs can be specified in several ways: in an implicit way (Scott, 1976), or in an explicit way and, in the latter case, as a function of the cash flow (Kim, 1978) or as a function of the payments promised to the debtholders (Castanias, 1983). In the present single-period context, the analysis is limited to an explicit specification of bankruptcy costs, viz. bankruptcy costs as a function of the cash flow. The incorporation of bankruptcy costs as a function of the payments promised to the debtholders into the model developed in the previous subsection can be shown to produce indeterminate results (Van der Wijst, 1986). Therefore, this case is not further elaborated here. An example of such an elaboration can be found in Castanias (1983) (7).

Although the concept of agency costs in broadly applicable, we shall confine ourselves in this study to the agency costs of debt financing. In models of optimal capital

(6) This result was first proved within a state-preference framework by Stiglitz (1969) and within the mean-variance approach by Rubinstein (1973).

(7) Castanias avoids inderminate results by assuming unlimited liability, although the consequence of riskless debt is omitted. See Van der Wijst (1986, p. 22) for a more detailed discussion.

structure, agency costs are expressed in almost the same way as bankruptcy costs [8]. A difference between the two, however, is that the former are only made in case of bankruptcy, while the latter are incurred regardless of the state of nature. Agency costs can be looked upon as being made at the beginning of a period (e.g. bonding costs) or during a period (monitoring costs) but in any case before the firm's financial results become known. It is therefore not in accordance with the nature of agency costs to define a broad category of leverage related costs, including agency and bankruptcy costs, that are only incurred in case of bankrupcty (as is done by Bradley, Jarrel and Kim, 1984 and implicitely by Jonkhart, 1980). In this study, agency costs are specified as an increasing function of the payments promised to the debtholders (cf. Barnea, Haugen and Senbet, 1981).

The effect of bankruptcy and agency costs

The introduction of bankruptcy and agency costs into the model developed in the previous subsection does not change the valuation of equity. So the valuation formula for equity remains as in (3.6). The valuation of debt changes with the amount of bankruptcy and agency costs: in costless capital markets, rational investors anticipate these costs and deduct them from the amount they would otherwise be willing to pay. At the end of the period, the debtholders receive the positive balance, if any, of these costs and $\tilde{x}$ or R:

$$\begin{aligned} Y_d &= -A(R) && \text{if} \quad \tilde{x} < 0, \\ &= \tilde{x} - B(\tilde{x}) - A(R) && \text{if} \quad 0 \leq \tilde{x} < R, \\ &= R - A(R) && \text{if} \quad R \leq \tilde{x}(= b) \end{aligned}$$

where $B(\tilde{x})$ represents bankruptcy costs as a function of $\tilde{x}$ (but no greater than $\tilde{x}$) which is positive in the bankruptcy zone and zero otherwise. $A(R)$ represents agency costs a function of R but no greater than R. (Both functions are assumed to be twice differentiable with first and second derivative ≥ 0.) The equilibrium value of debt is:

$$V_d = \frac{-A(R) + \int_0^b \tilde{x} f(\tilde{x}) \mathrm{d}\tilde{x} - \int_0^b B(\tilde{x}) f(\tilde{x}) \mathrm{d}\tilde{x} + R(1 - R)}{(1 + r)}. \tag{3.10}$$

The value of the firm is the sum of (3.6) and (3.10).

$$V = \frac{\int_0^\infty \tilde{x} f(\tilde{x}) \mathrm{d}\tilde{x} - \tau \int_b^\infty \tilde{x} f(\tilde{x}) \mathrm{d}\tilde{x} - \int_0^b B(\tilde{x}) f(\tilde{x}) \mathrm{d}\tilde{x} + \tau R(1 - F) - A(R)}{(1 + r)} \tag{3.11}$$

[8] Jensen and Meckling (1976), p. 342, consider bankruptcy costs an element of the agency costs associated with debt.

The firm's optimal capital structure is found by differentiating (3.11) with respect to R, which produces:

$$\frac{\partial V}{\partial R} = \frac{\tau(1-F) - B(R)f(R) - A'(R)}{(1+r)} \tag{3.12}$$

Optimal capital structure is reached if the present value of the expected marginal tax savings equals the present value of the expected marginal bankruptcy costs, plus the marginal agency costs. Because the marginal bankruptcy and agency costs are positive (by assumption), optimal capital structure is reached before bankruptcy is certain (i.e. $F < 1$). For normally distributed cash flows the second order condition for (3.12) can be shown to hold.

The foregoing shows the effect on the financing decision of two types of leverage related costs in combination with risky debt and limited liability. From this it becomes clear, that the number of leverage related costs (or leverage related benefits, for that matter) can be freely extended without consequences for the qualitative results. For instance, a term representing the agency costs of equity may be included, inversely related to the payments promised to the debtholders. The introduction of new cost categories will doubtlessly enhance the realism of the model, as well as the complexity. However, the qualitative results of the model will remain unaltered by these extensions. A more fundamental extension of the model is the introduction of information asymmetries by relaxing the assumption of homogeneous expectations. Such an extension can be shown to produce determinate results, albeit not in a closed form. See Van der Wijst (1986) for an elaboration of this.

4. Multi-period models

4.1. Introduction: additional assumptions and redefinitions

Modelling the valuation of corporate claims in a multi-period context requires some additional assumptions; also, some variables have to be redefined. The first assumption is that of a perpetual model, i.e. the firm can exist indefinitely as long as it does not go bankrupt. This means that the cash flow ($\tilde{x}$) and the payments to the debtholders (R) are redefined as perpetuities (cf. Haley and Schall, 1979, p. 299). The cash flow is assumed to have an intertemporally independent and identical probability distribution in each future period. The payments to the debtholders only comprise interest payments (no redemption of the principal sum) and are assumed to be fixed over time. The corporate tax rate (τ) and the risk free rate of return (r) are also assumed to be fixed over time. Note that these assumptions imply that the multi-period elements are kept at their minimum.

The multi-period redefinition of the bankruptcy condition requires a separate discussion. In the previous section, bankruptcy was assumed to occur whenever the contractual obligations to the debtholders exceed the firm's cash flow. In multi-period models, this condition is also necessary but not sufficient: the value of future income streams should be taken into account. The firm's owners would lose a possibly perpetual income stream if the firm would go bankrupt in case of a -possibly very small- loss in only one period. Hence, if in a given period a loss occurs which is not large enough to cause bankruptcy, funds to the amount of the loss have to be raised or the firm will as yet go bankrupt. In principle, the firm can raise funds by selling equity, debt or (physical) assets. In each of these cases, the limit on the amount that can be raised is determined by the value of these three items. This value is to be incorporated into the bankruptcy condition to account for the value in future periods. The possibilites to sell debt or physical assets may be restricted by covenants in the debt contract.

Note that, in the absence of these covenants, it may be optimal for the owners to expropriate debtholders by issuing new debt with claims not subordinate to those of the senior debt. In the long run, however, market participants are likely to find ways to protect themselves against this. Therefore, it is usually assumed that debtholders are protected against unanticipated transfers of their wealth to the owners by restrictive covenants in the debt contract. In this way, the firm's optimal capital structure becomes a Pareto optimum with respect to all the firm's security holders. In this study, debtholders are also assumed to be protected agains expropriation. If expropriation is ruled out, the question of how funds are to be raised in case of a loss becomes easier to answer. As Scott (1976, p. 37-38) argues, it is always optimal to sell equity because the protective covenants in the debt contract either prohibit the sale of debt and assets or require the debtholders to be compensated for the resulting decrease in value of the outstanding debt. In this way, Scott arrives at the bankruptcy conditions that has also been suggested by Stiglitz (1974): bankruptcy occurs if the cash flow is insufficient to meet the obligations to the debtholders and the firm cannot issue enough equity to cover the loss. Clearly, the proceeds of an equity issue cannot exceed the current value of equity, so the bankruptcy condition obtains when $R > \tilde{x} + V_e$. If the loss, $(\tilde{x} - R)$, is assumed to induce a tax rebate of $-\tau(\tilde{x} - R)$, that can be used immediately to pay the interest bill, the bankruptcy condition becomes: $R > \tilde{x} + V_e - \tau(\tilde{x} - R)$, which can be written as $\tilde{x} < R - V_e/(1 - \tau)$. This bankruptcy condition, also used by Scott (1976), is used in the sequel.

4.2. The MM-position

In the multi-period context, the MM-case relies on essentially the same assumptions as in the single-period context. All market participiants have equal and costless access to all relevant information. Bankruptcy is costless. Owners have unlimited liability and enough personal wealth to meet the contractual obligations to the debtholders if these cannot be met out of the firm's cash flow. This means that debt is riskless and that the owners always receive the -positive or negative- cash flow after interest and taxes. The valuation formulae for this case are developed as follows. At the end of the period, the owners receive the cash flow after the interest and taxes. If we assume that profits and losses are fiscally treated in the same way, this amounts to $(1-\tau)(\tilde{x}-R)$. In addition to the returns over the period, the owners's wealth also comprises the value of all future income streams. Since all relevant variables $(r, R, \tau$ and the distribution of $\tilde{x})$ are assumed to be fixed over the time, the value of equity, V_e, represents the end of period value of all future income streams. The end of period value of equity, Y_e, is:

$$Y_e = (1-\tau)(\tilde{x}-R) + V_e.$$

For risk neutral investors the equilibrium value of equity is the present value, discounted at the risk free interest rate, of the expectation of Y_e :

$$V_e = \frac{E(Y_e)}{(1+r)} = \frac{(1-\tau)\int_{-\infty}^{+\infty}(\tilde{x}-R)f(\tilde{x})d\tilde{x} + V_e}{(1+r)}, \qquad \text{which equals}$$

$$V_e = \frac{(1-\tau)(\bar{x}-R)}{r}. \tag{4.1}$$

Similarly, the end of period value of debt, Y_d, comprises the interest payments over the period, R, plus the value of all future interest payments. Since the latter are assumed to be fixed over time, their end of period value is given by Y_d, the value of debt:

$$Y_d = R + V_d.$$

For risk neutral investors, the equilibrium value of debt, V_d, is the present value of the expectation of Y_d :

$$V_d = \frac{E(Y_d)}{(1+r)} = \frac{R+V_d}{(1+r)}, \qquad \text{which leads to}$$

$$V_d = \frac{R}{r}. \qquad \text{Since } V = V_e + V_d, \tag{4.2}$$

$$V = \frac{(1-\tau)\bar{x} + \tau R}{r}. \tag{4.3}$$

The MM conclusion that the value of the levered firm equals the value of the unlevered firm plus the tax advantage of debt remains unchanged. So, optimal capital structure is reached at a hundred percent debt financing, as differentiating (4.3) with respect to R shows:

$$\frac{\partial V}{\partial R} = \frac{\tau}{r} > 0. \tag{4.4}$$

This result is equivalent to the single-period result in (3.4).

4.3. The effect of limited liability and the risk of default

The concept of limited liability and its counterpart, the risk of default, have already been discussed in section 3.2 and need no further elaboration in the present multi-period context. Under the assumption that all security holders have limited liability, implying that debt is risky, valuation formulae for the firm's securities can be derived as follows. If the firm does not go bankrupt, the end of period value of equity comprises the dividends (cash flows after interest and taxes) over the period, and the value of the expected future dividends. The latter equals V_e, since all relevant variables $(r, R, \tau$ and the distribution of $\tilde{x})$ are assumed to be fixed over time. In case of bankruptcy, the owners are protected by limited liability and receive nothing. So the end of period value of equity, Y_e, is:

$$\begin{aligned} Y_e &= 0 && \text{if} \quad \tilde{x} < b \\ &= (1-\tau)(\tilde{x}-R) + V_e && \text{if} \quad \tilde{x} \geq b, \end{aligned}$$

in which $b = R - V_e/(1-\tau)$, the multi-period bankruptcy condition developed in section 4.1. Given risk neutrality, the equilibrium value of equity, V_e, is the present value of the expectation of Y_e :

$$V_e = \frac{E(Y_e)}{(1+r)} = \frac{(1-\tau)\int_b^{\infty}(\tilde{x}-R)f(\tilde{x})\,\mathrm{d}\tilde{x} + V_e\int_b^{\infty}f(\tilde{x})\,\mathrm{d}\tilde{x}}{(1+r)}.$$

Defining the probability of bankrupcty as $F = \int_{-\infty}^{b} f(\tilde{x})\,\mathrm{d}\tilde{x}$, this can be written as:

$$V_e = \frac{(1-\tau)\int_b^{\infty}\tilde{x}f(\tilde{x})\,\mathrm{d}\tilde{x} - (1-\tau)R(1-F)}{(r+F)} \qquad (4.5)$$

Note that (4.5) defines V_e only implicity since V_e is also an element of b, which is the lower limit of integration.

The valuation formula for debt can be derived along similar lines. If the firm does not go bankrupt, the end of period value of debt, Y_d, consists of the interest payment over the period, R, plus the value of all expected future interest payments. Since the latter are assumed to be constant over time, the value of the expected future interest payments is given by V_d. The composition of the value of debt in case of bankruptcy is somewhat more complex than when the firm is not bankrupt. If the bankruptcy condition obtains, the firm is transferred from the owners to the debtholders. The value to be transferred consists of the proceeds over the period and the value of future income streams, if any, while limited liability for the debtholders requires only positive values to be transferred.

At this point, some additional assumptions regarding the distribution of a bankrupt estate are necessary. It is possible to assume that debtholders have absolute priority over all other creditors so that they receive all positive values. However, it seems more realistic to assume that debtholders find themselves in a position comparable with that of the owners, i.e. that they have to trade-off the proceeds over the period against the value of future income streams. The proceeds over the period consist of the cash flow and the tax rebate and are -in view of the bankruptcy condition- likely to be negative. If this «loss» exceeds the value of expected future income streams, the firm will be abandoned so that the debtholders receive nothing. If the loss does not outweigh the future value, it will be covered. One may think of this situation as one in which the operations of a bankrupt firm can be continued once the claims of other creditors than the debtholders (e.g. employees and suppliers) are satisfied. Note that, since there are no transfer costs, it is not necessary for the debtholders to actually continue the firm's operations; they may sell the firm.

So, it can be concluded that limited liability for debtholders in a multi-period context requires a «continuity condition» in addition to (and comparable with) the bankruptcy condition that ensures limited liability for the stockholders. This continuity condition specifies that the value to be transferred to the debtholders should be positive. The value to be transferred consists of the proceeds over the period (tax rebate and cash flow) plus the value of future income streams. Since all relevant variables (r, R, τ and the distribution of $\tilde{x}$) are assumed to be fixed over time, the value of future income streams is given by V, the value of the firm. This makes the «continuity condition»> $\tilde{x} - \tau(\tilde{x} - R) + V > 0$, which can be written as $\tilde{x} > (-V - \tau R)/(1 - \tau)$. So the continuity condition, c, is $c = (-V - \tau R)/(1 - \tau)$. Hence, the end of the period value of debt is:

$$
\begin{aligned}
Y_d &= R + V_d && \text{if} \quad \tilde{x} \geq b \\
&= \tilde{x} - \tau(\tilde{x} - R) + V && \text{if} \quad c \leq \tilde{x} < b \\
&= 0 && \text{if} \quad c > \tilde{x}
\end{aligned}
$$

In equilibrium, the value of debt, V_d, is:

$$
V_d = \frac{E(Y_d)}{(1+r)} = \frac{\int_b^{\infty}(R + V_d) f(\tilde{x}) \mathrm{d}\tilde{x} + \int_c^b (\tilde{x} - \tau(\tilde{x} - R) + V) f(\tilde{x}) \mathrm{d}\tilde{x}}{(1+r)}.
$$

Using a new symbol for the probability of bankruptcy $F_b = \int_{-\infty}^{b} f(\tilde{x}) \mathrm{d}\tilde{x}$ and defining $F_c = \int_{-\infty}^{c} f(\tilde{x}) \mathrm{d}\tilde{x}$, the above expression can be written as:

$$
V_d = \frac{R(1 - F_b) + (1 - \tau) \int_c^b \tilde{x} f(\tilde{x}) \mathrm{d}\tilde{x} + (\tau R + V_e) \int_c^b f(\tilde{x}) \mathrm{d}\tilde{x}}{(r + F_c)} \tag{4.6}
$$

The denominators in (4.5) and (4.6) are different and no simplification is reached by working out the terms of their sum. Hence, the value of the firm, $V = V_e + V_d$, is given by:

$$
\begin{aligned}
V = {} & \frac{(1 - \tau) \int_b^{\infty} (\tilde{x} - R) f(\tilde{x}) \mathrm{d}\tilde{x}}{(r + F_b)} + \\
& + \frac{R(1 - F_b) + (1 - \tau) \int_c^b \tilde{x} f(\tilde{x}) \mathrm{d}\tilde{x} + (\tau R + V_e) \int_c^b f(\tilde{x}) \mathrm{d}\tilde{x}}{(r + F_c)}.
\end{aligned} \tag{4.7}
$$

Differentiation of (4.6) and (4.5) with respect to R to find the optimal capital structure produces the following results:

$$\frac{\partial V_e}{\partial R} = \frac{-(1-\tau)(1-F_b)}{(r+F_b)} < 0\text{, and} \tag{4.8}$$

$$\frac{\partial V_d}{\partial R} = \frac{(1-F_b) + \int_c^b f(\tilde{x})\,d\tilde{x}\left(\tau - \frac{(1-\tau)(1-F_b)}{(r+F_b)}\right)}{(r+F_b)} \tag{4.9}$$

Equation (4.8) is strictly negative. The sign of (4.9) cannot be determined without further assumptions. Hence, the first order conditions for optimal capital structure may be satisfied. However, the second order condition for optimal capital structure cannot be shown to hold (see Van der Wijst, 1986). As can be seen from (4.6) and (4.9), the complexity of the effects of an increase in R on the component parts of the value of debt prohibits the on balance effect to be unambiguously determined. Hencc, even in this early stage of the analyses the computational complexity of valuing corporate claims in a multi-period world prevents clear-cut results.

4.4. The effect of bankruptcy costs

In view of the results obtained in the previous subsection, the choice of the bankruptcy costs specification is limited. The addition of an explicit bankruptcy costs function to the formulae developed in section 4.3 would not alter the -indeterminate- qualitative results. So the obvious way to proceed with the analysis is to introduce implicit bankruptcy costs. Implicit bankrupctcy costs occur when, upon bankruptcy, the firm's productive assets are sold in imperfect secondary markets at a pricc below the market value of an equivalent, well managed, non bankrupt firm. It should be noted that implicit bankruptcy costs require liquidation. This is a stronger assumption that bankruptcy, which only requires the firm to be transferred to the debtholders. If the firm is liquidated upon bankruptcy, the case of continuity under the bankruptcy condition is not accounted for so that the continuity condition is redundant. This simplifies the distribution of a bankrupt estate because there are no future income streams to be traded-off agains the loss in a period. Hence, the debtholders may be assumed to receive all positive values, while the negative values are not taken into account.

Neither the composition nor the distribution of a bankrupt estate affects the value of equity, which is zero under the bankruptcy condition. So the value of equity remains as in (4.5). Using implicit bankruptcy costs, the valuation formula for debt is developed in the following manner. If the firm does not go bankrupt, the end of period value of debt, Y_d, consists of the interest payments over the period, R, and the value of the expected future interest payments, which can be represented by V_d. Upon bankruptcy, the firm is liquidated and its assets are sold in imperfect secondary markets, the proceeds of which are represented by L. In addition to the liquidation value there are also the proceeds over the period, i.e. the cash flow and the tax rebate. The latter is always positive but the former may take negative values. Limited liability for debtholders requires negative payments to be excluded, so the end of the period value of debt is:

$$\begin{aligned} Y_d &= R + V_d && \text{if} \quad \tilde{x} \geq b \\ &= L - \tau(\tilde{x} - R) + \tilde{x} && \text{if} \quad 0 \leq \tilde{x} < b \\ &= L - \tau(\tilde{x} - R) && \text{if} \quad \tilde{x} < b < 0 \end{aligned}$$

in which L is the liquidation value of the firm ($L < V$) and b is the by now familiar bankruptcy condition. For risk neutral investors, the equilibrium value of debt, V_d, is the present value of the expectation of Y_d :

$$V_d = \frac{R(1 - F) + LF - \tau \int_{-\infty}^{b} \tilde{x} f(\tilde{x}) \mathrm{d}\tilde{x} + \tau RF + \int_0^b \tilde{x} f(\tilde{x}) \mathrm{d}\tilde{x}}{(r + F)} \tag{4.10}$$

In the absense of a continuity condition the subscript of F is redundant. Note that (4.10) rests on the implicit assumption that the value of the bankrupt estate is insufficient to meet in full the debtholders' claims on the firm. If the value of the bankrupt estate exceeds the debtholders' claim, debt will be riskless and the owners may receive a liquidation payment, which would lead to a different set of valuation formulae.

The value of the firm, $V = V_e + V_d$, is the sum of (4.5) and (4.10):

$$V = \frac{\tau R - \tau \bar{x} + LF + \int_0^{\infty} \tilde{x} f(\tilde{x}) \mathrm{d}\tilde{x}}{(r + F)}. \tag{4.11}$$

Note that both the tax-levy on the cash flow and the tax advantage of debt are certain, because of the tax-rebate in case of bankruptcy. Differentiating (4.11) with respect to R to find the level of interest payments that maximizes the value of the firm we get:

$$\frac{\partial V}{\partial R} = \frac{\tau - \dfrac{(1 + r)}{(r + F)} f(b)(V - L)}{(r + F)}, \tag{4.12}$$

Equation (4.12) can be interpreted as follows: τ represents the tax savings associated with a marginal amount of debt financing, while the second term can be thought of as the decrease in firm value due to a marginal increase in debt. The loss of value in case of bankruptcy is represented by $V - L$, while $((1 + r)/(r + F) f(b)$, i.e. $\partial F / \partial R$, represents the marginal increase in the probability of bankruptcy. So the first order condition in (4.12) is met if the marginal benefits of debt financing equal the marginal costs of debt financing. However, as was the case in the previous subsection, the second order condition cannot be shown to hold (see Van der Wijst, 1986).

At this point the analysis wavers. The introduction of new variables in a model with indeterminate results is rather pointless. The possibility of an alternative (explicit) specification of bankruptcy costs is already excluded at the beginning of this subsection because of the results obtained in section 4.3. The only alternative is a different (simpler) specification. Such a specification is used by Scott (1976) and his model closely resembles the analysis in this subsection. The differences occur in the composition of a bankrupt estate. Scott assumes that the tax rebate is either lost upon bankruptcy of exhausted by the priority creditors [9]. A positive cash flow in case of bankruptcy is assumed to be used up in administrative costs. These assumptions do not affect the value of equity; the valuation formula for equity in the Scott model is the same as the one developed in this subsection. The valuation formula for debt is simpler because the tax rebate and cash flow are assumed not to occur in case of bankruptcy. Scott also leaves the case of fully secured debt out of consideration. The Scott model can be shown the produce an optimal capital structure at less than 100% debt financing, albeit not in a closed form (see Scott, 1979 or Van der Wijst, 1986). The Scott model can be extended with agency costs, using the same procedure as in section 3. However, if information asymmetries are introduced the Scott model can no longer be shown to produce an optimal captital structure, so that further extensions of this model are not likely to produce clear cut results. The reader is referred to the literature for these models (Van der Wijst, 1986).

5. Conclusion

Reviewing the theoretical exercises in this paper is likely to give rise to rather skeptical conclusions, as probably the most striking aspect of the exercises is the large number of models which produce indeterminate results. To illustrate, the step-by-step procedure used in the previous subsections is schematically represented in table 1 in the appendix. In this table, each step is represented by a block and the results of the models developed in each step are set at the bottom. An «internal» solution for optimal capital structure and corporate debt capacity is denoted by $MC = MR$. If optimal capital structure and corporate debt capacity cannot be shown to exist, the results are labelled «indeterminate». References are placed at the top of blocks.

As table 1 shows, there is no question of a tree-structured family of interrelated models. In fact, only one path in the table is practicable to the end, viz. the line of single-period models in which bankruptcy costs are specified as a function of the cash flow. But even this line of models does not produce a closed form optimum once information asymmetries are introduced. The other four paths peter out in indeterminate results, often

[9] Note that, although the tax rebate is not included in the bankrupt estate, it is still included in the bankruptcy condition used by Scott (as is explained in section 4.1). If the tax rebate would be eliminated from the bankruptcy condition, the Scott model would lose its well behaved character and produce indeterminate results (see Van der Wijst, 1986, p. 60-62).

in an early stage of the analysis. So, modelling the valuation of corporate claims, even within the simple and rather restrictive framework of assumptions adopted in this study, quickly leads to models involving derivations, the results of which are too complex to be evaluated, even in qualitative terms. The consequences of this complexity are not only that a comparatively large number of models produces indeterminate results (mainly because the second order conditions cannot be shown to hold), but also, and perhaps more seriously, that the models are sensitive for small and by themselves trivial changes in the specification of variables. For instance, the introduction of bankruptcy costs in single-period models produces an internal solution if these costs are specified as a function of the cash flow, but indeterminate results if these costs are considered a function of the payments to debtholders. In the multi-period setting, only the Scott-model and some of its extensions produce determinate results (although not in a «closed form»). However, if a slightly different bankruptcy condition would be used in the Scott-model, the results would become indeterminate. Hence, it can be concluded that the robustness of the various theoretical models leaves much to be desired, so that the prospects of extending the models with more realistic assumptions are questionable, to say the least. The complexity and indeterminate results of the models are presented with some emphasis, because these aspects are hardly reported on in the literature. Virtually all published models are «well behaved», but, as this paper shows, models of optimal capital structure are less firmly established than these well behaved models suggest.

REFERENCES

A. BARNEA, R.A. HAUGEN and W. SENBET: *An equilibrium analysis of debt financing under costly tax arbitrage and agency problems*, Journal of Finance, vol. XXXVI, no. 3, June, 569-581.

M. BRADLEY, G.A. JARRELL and E.H. KIM, 1984: *On the existence of an optimal capital structure: theory and evidence*, Journal of Finance, 34, 3, 857-80.

R. CASTANIAS, 1983: *Bankruptcy risk and optimal capital structure*, Journal of Finance, vol. XXXVIII, no. 5, December, 1617-1635.

A.H. CHEN and E.H. KIM, 1979: *Theories of corporate debt policy: a synthesis*, Journal of Finance, vol. XXXIV, no. 2, May, 371-387.

C. HALEY and L. SCHALL, 1979: *The theory of financial decisions*, (McGraw-Hill, New York).

M.C. JENSEN and W.H. MECKLING, 1976: *Theory of the firm: managerial behaviour, agency costs and ownership structure*, Journal of Financial Economics, vol. 3, October, 305-360.

M.J.L. JONKHART, 1980: *Optimal capital structure and corporate debt capacity* (J.H. Pasmans, B.V. Den Haag).

E.H. KIM, 1978: *A mean-variance theory of optimal capital structure and corporate debt capacity*, Journal of Finance, vol. 33, no. 1, March, 45-63.

M. RUBINSTEIN, 1973: *A mean-variance synthesis of corporate financial theory*, Journal of Finance, March, 167-181.

J.H. SOTT, 1976: *A theory of optimal capital structure*, Bell Journal of Economics, 7, 33-54.

J.E. STIGLITZ, 1969: *A re-examination of the Modigliani-Miller theorem*, American Economic Review, vol. 59, no. 5, December, 784-793.

J.E. STIGLITZ, 1974: *On the irrelevance of corporate financial policy*, American Economic Review, vol. 64, no. 6, December, 851-866.

D. van der WIJST, 1986: *Corporate debt policy and valuation of corporate claims*, Research Paper 8601, Research Institute SME, Zoetermeer.

D. van der WIJST, 1989: *Financial structure in small business, theory, tests and applications*, (Springer-Verlag, Berlin).

MIX
Papier aus verantwortungsvollen Quellen
Paper from responsible sources
FSC® C105338

If you have any concerns about our products,
you can contact us on
ProductSafety@springernature.com

In case Publisher is established outside the EU,
the EU authorized representative is:
Springer Nature Customer Service Center GmbH
Europaplatz 3, 69115 Heidelberg, Germany

Printed by Libri Plureos GmbH
in Hamburg, Germany